The Search for
An American Public Theology:

THE CONTRIBUTION OF JOHN COURTNEY MURRAY

by
Robert W. McElroy

1989

PAULIST PRESS
New York ◆ Mahwah

Excerpts from *We Hold These Truths* by John Courtney Murray are reprinted by permission of Sheed & Ward. The author also thanks *Theological Studies* for permission to quote from Murray's articles in that journal, and Georgetown University Library, Special Collections Division, for permission to quote from its Murray papers.

Library of Congress Cataloging-in-Publication Data

McElroy, Robert W.
    The search for an American public theology : the contribution of
John Courtney Murray / by Robert W. McElroy.
        p.   cm.
    Bibliography: p.
    ISBN 0-8091-3051-3
    1. Church and state--United States--History--20th century.
    2. Church and state--Catholic Church--History--20th century.
    3. United States--Church history--20th century.   4. Catholic Church-
    -United States--History--20th century.   5. Catholic Church-
    -Doctrines--History--20th century.   6. Sociology, Christian
    (Catholic)--History of doctrines--20th century.   7. Murray, John
    Courtney--Contributions in American public theology.   I. Title.
    BR516.M378   1989
    261'0973--dc19   88-27022
                                                               CIP

Published by Paulist Press
997 Macarthur Boulevard
Mahwah, New Jersey 07430

Printed and bound in the
United States of America

CONTENTS

TO MY PARENTS

INTRODUCTION

It is one of the great ironies of American history that the United States, which among the nations of the world has arguably been the most creative in its constitutional approach to the relationship between religion and government, finds itself in the twentieth century deeply uncertain about the role which religion should play in public life and discourse. The presidential campaigns of Jesse Jackson and Pat Robertson, the continuing role of the fundamentalist Right in national politics, and the new willingness of organized religious communities in the U.S. to speak out repeatedly and systematically on the issues of nuclear war and the American economy have raised serious questions about how spiritual values should function in a pluralistic society, and about how a nation which is committed to religious freedom should promote that freedom in the modern era.

This uncertainty about the public role of religion was not always present in American life. At the time of its birth as a nation, America was committed to the proposition that the promotion of religious values and religious vibrancy is intrinsically tied to well-being of democracy. In his 1749 "Proposals Relating to the Education of Youth in Philadelphia," Benjamin Franklin argued that civic virtue is the natural outgrowth of a religious upbringing, and that society should give its unhesitating support to the development of a flourishing body of religious communities.[1] George Washington repeatedly reminded the American people that their effort to build a just and democratic republic would certainly fail unless religion continued to occupy a prominent role in the social life of the U.S.[2] And the correspondence between John Adams and Thomas Jefferson testifies emphatically

1

to their conviction that only a transcendent order of values could provide enduring guidance for the new nation.[3]

But in the contemporary era, this belief that religion should play a vigorous and substantive role in American public life has increasingly come under fire. In part, as Richard Neuhaus has pointed out, this challenge to spiritual values in the public square is "part of the conceptual air we breathe" in a nation which prides itself on its dedication to pluralism, individualism, and rationality.[4] But increasingly, the challenge to a substantive public role for religious values in American life has taken the form of specific propositions which seek to show why public religion is antithetical to fundamental American beliefs. Douglas Wald has ably encapsulated these propositions: (1) politics in the U.S. consists of compromise and negotiation, while religious values do not lend themselves to either compromise or negotiation; (2) the style of debate encouraged by the introduction of religious values into the public sphere tends to be rigid and dogmatic; (3) the enduring religious divisions which have torn other nations apart testify to the dangers of allowing spiritually-based values to have a determining role in the formulation of public policy and the constitution of American society; (4) the accommodation of religiously-based values in American public life automatically alienates and violates the rights of those who do not share such values.[5] These are forceful arguments, and their appeal is enhanced by the commitment of American society to the preservation of a genuine pluralism in all spheres of public life. Even for most religious believers in the United States, the substantive public role which religion has historically played in American life now seems more the anachronism of a less tolerant past than the foundation for the construction of a just and free social order for the future. Public religion is on the defensive in the United States—not because of any secular-humanist conspiracy—but because advocates of a strong and substantive public role for religious values in the U.S. have not been able to construct a compelling case for their cause.

Certainly public religion is not on the defensive among fundamentalists in the U.S. The emergence and political activism of the fundamentalist right has been one of the most intriguing and politically important events of the 1980's.[6] It has not only energized a formerly quiescent segment of American society, but has also tapped the feeling among many non-fundamentalists that the complete secularization of public life can bring social ills no less threatening than the religious intolerance which secularization is meant to remedy. But in the end, for most Americans the scriptural warrants for the reform of public life which constitute the heart of the fundamentalist agenda offer little appeal; for they smack of the very rigidity, divisiveness, and refusal to compromise which has brought the public role of religion into question in the first place. If the case for a strong public role for religious values in American life is to be made effectively in the 1990's, it will have to be made in terms other than a literal interpretation of Scripture.

Robert Bellah has made an immense contribution to this debate on religion and society through the essays on civil religion which he and his collaborators have written over the past twenty-five years.[7] For Bellah, the transition of America from an agrarian to a bureaucratic society has accentuated all of the centripetal forces of individualism inherent in American culture. The biblical and republican traditions which unified the nation in its first century and a half of existence are now largely excluded from public discourse and no longer have the unifying capacity which they exercised for most of the country's history. As a result the United States, which has no common ethnic or cultural heritage to bind the nation together, has increasingly become a nation of individuals estranged from one another, without common bonds, common goals, or common values. Bellah and his associates propose a reappropriation of the spiritual values that have historically formed the heart of American culture, a reappropriation which recognizes that modern realities prevent a simple return to the Calvinist culture which predominated in the agrarian age, but which also recognizes that any effort to forge a new sense of community in American public life will have to place great stress on the public expression of religious values.

Bellah's work is a masterful analysis of what takes place when religion ceases to occupy a prominent substantive place in public life. But in the end, it fails to point the way toward a revivification of American culture. For the "civil religion proposals" that Bellah and his collaborators have put forth constitute what Perry

Miller has called "a jeremiad": they poignantly and eloquently describe the decline of American culture, but they offer little concrete prescription for bringing spiritual values back into the center of American public life. Bellah's stance is a sociological one, though in the broadest sense of that term. Because he operates out of a scientific stance rather than a theological one, he cannot adopt the explicit faith-stance necessary to project spiritual values onto the national stage in the way that Jonathan Edwards or Reinhold Niebuhr did for previous generations.

It is precisely because speaking from a theological stance offers a much stronger platform for addressing the decline of religion in American public life that a recent series of scholars has attempted to construct a "public theology" for the late twentieth century. The term "public theology" was coined by Martin Marty in a path-breaking article on civil religion written in 1974.[8] It refers to a self-consciously religious effort to form and mold American culture and politics so that they conform more fully with God's plan of salvation. Public theology is both celebrative and prophetic in its attitude toward American society; God is seen as blessing the American national enterprise but also as challenging it. Public theology opposes those forms of civil religion which seek merely to interpret American policies and cultural attitudes as divinely-sanctioned; instead it regards American society and indeed all societies as subject to an enduring order of justice which calls all nations to self-criticism and reform. The public theologian seeks a new cohesiveness for American society to replace the centripetal forces of individualism which Bellah points to, but this new cohesiveness is a substantive and specific one which calls the people of the United States to expand and deepen their quest for freedom, equality, and human advancement by seeing that each of these goals has a transcendent dimension. Public theology is dialogical, but not relativistic. It seeks to create a new unity among the American people through civility and discourse; but it proceeds from the belief that the ultimate measure of public dialogue is not its procedural quality, but rather its ability to restore to the U.S. as a nation a spiritually-rich vision of society. Public theology does not represent the imposition upon a religiously pluralistic society of a specific sectarian creed. Instead it seeks to formulate a common religiously-based frame of reference for the people of the United States, a frame of reference which brings to the most important debates on American public policy the spiritual values which can alone add unity and depth to cultural and political discussion.

The effort to construct a strong and alluring public theology for the America of the 1990's has cut across both sectarian and ideological lines. It has produced the liberal Catholicism of John Coleman's *An American Strategic Theology* and the conservative Lutheranism of Richard Neuhaus' *The Naked Public Square.*[9] Public theology ranges from the scholarly commentaries of Richard McBrien and A. James Reichley to the more visionary prescriptions of Robert McAfee Brown to the trenchant commentaries of Michael Novak.[10] In a very real sense, the statements of the National Catholic Conference of Bishops and the United Methodist Council of Bishops on war and peace represent public theology in its most potent form, as do the statements of the national leadership conferences of the Presbyterian, Lutheran, Catholic and Episcopalian churches on the need for justice in the American economy.[11] Public theology, then, is the effort of the mainstream Christian churches and theologians in the United States to articulate a substantive role for spiritual values in public life which does not violate the spirit of American pluralism.[12]

One of the most interesting elements of the leading public theologies that have been written in the past decade is that despite their sectarian and ideological diversity, they have almost uniformly drawn many of their central insights from the works of John Courtney Murray, a Catholic theologian who grappled with the thorny issues of religion and American society during the 1950's and 1960's. Murray, who was born in 1903 and died in 1967, was a Jesuit priest whose initial interest in the question of public religion came from a desire to forge an inter-faith coalition for social justice in the 1940's. As a result of his early writings on ecumenism, social justice and public religion, Murray was drawn into the internal Catholic doctrinal debate on the question of religious liberty; and after a period in which he was forbidden by his superiors to write further on religious freedom, he emerged at the Second Vatican Council as a major architect of the conciliar statement affirming the right of the human person to immunity from any state discrimination based upon religious belief. Much of Murray's life in the 1950's and 1960's was devoted to this doctrinal debate on religious liberty, but he never ceased to wrestle with the larger question of how spiritual values should function in a modern society such as the United States. In a series of speeches and articles that began in 1943 and culminated in the publication of his best-selling *We Hold These Truths* in 1960, Murray articulated a strong and vibrant public theology which caught the imagination of America's cultural and political leaders and which sought to chart a clear and substantive course for the role of religion in America's public life.

Murray's public theology was well-received in the 1950's. But when one reads his writings today, many passages seem dated and out of touch with the problems confronting contemporary America. How, then, can one account for the fact that contemporary public theologians have continually looked to Murray for guidance in confronting the most vexing questions of religion and society? How can one explain the fact that Murray is utilized by most current public theologians more than even Reinhold Niebuhr? The answer lies first of all in the depth and breadth of Murray's life-work. Robin Lovin has written that it is possible to place public theologians in three general categories: those who are concerned with the ordering function of religion in society, those who stress that religion can undergird enduring freedom in society, and those who argue that religion provides the possibility for social justice in the public realm.[13] One of the enduring attractions of Murray's work is that it would be impossible to place him in one of these categories; for he united the ordering, freedom-producing and justice-enhancing functions of public religion in a manner which was not superficial but penetrating. It is for this reason that Murray's work appeals to contemporary public theologians of such different ideological perspectives. But Murray's enduring appeal goes beyond his breadth of vision; for he saw with great clarity twenty years before Robert Bellah that the dislocation of religion from the public life of American society dramatically threatened the future well-being of the United States. Murray appeals to contemporary public theologians because his writings were prescient in forecasting the debilitating effects that the decline of public religion would produce in the U.S., and because they betray the sense of urgency which public theology must bring to the American people. Finally, Murray has been critical to the work of so many contemporary public theologians because his mind had two characteristics which all too seldom appear in combination: the facility for penetrating and creative insights and the ability to express those insights with precision, clarity, and consistency. More than a generation after his death, Murray's articulation of many of the central issues involved in the public religion debate are still unsurpassed both in their originality and in their forcefulness of expression. For all these reasons, despite the datedness of parts of Murray's public theology, and despite its tendency to often speak within an explicitly Catholic framework, Murray has remained an unrivaled source for public theologians of all ideologies and mainline denominations.

Unfortunately for those interested in Murray's efforts to construct an American public theology, there is no one source to which one can turn for Murray's complete views on the proper role of religion in society. Always a systematic thinker, Murray was seldom a systematic writer. In all of his scholarly career he never wrote a single book that was originally composed as a book; even *We Hold These Truths* was a compilation of earlier articles and lectures. Many of Murray's most important treatments of public religion are contained in unpublished sources—his major addresses, class lecture notes, and the voluminous correspondence he had with many of the leading political, cultural, religious, and academic leaders of American society. For this reason alone, a systematic presentation of Murray's public theology would seem in order. But the need to revisit John Courtney Murray's life-work does not arise first and foremost from a sense of history, or even from a desire to provide heretofore unpublished insights which Murray formulated.[14] No, the need to revisit Murray's life-work on religion and society arises from the very real possibility that the frequency with which contemporary public theologians borrow from Murray's writings is a sign that the Murray corpus should not be treated merely as a source from which to draw, but as the foundational framework and guiding force of contemporary American public theology. Only an effort to revisit Murray's explorations of the question of religion and society, only a synthesis of his argument and a critical evaluation of that argument in light of the contemporary needs of American society, can correctly identify the role which John Courtney Murray should play in the future of American public theology. This book is an effort to provide such a synthesis and evaluation.

To those who have been so supportive to me during the years in which I have been investigating the work of John Courtney Murray, I owe many thanks: to my family, who first brought to me the faith of which Murray spoke so eloquently; to Archbishop John Quinn, who not only asked me to study the field of social ethics, but inspired me to do so; to Father William Spohn, who initially directed my research into the work of John Courtney Murray at Berkeley, and to Father Charles O'Neill, who generously directed my dissertation at the Gregorian University, and who offered a host of useful suggestions. I also want to thank Father Walter Burghardt, S.J., Monsignor John Tracy Ellis and Monsignor George Higgins, who shared with me their recollections of Murray. For the unfailing assistance of the staff of the Special Collections Division of the Georgetown University Library, which houses the Murray papers, I extend my thanks. Finally, I want to extend my heartfelt gratitude to the many people who helped me along the way with their assistance, their commentaries and their friendship: Gerald O'Collins, Joseph Fuchs, John O'Donnell, Thomas Schubeck, Karen Lebacqz, Rich Gula, Warren Holleran, Bruce Dreier, Greg Ingels, Randy Calvo, Ray Sacca, Milt Walsh, Jim McKay, Tom Madden, George Wesolek, John Balleza, Dave Mulvihill, Dan Smilanic, John and Mary McKeon, Jane Holl and Don Flickinger.

1

A SPIRITUAL CRISIS
IN THE TEMPORAL REALM

John Courtney Murray was not sanguine about the cultural ethos of the twentieth century. In fact one of the most consistent and compelling themes in Murray's writings is the conviction that the modern world faced a moral and social crisis of immense proportions—a crisis that dwarfed the threats to humanity which had been posed in earlier ages. While previous centuries had produced movements which temporarily lured men and women away from the moral and religious beliefs that were fundamental for human flourishing, only in the twentieth century did it seem possible that whole societies in the West would forsake their spiritual and ethical heritage in order to build a culture which was secular in origin and scientific in orientation.

"The secularist crisis"—the phrase appears constantly in Murray's works—represented for Murray a massive assault upon the very fabric of religion and the social values which he believed necessary for human well-being. The secularist crisis meant the increasing acceptance of the theory that commitments of faith and prayer were private and personal choices which should not be allowed to enter the social arena. It meant the pseudo-scientific mentality which held that articles of faith were an affront to the thinking person, and that in building the new social order they should be relegated to the sphere of cult and superstition. The secularist crisis was for Murray the onrushing tide of indifferentism that threatened to empty Western civilization of its spiritual roots and to put in its place a shallow humanism that could only lead to ennui and despair.[1]

The secularist crisis had many forms and diverse advocates, but it had effected a social transformation in the Western world that made the culture of the modern era seem strangely alien to the believer. Murray lamented that

> . . . to the modern Christian the world is not his Father's house. In fact it represents more closely "the strong man's house" (Mark 3:27) with the strong man not yet bound. For decades, as Pius XII recently pointed out, "the progress of mankind has been without God, indeed against God, without Christ, indeed against Christ." The world today is alienated from the Church. It stands over against the Church, as a closed system of life. And the faith of the ordinary Christian gets hardly any support from his environment. On the contrary, his greatest temptation is to live in the world, over against the Church.[2]

This alienation of the world from the Church and indeed from all spiritual values that had a transcendent reference was to be a constant source of reflection for Murray. It formed the backdrop not only for his work on the relationship between Church and state, but also for his writings on American politics, ecumenism, and foreign relations. Murray believed that the world was literally being torn apart by this profound spiritual crisis in the temporal order, and that the question of the proper relationship between the spiritual and temporal orders was the most important question facing modern society. "No one stands aside from this problem," Murray wrote; "everyone must adopt some solution for it."[3] Murray's solution was a lifetime of scholarship dedicated to healing the alienation between religion and modernity, between temporal society and its spiritual roots.

The European Context

This conception of a spiritual crisis in the twentieth century did not come suddenly to Murray. Rather, it had developed over a number of years and had been heavily influenced by the time which he spent in Europe studying theology just before the outbreak of World War II. The Europe which Murray had seen was the victim of a "systematic de-Christianization." All of the Chris-

tian assumptions about the supernatural end of the human person and the importance of transcendent values in the process of
societal decision-making had been challenged, and they had been
challenged effectively. Murray wrote that he had witnessed a
shrinkage of religious life in European culture that had not only
diminished the public role of religious faith but had also shat-
tered the private religious beliefs of countless Christians who now
saw their faith as a sometimes consoling anachronism rather than
as a source of knowledge and meaning in the modern world.[4]

These first-hand perceptions of the European scene were
reinforced by the writings of two men who were to have a great
impact upon Murray's intellectual development: Henri de Lubac
and Jacques Maritain. In *Le drame de l'humanisme athée*, Lubac
traced the ways in which the intellectual elite of the West had
abandoned the Christian philosophical principles that had been
the foundation of Western thought and culture. Murray was fond
of quoting Lubac's contention that:

> Underneath the countless surface currents that are bearing in
> all directions the thought of our contemporaries, there is, it
> seems, a deeper current that long ago set in—one might per-
> haps better call it an enveloping drift: by the action of a con-
> siderable portion of its elite thinkers Western humanity is
> denying its Christian origins and turning away from God.[5]

This drift was partly caused by the attack upon the reasonableness
of faith which had been mounted by those who saw in the methods of natural science the model for all human rational inquiry.
But it went much farther than this. Christianity had faced many
attacks upon its truth-claims in the past and would be able to
answer the critique raised by modern science. The drift which
Lubac described was more threatening precisely because it represented not so much an attack upon Christian faith, but a decision to ignore that faith and to circumscribe severely the role
which it should play in society. Commenting on Lubac's analysis,
Murray asserted that the elite thinkers of the West were moving
toward a conscious and dynamic atheism that was bringing about
"a new organization of the world, without God and therefore
against man."[6]

Maritain echoed similar themes in his *Education at the Cross-roads*. Taking the position that Western culture and Christian values are linked not merely by historical accident but by logical necessity, Maritain stated that

> . . . theological problems and controversies have permeated the whole development of Western culture and civilization, and are still at work in its depths, in such a way that the one who would ignore them would be fundamentally unable to grasp his own time and the meaning of its internal conflicts.[7]

Yet, as Maritain concluded, European society *was* in the process of ignoring these fundamental theological questions and by doing so risked losing the spiritual heritage which formed the heart of Western culture. Even more distressingly, Murray noted in 1945, it was not just the intellectual elite which was falling victim to the organized unbelief that Maritain described, it was European society as a whole.[8]

If the writings of Lubac and Maritain confirmed Murray's own beliefs about the increasing alienation of Western society from its spiritual roots, it was the encyclicals and public statements of Pius XI and Piux XII that clarified for Murray what the secular drift meant for the Church and for temporal society. Pius XI had set the tone for Murray's reflections on the secular crisis when he wrote in *Laetus Sane Nuntius* (1929) that the growing de-Christianization of Europe represented a threat to the faith that dwarfed those encountered in previous ages:

> You see upon what times we have fallen, and what they clamorously demand of us. On the one hand, we have the sorrow of seeing how human society has been despoiled of the Christian spirit, and how the life of men is governed by a pagan ethic; in the minds of many the light of Catholic faith is being dimmed, so much that the religious sense is almost extinguished, and moral integrity and rectitude are being day by day more miserably undermined.[9]

For Murray, this text and indeed Pius XI's entire corpus dealing with the role of religion in society pointed toward an enormous social transformation that had taken place in Western society, a

transformation that had "effected what we ordinarily call the secularization of modern life, the gradual development of a complete separation and an active opposition between the spiritual
and the temporal, between the Church and human society."[10]

This opposition between the spiritual and the temporal
seemed even more pronounced during the pontificate of Pius
XII. Pius' 1939 encyclical *Summi Pontificatus* and his Christmas
messages of 1942 and 1943 reveal a grieving Pontiff who discerned beneath the pattern of military conflict which raged
around him a far more profound and dangerous combat: the
struggle for the soul of society in an age which increasingly
denied the existence of God and spurned even the most basic
respect for human dignity and sacredness:

> Today, as never before, the hour has come for reparation, for
> rousing the conscience of the world from the heavy torpor
> into which the drugs of false ideas, widely diffused, have sunk
> it. This is all the more so because in this hour of material and
> moral disintegration the appreciation of the emptiness and
> inconsistency of every purely human order is beginning to dis-
> illusion even those who, in days of apparent happiness, were
> not conscious of the need of contact with the eternal in them-
> selves or their society, and did not look upon its absence as
> an essential defect in their constitutions. What was clear to
> the Christian, who in his deeply founded faith was pained by
> the ignorance of others, is now presented to us in dazzling
> clearness by the din of appalling catastrophe which the pres-
> ent upheaval brings to man and which portrays all the terri-
> fying lineaments of a general judgment even for the tepid, the
> indifferent, the frivolous. It is indeed an old truth which
> comes out in ever new forms and thunders through the ages
> and through all the nations from the mouth of the prophet:
> All that forsake Thee shall be confounded; they who depart
> from Thee, shall be written in the earth; because they have
> forsaken the Lord, the Vein of Living Waters.[11]

Such statements of Pius XII had a profound effect upon
Murray's perceptions of the temporal order and the growing spiritual vacuum which lay at its heart. Murray wrote that Pius had
provided the spiritual leadership which the world needed by alert-

ing the conscience of all peoples to the root of the disorder in secular life. In Murray's words, Pius had shown that

> . . . the issue in this war of spirits is truly cosmic. It is a "war on the darkness that comes of deserting God, and on the cold-ness that comes from strife between brothers. It is a fight for the human race, which is gravely ill . . ." Christ, as Pius XII solemnly stated in *Summi Pontificatus,* is once again crucified, and a chill darkness covers the earth. By Christ he means his members, every human person; and the crucifixion is not sim-ply on the cross of total war but on the whole order of human life, dechristianized and dehumanized in its spirit and its insti-tutions, which made total war possible, and even inevitable.[12]

For Murray, World War II did indeed represent the crucifixion of humankind, not merely in the suffering which it unleased, but more profoundly because the forces which lay at its root threat-ened to rob the social soul of the human person and to leave him alone and alienated from his God.

Nor did this deeper crucifixion end when the guns of World War II were silenced. For in his Christmas Allocution of 1945, Pius XII made clear that a true and lasting peace could only be forged if the world returned to belief in God and in the order of law which he had created. Surveying the untold human tragedy which had been wrought during the past six years, Pius said: "Let it not be said that this is not realism in politics. Experience should have taught to all that the policy guided by . . . the laws of God is the most real and tangible of policies. The "realist" politicians who think otherwise only pile up ruins."[13] In his commentary on this text, Murray wrote that:

> The ruins around us surely have refuted the ancient sneer, uttered by what the Pope calls "a musty Liberalism." Its effort was to create without the Church, or in opposition to her, a unity built on lay culture and secularized humanism. What it did, together with the totalitarianism that moved into the vac-uum it created, was to bring about a world that "for its tragic disunity and insecurity has never known an equal."[14]

It was clear that this tragic disunity could be remedied only if the crisis of secularization were clearly recognized and forthrightly confronted. In Murray's view, "the Pope of Peace" had provided the analysis and leadership necessary to begin both tasks.

Thus as Murray surveyed the cultural scene of Europe in the 1940's he concluded that the Western civilization which had been built on Christian foundations was in great peril. There was indeed a drift toward atheism, not only among the elite of thinkers, but among the masses as well. And even more importantly, this drift toward atheism had been institutionalized in the most critical structures of modern society—the school, the media and the arms of government. It was this institutionalization of secularism that Pope Pius XII had stressed in his addresses on the spiritual crisis in the temporal realm, and it was this institutionalization of unbelief that most concerned Murray. Europe, in his mind, was on the edge of a cultural precipice, and it would only be prevented from going over that edge if the post-war period witnessed a dramatic reversal of the secularist drift which had characterized the first part of the twentieth century.

The American Scene

It was the growth of secularism in Europe that first aroused Murray's interest in the relationship between spiritual values and temporal life, but it was the attack upon religious faith in the United States that was to provide the context for his efforts to develop a public theology for the twentieth century. Murray returned from his theological studies in Rome attuned to the intellectual currents of the Continent; yet he recognized that the United States was not Europe, and that the phenomena which Maritain and Lubac had described in their analyses of the secular drift did not correspond fully with the process of secularization in America. Thus in the 1940's, Murray began to construct his own theory of the secular crisis that reflected American realities and American possibilities.

What struck Murray most about American culture was its practical orientation, its willingness to forego theoretical speculation in order to get on with the task of building the nation. The accomplishments of this practical orientation were manifold—the construction of a constitutional system that guaranteed both freedom and justice, the creation of a general material well-being that was the envy of the world, and the accumulation of sufficient military power to establish a true *Pax Americana* in the twentieth century. Murray consistently expressed his pride in these accomplishments, and he was quick to defend American society against those critics who would minimize them. But as he looked at American culture during the 1940's, Murray was concerned that this practical orientation had prevented the people of the United States from reflecting on the spiritual core of the civilization which they were building, and that as a result America faced a spiritual crisis of its own:

> Take Saint Thomas' statement of the essential twofold human endowment, that man "has reason and hands," and you will have the terms in which the crisis may be broadly stated: in the United States the traditional cultural emphasis has been on the hands, now an emphasis on reason begins to be needed. In the past we have been largely content to use our hands . . . in the work of building a City. . . . Now, however, the realization has struck home to many that in the course of all our furious building we have succeeded in erecting an immense structure that encloses—a vacuum. The intellectual, moral and spiritual vacuities perceptible in many regions of American culture have given rise to anxious reflection, How shall these hollow emptinesses within man, within his institutions, be filled?[15]

Murray believed that the United States was suffering from a spiritual anemia in which the mechanical perspectives of the American people had prevented the nation from reflecting on the values which grounded and guided its material progress. Murray called for a new period of reflectiveness in American society, a period in which the country would go beyond the slogans of "Manifest Destiny" and "The American Century" to assess the real direction of American civilization.[16]

Murray believed that such an analysis would reveal that the United States was increasingly falling victim to a creeping secularism that threatened to eradicate religious values from the public square. The American brand of secularism was less ideological than its European counterpart; it did not attack religion directly, but on the contrary was complimentary toward religious impulses, as long as they remained in the private realm.

> In America (the secularist) has traditionally had no quarrel with religion as a "purely private matter," as a sort of essence or idea or ambient aura that may help to warm the hidden heart of solitary man. He may even concede a place to religion-in-general, whatever that is. What alarms him is religion as a Thing, visible, corporate, organized, a community of thought that . . . is furnished somehow with an armature of power to make its thought and judgment publicly prevail.[17]

The forces of secularism in the United States opposed any public role for organized religion in society, and they opposed any appeal to substantial religious concepts in public discourse. For this reason, Murray argued, secularism in America was no less dangerous than Continental laicism; indeed because of the "quietness, brotherliness, and even good humor" with which it operated, it was all the more dangerous.[18]

In the late 1940's Murray encountered the writings of Paul Blanshard, a man who was to be an ideological adversary of Murray's for some twenty years and whose ideas represented to Murray the essence of secularism in the United States. In his book *Freedom and Catholic Power,* Blanshard attacked the role of the Catholic hierarchy in America, arguing that the bishops' cultural, political, and economic policies were un-American because they contradicted the nation's dedication to the principles of freedom and individual rights.[19] In his reviews of this work, Murray stated that Blanshard represented an American secularism which was the enemy not only of Catholicism, but of all religion.

Murray saw three ideas present in this American secularism. The first was that "the sole area of the Church's competence is that of devotional life. The Church belongs in the sacristy, as classical Liberalism put it."[20] Any effort of organized religion to pronounce on economic, social or political issues was an infringement upon these autonomous spheres of society. The second tenet of American secularism stated that the democratic state holds sway over all spheres of temporal life, and that the democratic process is valid for the just settlement of all issues of tem-

poral life. In this way, the claim of religion that there is a prior
order of values instituted by God was effectively nullified in social
discourse and decision-making. Finally, in Murray's view, American secularism claimed that "the singly valid guide of the individual or group in forming opinions is scientific method."[21] Thus
religious truth-claims and insights into the nature of humanity
and society would be considered invalid because they could not
be justified in terms of the methods of natural science.

It was this threefold structure of American secularism that
alarmed Murray, for he saw people such as Blanshard to be
merely the most visible manifestation of a cultural drift that was
eroding religious values in United States society. The spirit of
Christian humanism which had guided the founders of the American nation was being replaced by a secular humanism that denied
any place to God in public life. The vision that the human person
was part of a created order dependent upon an all-powerful God
was being replaced by the vision of the self-sufficient person,
dependent upon no other.

> Affirmation of the *res humana,* once made in the context of
> belief in God and an all-ruling moral order, has gone over
> into exclusive affirmation of the *res huius saeculi,* under igno-
> rance or even denial of the transcendent. Belief in man has
> proved, with some groups, to be an enemy of belief in God.
> The cultivation of human values by human energies, under no
> appeal to higher action or assistance, has found as its coun-
> terpart the theory that all values are simply immanent in man
> and have no transcendent reference. A mentality has been
> created to which the idea of the absolute is a horror. We have
> even heard from our highest court of law, supposedly the last
> rampart of the values by which our society lives, the dictum
> that our only absolute is the belief that there is no absolute.[22]

It was this rampant secularism in American society that posed the
real danger to the soul of the nation, and Murray called upon
Catholics and Protestants to unite against this common enemy.
"In the presence of this enemy," Murray wrote, "I consider the
Catholic-Protestant polemic to be an irrelevance."[23] Writing on
another occasion Murray reiterated his position that secularism
was the real danger to American culture:

There is a stand to be made against secularism, which makes freedom of religion mean freedom from religion, and which is particularly dangerous in its denial of the relevance of religion to social order and public life. The stand against this enemy can be made on the ground of human reason and the natural law, that define the nature of the human conscience and the nature of the State. On this ground, therefore, Catholics and Protestants can make a common stand, as an act of good will—a will that has for its object a common good.[24]

Murray was deeply troubled by secularism, but he recognized that it was far from having triumphed in American society. He believed that the American people still recognized that religion is not purely a private affair, and he believed also that the tide of secularism could be reversed in the United States.[25] But such a reversal would come about only if the religious people of America recognized the peril which confronted them, and, equally importantly, constructed a positive new theory of how religion should function in American society in the twentieth century. It was to these two tasks that Murray dedicated much of his life's work.

THE HISTORICAL DEVELOPMENT OF SECULARISM

In order to begin the twin tasks of alerting the American people to the spread of secularism and of developing a new theory of the role of religion in society, Murray undertook an extensive historical investigation into the roots of the secularist crisis: how had the progressive evacuation of spiritual values from public life begun, and how could it be reversed? The focus of this investigation was twofold; it concerned both the historical role of spiritual values in the formation of Western civilization and the institutional role of the Church in Western society. Neither of these facets could be ignored, because the secularist crisis had both a cultural and an institutional dimension. And Murray was determined that his historical inquiry should locate the origins of both of these threats.

In approaching Murray's theory of the role of religion in Western society, it is important to examine briefly the main sources from which he drew. Murray began his historical investi-

gation during the last years of World War II; the threat of totalitarianism in Germany and Italy was on the verge of being
defeated, but thoughtful people in the West were asking the question: How could totalitarianism have come to exist in these coun-
tries which lay in the Western democratic tradition? It was a question of central concern for Murray himself, and, just as
importantly, it was a question of central concern for the historians and social scientists writing during this period. Thus it is not
surprising that the chief sources which Murray utilized in his historical investigation framed their presentations on the development of Western political and social institutions against the backdrop of the rise of modern totalitarianism and the question of
where the Western tradition had gone wrong.

Many of the authors whom Murray consulted had known
first-hand the repression of life in a totalitarian state. A. P. D'Entreves had left his native Italy after the rise of Mussolini and had
watched from England as fascism became increasingly repressive;
his eloquent history of the role of government in society, entitled
The Medieval Contribution to Political Thought, was preoccupied
with the issue of limiting the role of the state in societal life, and
Murray drew substantially from it.[26] Similarly, Don Luigi Sturzo
was also a victim of fascist rule, and his book *Church and State* was
the source of Murray's belief that totalitarianism could only be
avoided in society if organized religion played a strong and out-
spoken role in public life.[27] J. L. Talmon had witnessed the Nazi
terror unleased against the Jews in Europe, and his *The Rise of
Totalitarian Democracy* located the totalitarian tendency not only
in Germany and Italy, but also in the secular democratic mystique
that pervaded England, France, and the United States.[28] The
works of Christopher Dawson, Eric Voegelin, and Romano Guardini pursued these same central themes, and Murray drew heavily
from all of them.[29] Each of these authors discerned in the totalitarianism of the modern era a fundamental break with the tradition of Western civilization, and each of them located that break
in the spiritual realm of public life.

The Rise and Fall of the Medieval Synthesis

The starting point for Murray's consideration of the growth
of secularism lay in the writings of Pope Gelasius I, who ascended

to the papacy just after the fall of the Roman Empire in the West. Gelasius was embroiled in a series of disputes with the emperors Valentinian II and Anastasius I, who were attempting to take full control of the Church in the East during the crisis in Rome. Gelasius vigorously resisted these efforts, and in the process he created a corpus of social theory which became the foundation for both the medieval doctrine on Church and state and Murray's interpretation of the political tradition of the West. Writing to Anastasius, the Pope said:

> Two there are, noble emperor, whereby this world is ruled in sovereign fashion. The consecrated authority of the priest-hood and the power of the king, and of these two the responsibility of the priests is by so much the weightier. . . .[30]

Such was the formulation of Gelasius' doctrine of "the two swords," a theme he developed extensively in several tracts on the nature of the Church and its role in society. Gelasius believed that divine things belonged in the care of the bishops of the Church, and that the order of public discipline was entrusted to the secular rulers. The higher dignity of the spiritual realm meant that the order of the sacred enjoyed a primacy in dignity. But this did not diminish the fact that the secular ruler received his authority directly from God and not through the Church. Both the Church and the state were in need of each other, according to Gelasius' teaching, for it was only in the intermixture of spiritual values and temporal activities that the work of Christ on earth could be accomplished.[31]

Murray believed that the "Gelasian thesis" represented the "Magna Carta" of the freedom of the Church and the spiritual health of society. "In a true sense," Murray stated, "the whole of Catholic theory and practice in the matter of Church-State relationships had taken the form of a speculative interpretation and practical application of this text."[32] Murray drew several important conclusions from the Gelasian doctrine. The first revolved around the fact that Gelasius did not use the same word to describe the power of the bishops and the power of the emperor. The Church enjoyed *auctoritas,* while the civil power held *potestas.* In this distinction of terms, Murray believed, Gelasius was pointing to the fact that the power of the state included the element of compulsion, while the power of the Church was one of inspiration:

> Authority leads where power drives. Authority leads by virtue of its own dignity and one follows it out of conviction. Power drives by virtue of force and one moves before it in consequence of coercion—a coercion that may indeed be just, legitimate, but remains coercion nonetheless.[33]

A second element of Gelasius' thought which was of enduring importance for Murray was the Pope's delineation of the two spheres of the temporal and the spiritual. The Gelasian texts did not demarcate the clear distinction between the natural and divine orders which the Middle Ages would produce, but they did suggest the existence of two separate orders of activities and values in this life. There were not simply two powers, there were two spheres. Hence there were elements of human life which lay beyond the reach of the state, just as there were aspects of political life which were beyond the reach of the Church.

Murray maintained that the introduction of the Gelasian thesis into practice during the post-Constantinian period represented a critical formative development in Western civilization. For it began the process whereby both the spiritual and civil powers in temporal society would exert positive yet countervailing influences upon the social life of the citizen:

> From the time of Gelasius onward, Church and state stood side by side as separate authorities, each claiming the right to regulate a portion of the total life of man. The earlier view of society as a single homogeneous structure was replaced by a radically new idea of the two-fold organization of society. With the possible exception of the concept of law itself, the concept of social dualism has done more itself than anything else to determine the specific character of Western civilization.[34]

Murray recognized, of course, that the Christian Empire of the post-Constantinian period did not represent a full realization of the Gelasian principles, but he maintained that from the fourth century onward "the Christian revolution" had begun, a revolution that relativized the political order by erecting a sacred order both in the life of the individual and the life of society.[35]

This concept of a "sacred order" in the individual and social life of the human person came to be a central tenet in Murray's thought. Defining this sacred order, he wrote, "this concept embraces all those things which have their roots within the temporal order of human life and are a part of it, at the same time that, in their finality or in their Christian mode of existence, they transcend the purposes of the political order."[36] These *res sacrae* included the unity of the human person both as Christian and citizen, the relationship of husband and wife, the relationship of parent and child, including the area of education, the employer-employee relationship, and the common cultural patrimony of humankind.[37] In sum, these *res sacrae* affirmed the sacredness of the human person, his transcendent value and destiny, and the immunity of certain areas of his personal and social life from the power of the state.

If the erection of this sacred order began in the fourth century, Murray believed that it reached a certain fullness in the medieval period, when "the medieval Christian Commonwealth achieved its stylistic unity by a nice balance of inner strains and stresses."[38] These "strains and stresses" included the feudal power of the lords, the national claims of the monarchy, the institutional authority of the Church, and the growing influence of the guilds and towns. In such a climate, the *res sacrae* were allowed to flourish precisely because the sheer number of mediating institutions in society prevented any one temporal power from exerting over-weaning control.

But Murray believed that there was a further and more profound reason for locating in the Middle Ages the institutionalization of the *res sacrae* in the political tradition of the West. For during the medieval period the whole of society was essentially Christian; thus the Church, seen as the Christian people, was virtually co-extensive with society, and freedom for the Church meant freedom for society:

> Since in medieval times the Church itself was the Great Society, free under its own law, there was inherent in the freedom

of the Church the concept of a free society, a whole area of human concerns—the sacred concerns of man and also those temporal concerns which have a sacred aspect—which had its own structure in terms of man's original rights and responsibilities. This area was marked off as being outside the legitimate sphere of interest of the secular power. The secular power itself stood within the Great Society, as a limited aspect of its administrative life, constituent of a minor order distinct from the order of the Great Society, set to serve the order of the Great Society.[39]

This was the great accomplishment of the Middle Ages. It declared that society was prior to the state in terms of authority and rights. Society embraced the *res sacrae,* while the state was meant to serve them. Society was not co-extensive with the state, but extended far beyond the boundaries of the state.

The medieval period, in Murray's view, generated two other significant advances in the proper structure of society. The first was the replacement of the Roman voluntaristic notion of law with the Thomistic notion that law is based upon principles discoverable in the created order. Thus the ultimate referent for the binding force of a particular law lay in the law of nature rather than the will of the legislator.[40] In addition, Murray argued that the Middle Ages developed an incipient notion of the principle of the consent of the governed. This principle was reflected in the king's obligation to obtain consent from the various legislative bodies for new laws and in the right of popular resistance to civil authority which violated the law.[41] Indeed, Murray went so far as to say on one occasion that "all that is best in modern democracy is a reviviscence of . . . 'the eternal Middle Ages.'"[42]

While such an analysis may seem blind to the defects of the constitutional structure of the Middle Ages, Murray was careful to point out that the medieval period was not a halcyon age. "The thirteenth was a magnificent century," he wrote, " . . . but for all its magnificences it had also its miseries."[43] One of the chief miseries was the exaggerated claim of the papal court for direct power over the temporal realm, a claim epitomized by Boniface VIII's encyclical *Unam Sanctam.* Murray endorsed the view of John of Paris that the proper role for papal and indeed all spiritual power in the temporal realm is through the conscience of the community. The failure to achieve this proper differentiation of roles was, he felt, the medieval betrayal of the Gelasian thesis, a betrayal that was to have ominous consequences.

> The dynamism native to the Gelasian Thesis should have led to a progressive differentiation of the two orders of human life—the sacred and the secular. It should have led to a fuller realization of the transcendence of the Church and to a commission of the whole secular cultural enterprise to lay hands. This differentiation would have accrued to the native good of the Church herself . . . and it would have afforded the opportunity for a more powerful irradiation of the whole temporal order. . . . As a matter of fact, this differentiation of the two orders has been left to very recent times and when it did come about it came about in the form of a tragic rupture. . . .[44]

The Middle Ages, Murray argued, had witnessed great progress in the establishment of a proper relationship between the spiritual and temporal powers in society; but its failure to go further laid the groundwork for the distortion of the power of the state which began in the sixteenth century and led to the Third Reich.

The Origins of Secularism

Even if Murray's analysis of the importance of the Gelasian thesis and its institutionalization into the Western political tradition during the Middle Ages was correct, he had still not answered the question which he had set out to address: How had secularism skewed the Western tradition? In Murray's theory of the rise of royal absolutism during the sixteenth century, he provided the beginnings of an answer.

> This corruption (of the Western political heritage) did not begin with "the principles of '89" or even with the Reformation. It began with the beginnings of that state absolutism which became the distinctive mark of the *ancien regime*, setting it off sharply from medieval polity, whether imperial, royal, or municipal.[45]

The absolutist monarchies of Philip II in Spain and Louis XIV in France purposely destroyed the power of the mediating structures in society precisely in order to submit all spheres of societal life to the political. The "strains and stresses" of the medieval period, in which the countervailing powers of the nobility, the monarchy, the Church, the guilds and the towns had prevented any supreme accumulation of power, were replaced by a pyramidal structure in which the authority of the monarch recognized no boundaries. Murray maintained that

> . . . the most fateful, corrupting consequence of absolutism was the development of the notion of sovereignty as one, indivisible, and omnicompetent. Absolutism enthroned the unchristian principle of the primacy of the political, the supremacy of the *raison d'Etat*. It led to the irrational idea of law as simply the command of the sovereign. It destroyed the Christian concept of an organic society whose several orders and institutions have their own autonomy and freedom. It cancelled out all distinction between state and society.[46]

In the rise of absolutism, the medieval principle of consent of the governed fell into disuse as the feudal legislative bodies were either ignored or suppressed. The right of the people to resist the unjust use of royal authority was buried under the military might of the crown. In Murray's view, "the medieval *homo liber et legalis,* who had an intelligible charter of freedoms . . . was turned into a passive unit who got lost in an undifferentiated mass of 'subjects.'"[47]

As a result of these changes, Murray said, the nation-state became the one all-embracing and omnicompetent form of human association. The *res sacrae* continued to exist, but their sacred and inviolable character was lost sight of as political authority claimed the right to adjudicate every form of human association. The Church, which had been a bulwark against the over-weaning claims of the state, now became domesticated by monarchs who cleverly used a combination of patriotism and force to insure that the national hierarchies placed their political allegiance before their fealty to Rome. Thus religion, instead of protecting the *res sacrae,* more often became a source of legitimation for the ever-extending power of the monarchies, a power which was seen as a divine right.

It was for all these reasons that Murray pointed to the rise of absolutism as the origin of modern totalitarianism. With absolutism society became the particular nation-state instead of the Great Society of Christendom. With absolutism the feudal rights which had taken centuries to build up were swept away, leaving only the unlimited power of the crown. And with absolutism the Church, divided by Reformation and nationalisms, became the ally of the state rather than its watchdog.

If the rise of absolutism signaled for Murray the institutionalization of the unified sovereignty of the political sphere over all forms of human association, it was the French Revolution which made that sovereignty demonic by linking it to a secularist philosophy of society. In the medieval period, the state had been seen as being incorporated into the spiritual purposes of society; both Church and state were engaged in the common *res publica* of serving the temporal and eternal welfare of the human person. Even during the absolutist period, although the state achieved an institutional power which exceeded its proper bounds, the ruling theory of society still held that the role of the state was based upon a transcendent referent, namely, the power and authority of God. But in the French Revolution, Western civilization was wrenched from its spiritual foundations, as the state came to be seen as the ultimate referent in society with an all-encompassing messianic significance.

For Murray, the Revolutionaries proclaimed an entirely new creed which contradicted the fundamental tenets of Christianity and which altered the entire course of Western history:

> This new secular faith proclaimed a new revelation with regard to the nature and destiny of man. It said that man's destiny was simply political, to be fulfilled within the earthly city; it said that the state is to be the author of whatever salvation man may hope for, and the means of salvation were really altogether simple. The sovereign people would save themselves and would erect the kingdom of God on earth. . . .[48]

This secularist ideology took the form of a religious faith as exclusive, as universal in its claims, and as fervently held as any creed which the world had ever known. Its high priests were Rousseau, Robespierre and St. Just, and its Inquisition was the roar of the crowd and the fall of the guillotine. It powered the Revolution but did not end with the rise of Napoleon; instead it filtered into the political tradition of the West and set the stage for the totalitarianism of the modern age.

The essence of this creed, according to Murray, was the new picture of human society which it presented. While the Christian era had previously been characterized by the assertion that men and women are part of a created order in which God is the Absolute, the philosophy of the Revolution made human society the Absolute and center of creation. Quoting Geoffrey Brunn, Murray said:

> For the first time in modern annals the *civitas humana* was set forth unequivocally as the ultimate reality in the place of the *civitas dei*. For the first time the authority of reason was unblushingly acknowledged as superior to the authority of revelation, and the doctrine of human perfectibility (shortly to be reformulated as the doctrine of progress) was substituted for the doctrine of miraculous redemption.[49]

The magnitude of this redemption was not in doubt to the leaders of the Revolution. For the doctrines of Rousseau had taught them that men and women had only to return to the "natural order" in order to find a social bliss that had been destroyed by organized society.

> The expectation of the advent on earth in full social fact of "the natural order" was truly messianic. And the main supports of this messianism were the belief in the natural goodness and rationality of man and the consequent belief in the omnipotence of education, especially as accomplished by legislation: Helvetius, Holbach, Mably, the Physiocrats and others, in the same way as Rousseau himself, believed that man was nothing but the product of the laws of the State, and that

there was nothing that a government was incapable of doing in the art of forming men.[50]

This abiding faith in the rationality and perfectibility of the human person, combined with the conception of the state as the vehicle for the achievement of citizens' ultimate destiny firmly placed the Revolutionary creed outside the Christian tradition of politics. It led to the formation of a society in which all centers of power that were rival to the government would be suppressed, and it set the stage for a confrontation between Church and state which was begun in 1789 but extended well into the twentieth century.

The Revolutionary Republic was quick to realize that the Church represented its strongest adversary in French society. The political power which the Church had wielded under the constitution of the *ancien regime* was of course significant, but that power could be neutralized just as the power of the nobility and the king had been vanquished. The real threat that the Church presented to the Revolution was, in Murray's view, much more formidable than this. It consisted primarily in two assertions of authority by the Church. The first was that "by proclaiming a religious ethic founded on the sovereignty of God, heterogeneous to the naturalist ethic founded on the sovereignty of reason, the Church presumed to deny the totality of the claims of the state upon the individual."[51] The second was the Church's claim to be independent from the control of the state, a claim which sharply challenged the state monism of Robespierre.

> . . . the Church presumed to demand the right to exist as a sociological entity and a spiritual sovereignty within the state, but independent of the state and indeed superior to it. It presumed at once to be a structural element of human society and an element altogether heterogeneous to the political order. As such, it again violated the basic totalitarian principle of social unity. It refused to be subsumed under the one general will; it represented a "partial interest" destructive of the unity of the one general interest. . . . This was the line taken by Rousseau: "You cannot be a citizen and Christian at the same time, for the loyalties clash. . . ." As a faith and as a

society, the Church was not "of the nation;" it was alien to the *republique une et indivisible*. Consequently, it was the enemy.[52]

The Church *was* the enemy of the Revolution precisely because it challenged the monistic theory of society which underlay the Revolution. By continuing its historic role of defining and protecting the *res sacrae* of society from the power of the government, the Church contradicted the New Republic's belief that the only *res sacra* was the state and that the only authority which must be obeyed was the will of the people.

If Murray saw in the French Revolution an ominous turning point in the history of Western civilization, he also saw it as a historical development which had made several positive contributions to the modern political tradition. The Revolution of 1789 effectively ended the order of political privilege symbolized by the divine right of kings, and it established the principle that sovereignty is from the people. In addition, the Revolution created new structures of popular consent that allowed the participation of the people in their own governance, structures which for all their defects did firmly place the concept of participatory democracy in the European political tradition.[53] Murray's evaluation of the Revolution was generally a critical one, but it was far from being blind to the democratic advances which the fall of the *ancien regime* had produced.

The same could be said of Murray's evaluation of nineteenth century liberalism, a movement that he viewed as a further significant step in the formation of the spiritual crisis of the twentieth century. The liberal movement had been responsible for establishing protection for human rights and introducing democratic reforms into many of the nations of Europe. Yet liberalism concurred with the *philosophes* in denying religion a meaningful role in defining the nature of the state. "The State, said the Liberals, is not subject to an order of justice, established by the law of God and containing certain imprescriptible human rights; on the contrary, the state itself establishes the order of justice."[54] This was the amoral state, rational and limited in its powers, bearing not the messianic significance of the Revolutionary French Republic, but rather the studied neutrality appropriate to a Darwinian age. This was the scientific state, which recognized not the spiritual claims of the *res sacrae*, but rather the "rational" claims of *laissez faire* economics and the scientific method.

Murray argued that the supposed neutrality of the nineteenth century liberal state masked a secularist agenda which sought to displace the traditional role of Christianity in Western society:

> (Liberalism) sought to effect, through the control and use of governmental power, the politico-social change known as "the separation of Church and state." This current phrase was pregnant both as an ideology and as a political and social program. It meant, first, the alteration of the Christian structure of politics, which had been characterized by the traditional duality of Church and state, in the direction of a juridical and social monism. It meant, secondly, the evacuation of the Christian substance of society through the establishment of a surrogate political religion which went by the name of "laicism."[55]

Christianity would be attacked directly on rational and scientific premises which undercut the authority of revelation and the notion of transcendence itself. For those whom this direct attack upon religion failed to convince, religion could be retained, but only as a private faith. It was to have no public role in society.[56]

It was this secularizing tendency of nineteenth century liberalism which generated the Church's antagonism toward the liberal movement, according to Murray. Pope Leo XIII recognized that the "neutral state," if left unchallenged, would evacuate the spiritual substance of society by undermining the *res sacrae*. Thus the relationships of husband and wife, parent and child, employer and employee, would still exist, but would lose their sacred character and their immunity from the power of the state. The parent-child relationship would be vitiated by the state's demand that all children be educated in secular curricula; thus if the state could not end the power of religion in the lives of the present generation, it could certainly promote a religiously sterile population for the next generation. The employer-employee relationship was to be seen, not as a sacred relationship bound by the principles of justice, but merely an exchange of the factors of production. The Church was to be seen, not as the divinely instituted bulwark of transcendent dignity, but merely as a voluntary association which lay completely within the jurisdiction of the temporal realm. For all of these reasons, Murray believed, Leo XIII fought continental liberalism in the nineteenth century, and although he recognized that the Church had made serious mistakes in its attack upon the liberal movement, Murray firmly held that the Church's reasons for challenging liberalism were both valid and prophetic.[57]

In light of this analysis, Murray believed that the defects of continental liberalism outweighed its merits. The liberal movement had indeed succeeded at times in its efforts to implement democratic reforms and to establish the legitimacy of the human rights to free speech, free association, and freedom of the press. But these rights were established on the shaky ground of a nominalist epistemology which did not acknowledge the transcendent order that could be the only durable ground for human rights and democratic processes.[58] Moreover, liberalism had loosened the ties between ethics and societal life by denying the sacredness of human relationships. Speaking from the vantage point of the twentieth century, Murray wrote,

> . . . all men living today have inherited the temporal order which liberalism, and all the reactions it inspired, managed to create; and all men view, as part of their heritage, the massive fact of a tremendous social apostasy—the escape of national and international life from the control of moral standards.[59]

The consequences of this apostasy would be realized only in the totalitarian state which liberalism's secular ideology would produce.

The Twentieth Century: Church and Society Confront "Modernity"

John Courtney Murray's efforts to reconstruct the historical role of religion in Western society had been generated by his concern with the secular crisis of the twentieth century. In the Gelasian thesis, he had found the principle which erected a powerful dualistic dynamic in society, with the political sphere being limited in scope by the Church's proclamation of the sacredness of the human person. In the medieval period, Murray had seen the

greatest institutionalization of the Gelasian thesis, an institutionalization that clearly differentiated between state and society. Yet
with the rise of absolutism, this distinction was replaced by a unified sovereignty of the state, and through the French Revolution
and the spread of liberalism, the sovereignty of the state became
avowedly anti-religious. Now Murray confronted his own age, and
he saw a bridge between the Western political heritage and the
twentieth century in the concept of modernity.

Murray saw "modernity" as the effort in Western civilization
to find a secular substitute for the historical role which religion
had played in society. Where Christianity had sought to protect
the rights of the human person by pointing to his transcendent
dignity, "modernity" sought to protect those rights through
political institutions. Where Christianity had seen itself as the
mediating principle between society and the state, "modernity"
saw only the individual conscience of the citizen, alone and
unaided:

> Modernity has maintained that (the *res sacrae*) are now to be
> known to be simply immanent in man; that man has become
> conscious of them in their mergence in historical experience;
> that, whatever may have been the influence of the Christian
> revelation on the earlier phases of this experience, these val-
> ues are now simply a human possession, a conquest and an
> achievement of humanity by man himself. Now that I have
> arrived, said modernity, Christianity may disappear. Whatever
> aesthetic appeal it may still retain as a myth, it is not needed
> as a dynamic of freedom and justice in this world. *Res sacra
> homo* is now under a new patronage, singly his own.[60]

Thus the Church's traditional role of using its institutional power
to limit encroachments by the state and of mobilizing the moral
consensus of the people was to be no more. The political institutions designed by modern societies would be a more than adequate substitute.[61]

Murray believed that the fallacy of this modern creed had
become evident in the rise of the Nazi state. For he saw Nazism
not as an aberration in the Western political tradition, but a consequence of the secularization of society which had begun in the
sixteenth century and had triumphed at the end of the nineteenth

century. The monistic tendency of the state, which had been can-
onized by the *philosophes,* had reached its apex in Hitler's brutal
dictatorship, where the sacred character of the human person lay
devastated in the ovens of Auschwitz and Buchenwald. The democratic political institutions which had been "modernity's" substitute for the Transcendent Order of Values were shown to be
unable to protect the dignity of the human person. And the individual conscience of the citizen, having scorned the authority of
religion in forming a moral consensus in society, lay impotent
before the allure of blind nationalism and the force of the storm-
troopers. Here at last was the answer to the question that had
driven D'Entreves and Talmon and Sturzo: the totalitarianism of
the twentieth century was the logical outgrowth of the effort to
remove the public role of religion in society.[62]

But if Nazism represented a particularly barbaric outgrowth
of modernity, Murray contended that it was communism that
constituted the most ominous threat posed by "modernity" in the
twentieth century.

> Communism is, of course, political modernity carried to its
> logical conclusion. All that is implicit and unintentional in
> modernity as a phenomenon in what is called the West has
> become explicit and deliberate in the Communist system. . . .
> The operations of the Communist system would seem to offer
> an empirical demonstration of the fact that there can be no
> freedom or justice where God is denied and where everything
> meant by the freedom of the Church is deliberately excised
> from the theorem on which the life of the community is
> based.[63]

By the time Murray formulated his theory of "modernity," Nazism had been defeated and the cold war had begun. The utter
incompatibility of Stalinist communism with a vital public role for
religion led Murray to conclude that the great battle between
"modernity" and the transcendent dignity of the human person
was being fought between Russia and the West, and it was not
clear that the West would be victorious. "Here is the new
Enemy," wrote Murray, "in whose shadow all other dangers
pale."[64]

Murray's doubts about the outcome of this battle did not rest upon an assessment of the relative strengths of the military machines of the Soviet Union and the United States, but upon the infiltration of the principles of "modernity" into the social and political life of the West. The locus of this infiltration was what Murray called "the democratic *mystique*," the proposition that "all issues of human life—intellectual, religious, and moral issues as well as formally political issues—are to be regarded as, or resolved into, political issues and are to be settled by majority vote."[65] It was this "democratic mystique," when combined with the tendencies toward state monism and secularism which had been introduced into the Western political tradition since the sixteenth century, that threatened to undermine the moral fiber of the West by creating a spiritual vacuum at the core of society.

> The inspiration of (this) democratic monism is partly a sentimentalist mystique—the belief that the power in the people, in distinction from all other powers, is somehow ultimately and inevitably beneficent in its exercise. But the more radical inspiration is the idea, unknown to modern times, which modern rationalism thrust into political history. Christianity has always regarded the state as a limited order of action for limited purposes, to be chosen and pursued under the direction and correction of the organized moral conscience of society, whose judgments are formed and mobilized by the Church, an independent and autonomous community qualified to be the interpreter of man's nature and destiny. It has been the specific of modernity to regard the state as a moral end in itself, a self-justifying entity with its own self-determined spiritual substance. The state itself creates the ethos of society, embodies it, imparts it to its citizens, and sanctions its observance with rewards and punishments.[66]

By challenging the validity of the Transcendental Order of Values established by God, the "democratic mystique" was eating away at the only secure foundation which the West had for its resistance to communism: the sacredness of the human person.

In Murray's view, the history of Western civilization demonstrated that without a substantive public role for religion in society, a nation cannot thrive morally; without a public consensus about the ultimate transcendent purposes and values of human life, a true society cannot be erected at all:

> Can a political society do without a public religion? So far, the historical evidence would seem to argue for a negative answer. It has been pointed out that the chief phenomenon of modern times has been the development of secular civil religions. We know about the political faith of Jacobin democracy; we know about the racist faith of German National Socialism; we know more about the materialistic faith of Russian communism; and we know something, or are beginning to know something, about the more idealist faith in democracy as man's way of life and salvation. . . . (These examples teach that) a political society is normally incomplete without some spiritual bond of unity. Society—secular society—must have some spiritual substance that underlies the order of law, the order of public morality and all other orders and processes within society. And if there is no such spiritual substance to society, then society is founded on a vacuum; and society, like nature itself, abhors a vacuum and cannot tolerate it.[67]

The way to avoid such a vacuum in the twentieth century was to respiritualize the whole social order, bringing the insights of religious faith not only to political society, but to all manner of social relationships and institutions. Only such a renewal of the *res sacrae* could reverse the secular drift which had enveloped Western society in the era of "modernity."[68]

In arguing that the history of the West demonstrated the need for a respiritualization of society, Murray fully recognized that this could not mean a return to the Middle Ages, or to a society in which the Church had a direct role in controlling the actions of the state. This had been the great defect of the medieval period, which had been corrected by the rise of absolutism, the Enlightenment, and liberalism. Murray argued that in the modern era the Church must respect the legitimate autonomy of the secular sphere, for in doing so it would be safeguarding two freedoms essential to the *res sacrae* of the human person:

> The first is her own spiritual freedom, which demands that she should not be compromised in her essential mission by

engagement in the inevitable uncertainties that attend every directly political and economic manoeuvre. The second is the freedom of the secular order itself and of its controlling agencies—notably the State—a freedom which is based on the distinction between the spiritual and the temporal, and on the sovereignty and autonomy in its own order that the temporal, now evolved to full self-consciousness, can legitimately claim.[69]

It was these two freedoms which the ultramontane Church had ignored in its fight against the secularizing tendencies of liberalism, and it was these two freedoms which Murray sought to restore to the Church's doctrinal tradition through his path-breaking work on religious liberty.

But Murray's agenda was larger than this. It was not merely to reform the doctrine of the Church, but also to reform the structure of society. And to accomplish this, the autonomy of temporal and spiritual spheres would have to be maintained while the respiritualization of the temporal order was accomplished:

A work of differentiation between the sacral and the secular has indeed been effected in history. But differentiation is not the highest stage in human growth. The movement toward it, now that it has come to term, must be followed by a further movement toward a new synthesis, within which the differentiation will at once subsist, integral and unconfused, and also be transcended in a higher unity.[70]

As Murray looked out into America at mid-century, he saw a formidable array of fundamental problems. "The problems are endless," he wrote in 1950, "and every one of them is basically a spiritual and moral problem, and no one of them can be solved except by the whole American people."[71] The American people had the spiritual heritage with which to address these fundamental problems, but there was need for that heritage to be revitalized, to be restored to its roots. In Murray's view, it would fall to believing men and women to ignite that revitalization, to bring America back to the true ideals of the Western political and social tradition:

If you do not take into your hands that task, I do not know into whose hands it will fall. Or, rather, I do know. It will fall into the hands of a group, motley enough in its complexion, but whose members have at least this in common: that they are of today, wholly of today, with no roots in humanity's Christian past and no sense of continuity with it; nor gratitude for its cultural heritage; men and women whom Bertrand Russell described as "ignorant of the past, without tenderness for what is traditional, without understanding of what they are destroying." And, I may add myself, with little concept of what they are trying to build.[72]

This was the fundamental issue of the twentieth century: the decision as to whether the West would follow the path of secularism or return to its spiritual roots. This was the task for the believer of the modern age.

2

RECLAIMING
THE CULTURAL ORDER

John Courtney Murray firmly believed that the most important focus for the fight against secularism lay not in the political realm, but in the order of culture. Just as society was a far broader concept than the state, so too the order of culture was for Murray a far broader concept than the order of politics. Culture, in Murray's mind, was the formative principle of society. It distinguished a true human community from a formless mass of people. It represented the heritage of ideas, customs, and traditions that marked one society from another:

> The masses are amorphous; their principle of direction is external to themselves. A people is a structured moral community, fashioned by a consciously shared consensus; it is capable—both as a collectivity and in its individual members—of protecting its own moral identity and directing its own social life.[1]

It was the formation of this consciously shared consensus that Murray labeled "the cultural enterprise." The consensus would differ in form from society to society, but the primary objective of the cultural enterprise would always be the same: the protection of the moral bases of the community and the conservation and development of the human heritage.[2]

Precisely because the cultural enterprise sought to establish a *moral* consensus, Murray believed that it represented a spiritual reality:

> Culture is essentially a spiritual thing, for its home is in a soul.
> It is to the life of an individual or a nation what the soul is to
> the body: a "form" that animates, organizes, humanizes what
> otherwise would be brute matter, inert disorganized. Culture,
> then, means man's effort to be fully human, and hence his
> effort to bring spiritual order and spiritual purpose into his
> life.[3]

It was just this effort to bring spiritual order and spiritual purpose into the social life of America that Murray believed was at
risk in the twentieth century.

Murray believed that the cultural enterprise in the United
States had historically been a uniquely successful one. In large
part this was a result of the American dedication to the principle
of freedom in society. "Our American idea," wrote Murray,
"puts the creative forces of value and all the creative forces of
the spirit not in the state or the government, but in society, which
is distinct from both."[4] The culture which had been generated
from this atmosphere of freedom was one of pluralism that
allowed the citizens of the United States to follow diverse religious, ethnic, and intellectual traditions. Yet it was also a culture
which stressed the need for the development of common virtues
in society, the virtues of service, civility, justice, and tolerance.[5]
At the core of these common virtues lay a belief in the existence
of God and of a divinely-created order of values which men and
women sought to realize in all facets of their life, both personal
and societal.

But, Murray argued, this cultural accomplishment was in
jeopardy in the post-war era, for the twentieth century had witnessed the disappearance of the concept of public morality in
America. "There are no organized social habits based on moral
ideas," he wrote in 1952, "and as a result the bonds which tie
American society together are being destroyed, only to be
replaced by a counterfeit and surface humanitarianism."[6] At the
base of this disappearance of public morality lay a profound confusion about the order of truth itself:

> . . . today in America there is really no such thing as a genuine
> intellectual community. . . . In other words, our culture does
> not rest upon any genuine and commonly accepted order of

truth. There is no spiritual community based on commonly shared religious truth. And even the old humanist "republic of letters" in which there was a certain principle of cohesion, has pretty well perished. And nothing has taken its place. Our culture is heterogeneous to the point of being chaotic, and 'truth' is what every man individually thinks it is.[7]

Such an intellectual chaos posed a grave threat to the order of culture in American society, for if culture truly represented "man's effort to bring spiritual order and spiritual purpose into his social life," then that order must be founded upon certain commonly accepted principles of truth. As the twentieth century progressed, Murray became more and more skeptical about the ability of American society to reach agreement on any substantial principles of truth. And in the absence of such an agreement, the cultural achievement of the United States could not possibly endure.

Faced with this dilemma, Murray turned to the religious communities of the United States in search of leadership for the campaign to restore America to its cultural roots.[8] Murray believed that as the era of "modernity" was drawing to a close, the people of the U.S. would be making fundamental choices about the future of society. New, secular alternatives were being proposed as the fundamental ordering principles of American society, and unless the nation's religious communities took the lead in defending the existence of the *res sacrae* in society, America might lose the balance between freedom and order, between justice and liberty, which had characterized the American cultural experiment. Speaking to a group of Catholic lay leaders about the religious concept of culture, Murray made clear his view of their responsibilities in this crisis of "modernity":

My desire is to present you not merely with a thesis, but with a task. . . . It is not enough to have grasped the idea of a Christian culture; that idea must be given shape in the world of human life. And it is for you to give it shape: on that point I must insist. The most superficial observer of the American scene cannot fail to recognize that our greatest need today is the need for cultural leadership. Without it, political leadership or economic leadership of the most inspired kind would

avail us little, even if we could find them; of what use is a
prophet, if the ears of the people are dull, and their souls
dead?[9]

The message was clear. The religious communities of the nation
must be the architects of a cultural revival in the U.S., and the
culture which they were to produce must be spiritual in orientation and American in form.

THE SEARCH FOR CONSENSUS IN AMERICAN SOCIETY

The effort to produce a cultural revival in the United States
was necessary, according to Murray, because the two traditional
formative principles of American society were no longer able to
carry out the unifying function that they had fulfilled in the first
one hundred and fifty years of American national life. The first
of these principles had been the republican tradition of virtue, a
worldview that was particularly strong at the time of the writing
of the Constitution. The founders of the United States saw themselves as the intellectual descendants of Cicero, Scipio, and the
Gracci, and many of the social institutions designed at the time
of the American Revolution owed their origin to the Roman
Republic. This republican ethos continued to be strong long after
the passing of the revolutionary generation, and the heritage of
integrity, public service, civic unity and social dialogue that represented the best of the republican tradition had contributed
greatly to America's self-understanding. But the republican heritage seemed strange and anachronistic in the modern age; its
exhortations to self-sacrifice and civic unity seemed out of place
in an era of material plenty and cultural diversity, and as a result
Murray believed that it could no longer serve as a cementing and
guiding force in American society.[10] The second traditional formative principle of culture in the United States had been the Calvinist morality which dated from the colonial era. America had
historically been a Protestant nation, and the form of Protestantism that had been dominant in the formation of America's
self-understanding was the high Calvinist theology that influenced almost every strain of American religious thought. Calvin-

ist morality was scriptural in foundation and voluntaristic in style; its command to believers to follow the will of God in their lives produced a strong sense of social virtue and self-sacrifice in the United States. But now, Murray believed, that morality was losing its hold on the American psyche and its power to act as a formative principle for American culture; the tradition of Calvin and Jonathan Edwards, with its rigid morality of intention, was seen as too simplistic to cope with the escalating complexity of industrial society.[11]

Thus the two cultural strains which had been dominant in the development of American society had been weakened by the spirit of modernity and by the transformation of the United States from an agricultural to an industrialized nation. Neither one could effectively serve as a key to the ongoing growth of American culture in the post-war era. But such a key had to be found if the cultural enterprise was to continue in American society, if the United States was to remain truly a free and moral people and not merely a mass of individuals occupying the same geographical territory:

> What is at stake is America's understanding of itself. Self-understanding is the necessary condition of a sense of self-identity and self-confidence, whether in the case of an individual or in the case of a people. (The American people must) find other, more reasoned grounds for their essential affirmation that they are uniquely a people, uniquely a free society.
> Otherwise the peril is great. The complete loss of one's identity is, with all the propriety of theological definition, hell. In diminished forms it is insanity. And it would not be well for the American giant to go lumbering about the world today, lost and mad.[12]

America was faced with the real danger of losing its moral identity, its national self-understanding. That is why Murray believed the cultural enterprise in the United States had reached a critical juncture. It was not that there were no alternatives to the traditions of republican virtue and Calvinist morality which had previously mediated America's self-understanding; there were in fact several cultural principles which Murray pointed to in his various writings as contenders for the soul of American society. But Murray believed that most of these competing cultural principles were secularist both in tone and in substance, and that they were incapable of defending the *res sacrae* in the twentieth century. Murray's writings on the cultural crisis were an effort to convince the American people that they must choose a new formative principle for their culture, and that that principle must acknowledge and enhance the transcendent dignity of the human person.

Technological Secularism

In order to accomplish this task, Murray undertook to examine each of the secular principles of culture that seemed likely to dominate American society in the post-war era, and then to show how each would, far from protecting the dignity of the human person, lead in the end only to dehumanization, emptiness and despair.

None of these formative cultural principles seemed more alarming to Murray than the technological principle, the idea that "the hope of society depends upon the extension of the habits of the scientific intelligence to every stratum of communal life and every form of social organization."[13] The republican tradition of virtue and the Calvinist ethical heritage had become outmoded because they were unable to grapple with the overwhelming complexities of life in the modern age: international economic penetration, the worldwide revolution in knowledge, and the advent of the psychological and sociological sciences. In contrast, the technological principle of culture seemed ideally fitted to an age where the accomplishments of scientific method had produced the ability to cure those afflicted with incurable diseases, the capacity to produce abundant surpluses of food, and profound new insights into the nature and composition of the human person. The claims of the technological principle were simple, according to Murray. They said that "ours is an industrial and technological society . . . such problems as confront us were created by technology, and they are to be solved by technology, either by more technology or less."[14] Thus the basic task of the cultural enterprise in America consisted of finding the best scientific and managerial minds in the United States and placing them in charge of education, resource allocation, and social development. Value formation was to be replaced by social engineering, and the "objective" standards of science would decide all important societal questions.

Murray was scathing in his critique of the technological principle in American society, both because he believed that it was subtly gaining ground in the culture of the United States and because he believed that it contradicted the very meaning of the word culture in its denial of the deepest values of civilization:

> What is our contemporary idiocy? What is the enemy within the city? If I had to give it a name, I think I would call it "technological secularism." The idiot today is the technological secularist who knows everything. He's the man who knows everything about the organization of all the instruments and techniques of power that are available in the contemporary world and who, at the same time, understands nothing about the nature of man or about the nature of true civilization.
>
> And if this country is to be overthrown from within or from without, I would suggest that it will not be overthrown by communism. It will be overthrown because it will have made an impossible experiment. It will have undertaken to establish a technological order of most marvelous intricacy, which will have been constructed and will operate without relation to true political ends; and this technological order will hang, as it were, suspended over a spiritual vacuum. This would be the real danger, resulting from a type of fallacious, fictitious, fragile unity that could be created among us.[15]

The cultural enterprise was for Murray essentially a spiritual endeavor. And the greatest fallacy of technological secularism was precisely that it excluded the spiritual realities of the human person from consideration.

In part this exclusion resulted from the epistemology inherent in the utilization of the scientific method as the sole criterion of truth. Such an epistemology proclaimed that "the highest form of human rationality is displayed in the methods of science, the life of reason is par excellence the life of the scientific intelligence."[16] This approach to reason denied the intellectual content not only of religious experience, but of all metaphysics, and it represented to Murray the decadence of the notion of intelligence in the modern world.

> The consequences of succumbing to the scientific temptation—whose power I freely acknowledge—have been many and grave. I am here concerned only with one of them—perhaps the most basic one, and the one that frightens men most. I mean the devaluation of the intellect, what has been called the "tragic disdain of the intellect." Science has created for our age such an illusion of knowledge that in a strange paradoxical fashion man has lost contact with the fundamental thing in him that knows, and that knows fundamentals. He has come to suffer from an hypertrophy of one part of his reason—the part that deals with the physical, the temporal, the historical, the relative.[17]

Murray believed that this hypertrophy had produced a schism in the soul of Western civilization.[18] On one side of this schism lay "scientific truth," all of the knowledge which had been accumulated through the use of the scientific method. On the other side lay the humanistic tradition of the West, the most profound insights into the nature of the human person and God's plan for the universe, insights which were now suspect in their authenticity because they could not be validated by science.[19]

The consequences of this schism were already becoming apparent in American society. The great artifice which science had created, unmediated and unrestrained by the traditional spiritual values of Western civilization, had become a Frankenstein which was crushing the sacredness of the human person rather than serving it:

> Was man not apprenticed in all the arts of Promethean sorcery, able to release the forces of scientific technology, able to create by them a new civilization, able to make this industrial civilization subserve the welfare of humanity? But now he sees his own creation seemingly emancipated from him, as he once emancipated himself from his own Creator. This creature, this creature of man's own mind and body and brain, our scientific industrial and technological civilization seems to have acquired an autonomous life of its own. It has

its own laws and its own logic. It seems not to care greatly for human welfare. It seems not to be amenable to the requirements of the deepest feelings in the spirit of man.[20]

In the spheres of economics, medicine, weapons development, and social organization, modern society was indeed faced with a technological civilization which seemed not to care greatly for human welfare. For the technological principle did not take into account the most profound dimension of the human person: the transcendence which made him not merely another part of the technological civilization, but its end and controlling principle. Looking forward to the coming century, Murray observed:

> The question is "What will be the human experience characteristic of the Post-Modern Age?" It's hard to say. But if the experience of man in the present moment is any sure indication, I venture to say that the experience of the Post-Modern Age will be something like this: man will have an experience of great impersonal forces that he has not quite got control of, and that this experience will be that of somehow feeling that the whole course of human events is not only uncertain, but that man's hold upon the course of events is extremely precarious.[21]

The legacy of technological secularism was already becoming apparent in American society; it led not to the panacea of human welfare which it promised, but to a world emptied of human values and to a sense of enslavement.[22] For this reason, Murray argued, the people of the United States must reject it as a formative cultural principle and search for another.

Practical Materialism

But if technological secularism in its naked form was already revealing itself to be demonic as a formative principle of culture, Murray believed that the people of the United States might yet succumb to the allure of a related cultural principle that was less doctrinaire, but no less dangerous—the philosophy of practical materialism that had always been present in American life but was becoming more powerful as the wealth of the nation increased. Murray was an ardent defender of the free enterprise system, and he believed that one of the great cultural accomplishments of the United States had been the establishment of relative freedom in the economic sphere. From this freedom had come a standard of living that was the envy of the world, but from it had also come an alarming preoccupation with economic competition and the accumulation of wealth.

It was not that either economic competition or the accumulation of wealth was evil; on the contrary, Murray believed that both contributed to the well-being of humanity. But in the United States the pursuit of material goods had become intermeshed with a philosophy which asserted that material goods represented the highest attainment of human endeavor, that the accumulation of wealth would bring to the individual and to society a happiness greater than had ever been known before:

> (American practical materialism) has had, in fact, one dominating ideal: the conquest of the material world. . . . It has made one promise: a more abundant life for the ordinary man and woman, the abundance being ultimately in physical comfort. It has had one technique of social progress: the exploitation, for all they were worth in cold hard cash, of the resources of land and forest and stream, and of the mechanical inventiveness of its citizens. It has recognized one supreme law: supply and demand. It has had one standard of value: the quantitative, that judges that best which is biggest. It has aimed at one order: the economic. It confers one accolade on those who serve it: wealth. It knows one evil: poverty. . . . It turns out one typical product: the *homo economicus,* the businessman in the business suit, whose dreams of paradise are of a land in which there is no red ink.[23]

Materialism as it existed in the United States did not have the ideological fervor of its Marxist counterpart, nor did it have the intellectual power and coherence of technological secularism. But it did have the potential to lure American culture away from the development of the personal and spiritual dignity of the human person and toward a one-dimensional scale of values that in practice registered only economic criteria.

In large part, Murray laid the blame for the prevalence of materialism in American culture at the door of business, especially big business. Speaking to a Harvard audience in 1952, he said, "Business is the greatest single secularizing force in the United States. It is organized materialism. Organized in a struggle for power."[24] The struggle which the leaders of big business saw themselves involved in was the struggle for profits. The struggle which Murray saw them involved in was the struggle for the cultural heart of American society: Would the American people trade in their religious and social heritage for a new car every year?

The consequences of the triumph of materialism in America would be twofold in Murray's view. The first consequence would be the destruction of the dignity of the human person; men and women would be treated either as factors of production or as potential consumers. The most fundamental aspects of civilization—education, the arts, intellectual attainment and moral uprightness—would be seen as unrelated to the material progress of society and thus as unimportant in the priorities of the nation. The equal dignity of all persons would be lost sight of as personal net worth became the most important determinant of interpersonal relations. In short, America would become "a body without a soul . . . that is literally without a spiritual principle to animate its program of economic and material organization."[25] The second consequence of the triumph of materialism in American culture was just as ominous, and became clear to Murray at the beginning of the Korean War. Murray believed that Korea represented not merely a war with a communist country, but one facet of an ongoing war with communism itself. And in that war of ideologies, the flaccid materialism of the U.S. would stand no chance against the dynamic ideology of Marxism:

> We are engaged in a spiritual, political, and military conflict with a materialism. But it is a materialism that is offered as a total explanation of life, a complete guide to human conduct, and the adequate dynamic of human history. It is a materialism that has been raised to the status of an idea of the dignity of a religion. And as Miss Barbara Ward has well said: "In a conflict between religious materialism and practical materialism, it seems certain that the religious variety will have the strength to prevail. An idea has never yet in human history

been defeated by no idea at all." American practical materialism has no status as an idea. It has no dignity. It has not the
strength to prevail.[26]

Practical materialism could not serve as an adequate formative
principle for American culture because it was not a principle at
all. It was merely an accommodation to the American preoccupation with the accumulation of wealth. As such it could neither
build a real culture nor provide a bulwark against the ideological
power of communist materialism. Those who thought otherwise
were merely deluded.

Philosophical Pluralism

Having located the fallacies inherent in technological secularism and practical materialism, Murray still faced a third formative principle of culture in the credo of modern pluralism.
This was perhaps the most formidable secular force in the cultural arena, for it appealed to the strong American prejudice in
favor of pluralism and tolerance. Indeed, it was the philosophical
embodiment of the ethnic, religious, economic and intellectual
pluralism that was the hallmark of American society and that
Murray himself celebrated as a great national treasure of the people of the United States.

But if Murray accepted pluralism as a sociological reality, he
did not accept it as a philosophical proposition. For pluralism in
the order of truth meant sacrificing either the belief that there
really was an objective order of truth or the belief that it was possible to attain some access to that order in this world. Murray was
willing to dispense with neither:

> Our current American pluralism has its own quality. Basically,
> I should say that it is related to the kind of Ultimate Questions
> that have become the typical concern of modernity as such.
> All of them are related to the central question, what is man?
> Thence they proliferate. . . .
>   All these questions, and others related to them, concern the
> essentials of human existence. The multiplicity of answers to
> them, and of the ways of refusing them, is in general what we
> mean by modern pluralism. Integral to the pluralism is the

agnostic view that it is useless or illegitimate even to ask questions that are Ultimate.[27]

Murray would have none of this American agnosticism. For it was the very essence of the cultural enterprise to ask the ultimate question: What is the human person and what is his role in the world? And it was the essence of the cultural enterprise to come to some societal answer to that question and embody that answer in public life.

The prophets of philosophical pluralism claimed that a refusal to ask the ultimate questions in society would produce a free and vital civilization, but Murray recognized that instead it would lead to cultural decadence and to losing touch with the classical heritage of the West:

> . . . it used to be assumed that an ever-expanding variety of conflicting religious and philosophical views was per se an index of richness, a pledge of vitality, a proof of the values of individualism, a guarantee against stagnation, and so on. But history has not left this assumption intact.
>
> In a word, it used to be assumed that pluralism represented "progress." But now the question has arisen, whether its proliferation may be causatively related to certain observable decadences within the area of intellectual life.[28]

The first of these intellectual decadences was "solipsism," the idea that an individual's insight belonged solely to him and could never be shared with a single other person, let alone an entire society. Murray called this intellectual perversion "the destruction of the classical and Christian concept of reason," and he argued that it would bring about "the consequent dissolution of the idea of truth itself to the point where no assertion may claim more than the status of sheer opinion, to be granted an equality of freedom with any other opinion."[29] A second intellectual decadence that accompanied the glorification of pluralism was a new dogmatism which held suspect any strongly held philosophical, religious or ethical opinions; the relativism of all truth was to be the sole legitimate dogma of modern culture in America.[30] A third consequence of philosophical pluralism could be found in certain distressing characteristics of intellectual debate in the twentieth century, namely "the decay of argument and the corruption of controversy, amid the sterilities of stock polemical attacks and counterattacks, or amid the bottomless morasses of semanticism."[31]

But intellectual decadence was not the greatest threat which Murray saw in philosophical pluralism. No, the most damaging effects of this creed lay not in the order of the intellect, but in the social order. For the refusal to ask ultimate questions in society, which was prompted by the desire to avoid conflict, could lead in the end only to deeper divisions within society and to the annihilation of the reality of society itself:

> . . . perhaps the ultimate tendency of the pluralisms created by the era of modernity is felt rather in the realm of affectivity than in the realm of reason as such. The fact today is not simply that we hold different views, but that we have become different types of men, with different styles of interior life. We are therefore uneasy in each other's presence. We are not, in fact, present to one another at all; we are absent from one another. That is, I am not transparent to the other, nor he to me; our mutual experience is one of opaqueness. And this reciprocal opaqueness is the root of an hostility that is overcome only with an effort, if at all.[32]

Pluralism was the intellectual offspring of the spirit of "modernity." Just as "modernity" had sought to find a secular substitute for the role that religion had played in society, philosophical pluralism had sought to find a secular and tolerant substitute for the classical role of metaphysics and ethics in social thought. In the end, both had left the individual impotent and alone before his own passions.

Murray believed that these shortcomings of modern pluralism were already being recognized both in American and European society. The works of Romano Guardini, William Ernest Hocking, Eric Voegelin, and Geoffrey Barraclough had demonstrated that the spirit of "modernity," for all of its promise, had left a legacy of cultural confusion and societal disorganization.[33] It was necessary for America to embark on a new chapter of its cultural enterprise: the effort to salvage those elements of truth which had given rise to the spirit of "modernity," while simultaneously achieving a new unity in society that would allow the United States to act responsibly in history.[34] Such a unity could not be achieved by force or by the false pressures of conformism; instead, it would have to be the product of faith, reason, freedom, justice, law and love. "Within the social unity created by these forces, which are instinct with all the divinity that resides in man, the human personality itself grows to its destined stature of dignity at the same time that the community achieves its unity."[35] Unity amidst pluralism. Justice amidst love. Law amidst freedom. These were the values that American culture needed to nurture in the second half of the twentieth century, and it was clear to Murray that they would not be found in technological secularism, practical materialism, or modern pluralism. The United States must seek elsewhere for the answer to its cultural dilemma, and Murray proposed the answer that lay at the heart of the Catholic theological tradition, in the concept of natural law.

The Natural Law

Murray recognized that in proposing natural law as the fundamental formative principle for American culture, he was directly contradicting some of the most powerful intellectual and social currents in United States society. While America prided itself on dynamism and openness to new ideas, the concept of natural law evoked images of rigidity and archaism. In an age of inter-subjectivity and renewed stress on the uniqueness of the human person, natural law seemed to see only the generic "person" and not the unique individual. And most distressingly of all, in a society where the last vestiges of virulent anti-Catholicism had not yet been erased, natural law represented to many a peculiarly Catholic perspective on the moral life.

Murray decided not to ignore these societal predispositions against natural law, but instead to face them head-on. In part he accomplished this by pointing out that many of the objections to natural law were objections not to natural law itself, but to caricatures of natural law which had been fashioned by its opponents. The first of these caricatures Murray labeled "the Kantian construct." Simply put, it held that "In Natural Law you start out with a formula that is something like a magician's hat, and out of it you pull all sorts of complicated moral precepts of one sort or another."[36] This Kantian construct, which accused natural law of the grossest kind of moral and philosophical simplism, had heavily influenced the intellectual tradition of the West. In response to it, Murray explained that any theory which did not recognize the contingency of specific moral conclusions and the complexity of ethical decision-making was not in reality natural law at all. A second caricature which Murray focused upon was "the objectivist-rationalist interpretation," the notion that the essence of the human person could be isolated from his concreteness and historicity. "In point of fact," Murray wrote, "the theory (of natural law) never forgets that the 'nature' with which it deals has no existence except in the person, who is a unique realization of the nature, situated in an order of other unique realizations."[37] Thus the historicity and individuality of the human person, far from being alien to natural law, were intrinsic to a proper understanding of it. The third pseudo-theory of natural law which Murray sought to correct sprang from the doctrines propounded by Rousseau and Locke in the Enlightenment. Such a view of natural law held that it was possible to reconstruct a past "state of nature" that could be used as a starting point from which to derive postulates about the identity of the human person and his role in society. Apart from the individualism and nominalism which he detected in these theories, Murray regarded them as outside the true natural law tradition because they relied for their content not upon what the human person really is, but upon Locke's and Rousseau's purely speculative interpretations of what the human person might have been in the age when social interaction first took place.[38]

Such arguments were helpful in dispelling many of the misimpressions about natural law which had crept into the mainstream of American intellectual life. But Murray's objective was not merely to demonstrate that the theory of natural law had been misunderstood in the past; it was to show that the true theory of natural law constituted the soundest foundation on which America could base its cultural enterprise. And in order to accomplish this, it was necessary to present natural law to the American people in a way which was coherent, non-parochial, and attractive. In a series of articles that spanned the period 1948–1963, Murray attempted to do just this.

The first step in this process was to establish clearly that the theory of natural law was not a "Catholic" theory, but rather was a valid description of the moral experience of all humankind:

> It is sometimes said that one cannot accept the doctrine of natural law unless one has antecedently accepted its "Roman Catholic presuppositions." This, of course, is quite wrong. Its only presupposition is threefold: that man is intelligent; that reality is intelligible; and that reality, as grasped by the intelligence, imposes on the will the obligation that it be obeyed in its demands for action or abstention. Even these statements are not properly "presuppositions," since they are susceptible of verification.[39]

In order to stress the fact that the theory of natural law was not sectarian in its claims or origins, Murray would often use the term "the tradition of reason" or "the tradition of civility" as a substitute for natural law. He would also emphasize that it dated, not from the founding of the Catholic Church, but from the age of the Greek and Roman philosophers, and that natural law represented not the accomplishment of a particular culture, but the *philosophia perennis* of the human heritage.[40]

The reason for this pervasiveness of natural law in human history, according to Murray, lay in the fact that it rested upon propositions which were readily discoverable by all people. The first of these was the assertion of a realist epistemology, the notion that the real is the measure of all knowledge and that it is possible for human intelligence to reach the real. The second proposition was the teleological conception of nature, the idea that "there is a natural inclination in man to become what in nature and destination he is—to achieve the fullness of his own being."[41] A third presupposition of natural law lay in its natural theology, the assertion that God is the author of nature and that he wills that the order of nature be fulfilled in its purposes. Finally, Murray stated, natural law presupposes a morality which sees the individual's highest moral activity not in an order of necessity which he fulfills blindly, but in an order of reason and freedom. "The order of being that confronts his intelligence is an order of 'oughtness' for his will; the moral order is a prolongation of the metaphysical order into the dimensions of human freedom."[42]

Murray recognized that these four assertions, while comprehensible to philosophers and theologians, would seem very complex to the average person. And since he was writing not merely for the theologian and the philosopher, but for the American people as a whole, Murray sought to make these philosophical presuppositions more clear:

> This sounds frightfully abstract; but it is simply the elaboration by the reflective intelligence of a set of data which are at bottom empirical. Consider, for instance, the contents of the consciousness of a man who is protesting against injustice, let us say, in a case where his own interests are not touched and where the injustice is wrought by technically correct legislation. The contents of his consciously protesting mind would be something like this. He is asserting that there is an idea of justice; that this idea is transcendent to the actually expressed will of the legislator; that it is rooted somehow in the nature of things; that he really knows this idea; that it is not made by his judgment, but is the measure of his judgment; that this idea is of the kind that ought to be realized in law and in action; that its violation is injury, which his mind rejects as unreason; that this unreason is an offense not only against his own intelligence, but against God, Who commands justice and forbids injustice. Actually, this man, who may be no philosopher, is thinking in the categories of natural law and in the sequence of ideas that the natural-law mentality (which is the human mentality) follows.[43]

Murray's argument was forceful, clear and consistent: the moral life of the human person must correspond with his own nature, and that nature is directed toward the purposes for which it was created by God. In seeking to fulfill his ethical obligations, the individual must look for guidance not to the messianic state, as the French Revolution had claimed, nor to a biological model of society, as the nineteenth century had claimed, nor to an atheistic vision of the human person, as the spirit of "modernity" had claimed. Rather, in seeking to fulfill his moral identity the individual must look to his own divinely created nature and discern therein the grounding for all actions, both individual and societal.

But it was one thing to assert that the nature of the human person is the foundation of the moral life. It was a far more complicated task to explain how one could discern from that nature specific ethical rules of conduct. Murray clearly recognized this, and in his many discussions of the role of moral discernment vis-à-vis the natural law, he stressed both the complexity of formulating ethical rules and the need to ground moral discernment in an experiential approach which avoided any rationalistic deductionism:

> What is the good that ought to be done? What is the evil that ought to be avoided? To answer these questions you refer to experience. To take a basic thing—that parents are to be honored—the third precept of the Decalogue—how do I know that this is true? I know it by understanding what a parent is. I acquire through experience an idea of the relationship between myself and my parents. I also get to know as a child the basic content of the word "honor" and I see this not intuitively. There is a certain amount of reasoning here. I have to experience parenthood or childhood or the relationships within the family. I have to do a very simple sort of reasoning, such as a child is capable of. I then arrive at the decision that this is a dictate of my nature, and I thus, simply because of the fact that I am a man, and a man in the status of a child, am morally obliged to honor my parents.[44]

Thus it was through the process of human experience and reflection that the principles of natural law were discerned. Contrary to the image of the "magician's hat" of the Kantian construct, the tradition of reason provided no simple answers to complex questions; rather, it represented the heritage of humankind's effort to discover in the nature of the concrete individual the ethical principles which God had ordained. In all stages of this process of discovery, both the fallibility of the human person and the limited nature of natural law claims had to be recognized.

At the same time, Murray argued, the ability of people to come to some clear understandings of their ethical obligations must not be underestimated. "The permeability of reality, especially moral reality, to intelligence is limited, as human intelligence itself is limited. But the limitations do not destroy the capacity of intelligence to do three things, in order of diminishing ease and certainty."[45] The first and most basic of these was the truth that good is to be done and evil avoided. Murray called this the "ethical a priori," and he stated that it did not come to human consciousness through argument, but "dawns, as it were, as reason itself emerges from the darkness of infant animalism."[46] A second level of moral discernment lay in the simple ethical reflection which takes place after some minimal experience of the basic situations of life, through which the intelligence can grasp how good is to be done and evil avoided in these situations. Murray's description of the process of coming to recognize the ethical obligations of a child to be respectful to his parents is an example of this second level. The third level of moral discernment concerns the establishment of general ethical norms for human life. Through simple reflection upon lived experience, men and women can derive a set of natural law principles that are obligatory and known to be obligatory. Such natural law principles provide the content of the natural law theory in most human situations, but they are always to be interpreted within the context of the more fundamental command to do good and avoid evil.[47]

Murray explained that these three levels of moral discernment were attainable by all reasonable people, since they required only common human experience and a limited intelligence. But there was a fourth level of moral attainment that was reserved for those gifted with a greater intelligence. This fourth level concerned the precepts of natural law as they applied to more complicated human situations and relationships. As an illustration of this fourth level of moral reasoning, Murray offered the example of the establishment of a just wage in society. Because such an issue demands an extensive amount of specialized knowledge regarding economics, law, and ethics, it cannot be addressed by the average person, but can be understood only by the wise and the learned in society.

This fourfold schema of moral discernment is, of course, borrowed wholesale from the writings of Thomas Aquinas; and in speaking of Murray's theory of natural law it is important to recognize that it was fundamentally an effort to apply Thomas' theory within the context of American life and institutions in the twentieth century. Murray was willing to acknowledge his intellectual indebtedness to Thomas, but he more often stressed that the natural law approach represented not the work of one man, or even one culture, but rather the common ethical patrimony of human civilization. "It represents the acquisitions of the human mind and spirit reflecting on the meaning of human life as it has historically developed," Murray wrote. "It represents the highest achievements, in its best moments, of the human spirit as it has reflected upon the basic problems of human, social, and political living together."[48]

Murray viewed the heritage of natural law as an intrinsically dynamic one, even though it was built upon certain enduring truths that are rooted in the very nature of being human. His approach to the tradition of reason skillfully mixed elements of continuity and change, so that it escaped the twin dangers of archaism and ethical relativism:

> History does not alter the basic structure of human nature, nor affect the substance of the elementary human experiences, nor open before man wholly new destinies. Therefore, history cannot alter the natural law, insofar as a natural law is constituted by the ethical *a priori*, by the primary principles of the moral reason, and by their immediate derivatives. . . . But history does change what I have called the human reality. It evokes situations that never happened before. It calls into being relationships that had not existed. It involves human life in an increasing multitude of institutions of all kinds, which proliferate in response to new human needs and desires, as well as in consequence of the creative possibilities that are inexhaustibly resident in human freedom.[49]

In Murray's view, the nature of the human person was open to change in history, while at the same time his fundamental structure and destinies continued unaltered. This highly nuanced balance allowed the natural law to be an anchor for enduring human values while simultaneously adapting to each new situation in which people find themselves.

Murray proposed the theory of natural law as the foundation for America's cultural enterprise because he believed that it represented the most illuminating description of humankind's moral experience and destiny. But he also recommended it because he believed that it could meet some of the most severe deficiencies in American culture in the twentieth century. In the first place, amidst the philosophical pluralism which was rampant in American society, natural law provided "a secure anchorage in the order of reality, the ultimate order of beings and purposes."[50] The cultural creation of philosophical pluralism would be an agnostic moral vacuum; the cultural product of natural law would be a public consensus rooted in the order of truth. A second benefit of the natural law approach was its acknowledgment of the transcendent dimensions of human nature. While technological secularism sought to banish the role of religious insights in public discourse, the tradition of reason frankly acknowledged its dependence upon an order of values that was created by God and that is obligatory for both individuals and societies.[51] Third, the principles of natural law provided a full-bodied theory of human ethics. Unlike the one-dimensional practical materialism which was so pervasive in the United States, the tradition of reason provided a method of moral reasoning which saw the richness and complexity of the human person and sought to develop that richness and complexity to the fullest. Fourth, the theory of natural law vindicated those principles of society which had been central to the Western liberal tradition and had been undermined by the French Revolution, continental liberalism, and totalitarianism— the notions that society is prior to the state, that law is measured by its conformity with reason, that the political realm is sharply limited in scope, and that the consent of the governed is necessary for legitimate government.[52] For all these reasons, Murray believed that the ancient tradition of natural law constituted the ideal cultural principle for American society, and that if the United States was to thrive in the post-war era, the tradition of reason would have to be integrated into all sectors of public life.

DEFINING THE PUBLIC CONSENSUS:
THE CULTURAL ENTERPRISE

John Courtney Murray was an ardent and articulate defender of the natural law as a formative principle of culture.

His analyses of the three principal secular proposals for the cultural enterprise in the United States had clearly delineated their moral and spiritual bankruptcy; and his skillful elaboration of the Thomistic theory of natural law presented the tradition of reason in a manner which not only did not seem alien to most Americans, but seemed to reflect the common sense approach which was a hallmark of American culture. Yet Murray's effort to formulate a contemporary public theology for the United States could not be content with merely demonstrating the conceptual superiority of natural law; it also had to demonstrate how natural law could function as an active and practical principle of culture in a society which was intensely anti-ideological. The key to this task lay for Murray in the concept of "the public consensus," a body of basic moral truths which was accepted in the society as a whole and which could be appealed to in cases where the natural law was violated.

Murray's notion of the public consensus did not emerge in its fully developed form until the 1960's. But during the period 1952–1956, as he wrestled with the question of how a society could establish and maintain a truly moral sense of community, one could begin to detect in his writings the origins of a theory of public consensus. This was the era of Dwight D. Eisenhower and "The American Century"; the divisive issues of race, economic justice, and war and peace which would rend the social fabric of the United States during the 1960's had not yet come forcefully to the surface, and America's post-war prosperity and military might bred a new confidence in the validity of American institutions and the cohesiveness of American society. Within this context, historians and social scientists undertook to examine the root of America's success, the source of its ability to avoid the divisive ideological struggles which had characterized social and political life in the Old World. The answer they produced was the notion of the American consensus, the idea that American society had become great because it rested upon an unwritten social compact concerning the function and limits of government, the non-ideological nature of social life, and the freedom of the economic order. This "consensus school" of the social sciences, characterized by writers such as Richard Hofstadter, Daniel Boorstin, and Seymour Martin Lipset, subscribed to the view that the pub-

lic consensus in the United States had set the American people
on a clear and correct social course, and that it would continue
to do so in the future.[53]

Murray did not share the complacency of the "consensus"
school about the direction of American culture in the twentieth
century. But he did believe that the notion of a societal consensus
on basic moral questions was important for the future of the cultural enterprise in the United States. For this reason, during the
decade 1953–1963 he picked up the theme of the American consensus and substantially modified it to reflect his own understanding of the challenges which were facing the United States in the
modern era.

In the early period of his writings on the American consensus, Murray drew heavily from Walter Lippmann's *Essays in the
Public Philosophy*.[54] Lippmann held with the "consensus school"
that there had traditionally been a public philosophy in the
United States that had mediated American social, economic, and
political life in a non-ideological manner. But Lippmann differed
from most of the "consensus" writers in affirming that the basis
of this public philosophy in the United States lay in the principles
of natural law. He also differed with the "consensus school" in
arguing that the public philosophy, which had been vital and alive
for most of the history of the United States, had begun to atrophy
in the twentieth century and was no longer the received wisdom
for most of the American people:

> In our time the institutions built upon the foundations of the
> public philosophy still stand. But they are used by a public
> who are not being taught, and no longer adhere to, the phi-
> losophy. Increasingly, the people are alienated from the inner
> principles of their institutions. The question is, whether and
> how this alienation can be overcome, and the rupture of the
> tradition of civility repaired.[55]

The source of this alienation could be found in the positivist philosophy which was being taught in the great universities of the
West and which was seeping into American society. Such a posi-
tivism, while capable of providing a practical orientation for society, could not provide the objective order of values that society

needed to avoid the various forms of totalitarianism and social ennui being produced in the modern era. Nor could it provide a true order of justice and peace in society, because its standard of value was the popular rather than the true. Only if there was a return to the high philosophy of Aristotle, Thomas, and the natural law tradition, Lippmann argued, could the public philosophy of the West retain its vitality. And only if that high philosophy was transmitted to the people of the United States as a whole would the free institutions of American society endure.

It was not surprising that Murray found Lippmann's analysis compatible with his own beliefs, for Lippmann had utilized Murray's writings on American philosophical pluralism in preparing *Essays in the Public Philosophy*. But Lippmann had gone a step beyond Murray in developing the notion of the public philosophy and in articulating the cultural crisis of the modern era. It was Lippmann who outlined the natural law roots of the public philosophy in the American tradition. It was Lippmann who pointed to the apostasy of the intelligentsia from the public philosophy as the source of cultural decline in the United States. And it was Lippmann who argued forcefully that the key issue in the cultural enterprise of the United States lay in the ability of those who still held to the public philosophy to communicate it to the next generation of Americans. All of these themes were to occupy a central place in Murray's evolving notion of the public consensus and of the role which it must play in American society in the post-war era.[56]

But while Walter Lippmann's conception of the public philosophy was instrumental in stimulating Murray's thought on the cultural enterprise in the United States, it was Adolph Berle's *Power Without Property* which more forcefully shaped Murray's notion of the public consensus.[57] In one sense it was odd that Berle's work should have had such a dramatic impact on Murray's thought, for *Power Without Property* was a book about the economic power structure in the United States, and economics was one area which the intellectually far-ranging Murray assiduously avoided in his writings and speeches. But Berle's analysis of the economic system in the United States happened to include a description of the American public consensus which Murray found to be powerful, attractive, and valid.

It was Berle's thesis that the American economic system had been able to achieve immense prosperity, economic freedom, and relative justice in the commercial sphere because there had existed throughout American history a public consensus regarding the nature of the economic system in the United States and the need for it to serve the many, rather than the few. The content of this consensus was "a set of value judgments so widely accepted and deeply held in the United States that public opinion can energize political action when needed to prevent power from violating these values."[58] The consensus had not arisen full-blown at the beginnings of the nation's history, but was the result of experience and reflection; neither would it ever be completed, for new historical developments would demand growth in the public consensus. While the consensus itself was inchoate and unwritten, it was "sufficiently expressed in one form or another so that its principles are familiar to and have become accepted by those members of the community interested in the given field."[59] For this reason, it acted as the final arbiter of the legitimacy of economic power in American society and demanded a corporate ethical standard of conduct that business would violate at its peril. At times, the public consensus could make its power felt through direct legislative action, but more often it used the economic leverage of the consumer to punish those who violated its principles. The repository of the public consensus, according to Berle, was in the conscience of the community as a whole, but the responsibility for its development lay not with the masses but with learned leaders of public opinion who could adapt the public consensus to the new situations which economic progress would produce.

Berle's elaboration of the public consensus seemed ideally fitted to Murray's project of reclaiming the cultural order in America. For Berle was describing the manner in which a true moral community could be established and maintained in the United States without allowing the political sphere to swallow up society. *Power Without Property* certainly saw a significant role for government in curbing the power of corporate elites. Yet the greatest power in society lay not in the role of government, but in the conscience of the community, which had the obligation to criticize both the business system *and* the actions of government itself. The conscience of the community, founded upon principles derived from experience and the intelligent reflection on that experience, was to be both the binding force and the corrective force in society. It was to provide the direction for the American people and set the parameters for public life in the United States. The continuing authority of the public consensus would be assured by its existence in the minds of the masses, while its continuing vitality would be assured through its refinement by the learned and wise.

Murray saw in such a conception of the public consensus the blend of practical dynamism and moral substance which was needed to translate the principles of natural law into the public life of the nation. The grounding of the public consensus in the contingencies of economic, social, and intellectual life assured that the consensus would be rooted in reality. And the need for the consensus to determine the central questions of value for society assured that moral reflection would continue to be part of the public consensus:

> Only this moral element will enable the consensus to transcend sheer experience, and impart some system to it, and do this in terms of non-contingent principle that is capable of coping with the issue of ends as well as of means. In a word, the very conception "public consensus" is a moral conception. Morality and the consensus have at least this in common, that they are not simply reflections of fact, as if whatever is must be considered right; nor are they mere techniques of success, as if whatever works must be considered true and good.[60]

Murray believed that the moral nature of the public consensus would be evident to most Americans. What would not be so evident was the truth that the public consensus was grounded in the principles of natural law. "Only the theory of natural law is able to give an account of the public moral experience that is the public consensus. This consensus is the tradition of reason as emergent in developing form in the special circumstances of American political-economic life."[61]

Murray defended this assertion by analyzing the public consensus in light of the traditional categories of the tradition of reason. The contents of the public consensus, he explained, constitute an example of Thomas' "remote" principles of natural law. They are not immediately self-evident to the average person, but are the product of communal and learned reflection upon the historical situation of American society. Thus the elaboration of the public consensus belongs to the well-educated; it represents the fourth level of moral discernment in the traditional Thomistic schema:

> This is not the work of the people at large. It is not a job for sheer common sense. The public consensus is not formally public opinion. Its elaboration is the task of the wise and the honest. The "careful inquiries," the "rather subtle reflection," the analysis of "circumstances," the exact formulation of the "precept"—these tasks lie beyond the competence of the generality. It is for the wise, who develop the consensus, to give "instruction" to the generality, in the meaning of its principles as "matters of necessary observance," and also in the manner of their application. Public opinion, thus instructed by the wise, conspires to effect these applications.[62]

But if the public consensus is given force because of its general acceptance by society as a whole, it is given validity only if it is in accord with the fundamental order of values created by God. Here Murray departed from Berle's notion of the public consensus. For while Berle *descriptively* rooted the binding force of the consensus in its acceptance by the community, Murray *prescriptively* rooted its binding force in its accord with the tradition of reason.

> This quality of being in accord with reason is the non-contingent element in the body of thought that constitutes the consensus. Brute fact (and) sheer experience have no virtue to elaborate themselves into controlling rules of public conduct. The transcendence of experience and the transformation of fact is the work of reason. The act whereby the doctrine of the consensus is formulated is not the act of inquiry into the facts, nor the act of reflection on the experience. It is an act of judgment, an exercise in moral affirmation or denial.[63]

In thus linking the public consensus to the principles of natural law, Murray transformed the conception of the word "consensus" as it had been used not only by Berle, but by the entire "consensus school" of the social sciences. The "consensus school" had been describing the public philosophy that actually existed in the United States and how it had come to be; Murray was describing the public philosophy as it *should* be in the United States and how it *could* come to be. Murray's final definition of the public consensus reflected this theme:

> The consensus is an ensemble of substantive truths, a structure of basic knowledge, an order of elementary affirmations that reflect realities inherent in the order of existence. It occupies an established position in society and excludes opinions alien or contrary to itself. This consensus is the intuitional a priori of all the rationalities and technicalities of constitutional and statutory law. It furnishes the premises of the people's action in history and defines the larger aims which that action seeks in internal affairs and external relations.[64]

But it was just this prescriptive notion of the public consensus that was being rejected by "the learned and the wise" in American society, as opinion-makers rejected the tradition of natural law in favor of technological secularism, practical materialism, and philosophical pluralism. Murray's goal was not merely to maintain the existing consensus in the United States, but to reclaim and revitalize it. And for that to occur the mediating institutions of American society would have to return to the tradition of reason which they had forsaken.

FORMING THE PUBLIC CONSENSUS

Murray's theory of the public consensus was not wholly an elitist one; indeed he maintained that the masses in the United States had been more faithful to the tradition of reason than the "wise and the honest" had been.[65] But since the elaboration of the public consensus was in Murray's mind a complex process of moral discernment, it fell to the elites in the United States to redefine the public consensus for the post-war era. For this reason, in a series of speeches and articles spanning the decade 1955–1965, Murray focused upon the three major institutions which he saw as central to the process of elaborating the public consensus and challenged them to renew the commitment of American society to the tenets of natural law.

The first of these institutions was the university community. Murray himself was a teacher for all of his adult life, and he was passionately committed to the intellectual enterprise. Moreover, Murray had been a pioneer in reaching out from the Catholic university community to the secular universities; his distinguished record as visiting professor of medieval studies at Yale and his ongoing dialogues with Robert Hutchins, Kingman Brewster, and Reinhold Niebuhr had done much to break down the secular suspicion of Catholic universities and Catholic theology. But enmeshed as he was in the academic elite of the United States, Murray was nonetheless convinced that the university communities had betrayed their identity and their heritage by embracing philosophical pluralism and by banishing the great high philosophy of Aristotle and Thomas from the classroom and the scholarly journal. Speaking to the John Carroll Society in 1961, Murray said:

> I wouldn't for a moment throw rocks at the American University Community largely because I belong to it. I've pledged my allegiance to it. I belong to the fraternity and they are my brothers. Nonetheless, the fact of the matter is that there is a problem here. . . . It's the vacuum. It's this vacuum intellectual forces have created by their corrosive skepticism and positivism and pragmatism and relativism—all the other isms that are abroad today in the intellectual world. It's the vacuum created by these forces which these forces cannot themselves fill.[66]

The university community in the United States had, far from clarifying and solidifying the public consensus in America, actually undermined that moral consensus by endorsing a nihilistic relativism.

But wasn't it the role of the university to be skeptical? Murray thought not. In a 1958 address on the theme of moral excellence in society, he stated:

... I should think that the function of the university within society might be fairly compared to the function of reason in man himself. Man is more than reason. But reason in man is supposed to be the clarifying function, the ordering function. Unless a man accepts the theory of sheer passionate existence, he must recognize these essential functions of his reason. By analogy, society is more than the university. But within society the essential function of the university ought to be a clarifying, ordering function. For the university represents the reason of man in all its various modes of exercise, and in the order and unity that ought to prevail among them.[67]

Murray's idea of the order and reason that ought to prevail in the intellectual community was not the imposed and uncritical order of authoritarian societies. And he would have vehemently rejected any effort to regulate thought within the university communities. But he was convinced that in substituting philosophical relativism for the tradition of reason, the universities of the United States had left society naked in the face of the technological challenge and had sacrificed much of their moral legitimacy:

May the community not legitimately indict the university for failing in its conservative function and thus powerfully contributing to the spiritual crisis of our times—I mean the crisis induced by the imbalance between the inner and outer life of man, by man's enormous progress in the scientific understanding and control of the processes of nature coupled with a decay in spiritual resources and an abandonment of traditional moral values?[68]

Murray agreed that the revolutionary advances in knowledge wrought by the modern university had greatly benefited the human person; but he argued that the legitimacy of the university in society must in the end be based not merely upon technological advances, but upon the contribution of the university toward helping society to face the momentous moral choices produced by the age of "modernity." And in assessing this moral contribution, Murray concluded, the universities had failed miserably.

The consequences of this failure might not have been so alarming for Murray if he had not assigned to the university the primary role in the continuing elaboration of the public consensus. It was the university which had the task of updating the public consensus by interpreting the principles of natural law in light of the new situations created by technological progress and historical change. And it was the university which had the primary responsibility of communicating the contents of the public consensus to each new generation of Americans.[69] Thus the apostasy of the university did not represent merely a disconcerting sidelight in the American cultural enterprise; it represented a seemingly insuperable challenge to those like Murray who sought to anchor American culture in the objective order of values created by God and discernible to reason.

But Murray did not shrink back from this challenge, for he did not believe that it was possible to shrink back and yet still continue the cultural enterprise in the United States. Instead, he countered the direction of the American university community on its own terms. He called for a renewed debate on the bases of knowledge and order in society, a debate which would reveal the presuppositions that lay behind the ethos of the modern university, as well as the alleged "biases" of natural law:

> Is the university, as a matter of fact, uncommitted? And in what senses or in what directions? Is "non-commitalism" an intellectual virtue or is it a vice of the whole personality? Is a commitment to "freedom," understanding "freedom" to be a purely formal category, any more a valid premise of the intellectual life than a commitment to the Kantian *Moralprinzip*, understood as a purely formal category, is a valid premise for the moral life?[70]

Such a debate would also address the social functions of the university, and the societal consequences of the universities' decision to banish religious viewpoints and to adopt the dogma of philosophical pluralism. In Murray's mind such a fundamental and far-reaching debate in the intellectual communities of the United States could reveal the moral bankruptcy of social thought in the nation's universities. It could also stimulate an alteration of the academic ethos that would, if not granting authoritative status to religion and the tradition of reason, at least grant them admission into the academic arena. And with such an alteration a significant step in the process of reclaiming the cultural order would have been accomplished.

Murray realized that such a change in the intellectual ethos of the United States would largely depend upon the willingness of the secular universities to change their philosophical premises. But he believed that the religious university also had a critical role to play in the cultural renewal of the United States. For the religious university could bear witness to the truths that secular universities dared not utter in twentieth century America: the explicit grounding of the order of truth in religious language and religious concepts. The extreme secularity which had come to characterize all too many of the great universities in America was the academic manifestation of *l'esprit laïque,* the assertion that "all that is transcendent to this terrestrial orb has, by that same token, been regarded as beyond intelligence and therefore no object of concern."[71] But it was the very nature of the religious university to continually assert the unity between reason and transcendent truth, and to assert this unity in the most rigorous intellectual manner. In doing so, it could considerably advance the cultural enterprise by establishing the intellectual foundations for both natural law and the transcendent dignity of the human person. For this reason, the renewal of the cultural order in the United States was the exclusive province of neither the secular nor the religious university; rather, the collaboration of both institutions would be necessary.

If Murray saw the universities as the primary elaborators and communicators of the public consensus, he believed that the legal community also occupied a strategic position in the formation of the public philosophy. "The corporate body of lawmen bears a special responsibility for the effective guardianship and for the periodic renewal of the public philosophy,"[72] Murray wrote in 1958; and in a series of lectures and articles directed at the American bar he made clear its obligation to strengthen the cultural order in the nation by reinforcing the precepts of natural law.

Murray centered his argument to the legal community around the theme that only the natural law tradition could adequately ground the American conception of jurisprudence and the public philosophy:

> The public philosophy derived from the ancient tradition
> whose central assertion was the existence of a rational order
> of truth and justice, which man does not create, since it is the
> reflection of the Eternal Reason of God. . . . From this phi-
> losophy we drew the moral concept of freedom, under law,
> both divine and human, and the concept of justice, and the
> concept of human equality.[73]

Historically the legal community in the United States had played
a central role in elaborating and renewing the public consensus;
theirs was the language of justice and freedom, of equality and
law. From the time of the Revolution onward, lawyers had stood
in the first rank of American statesmen, addressing the great public issues of their time and seeking the fundamental questions
which lay behind these issues. But in the late nineteenth century,
Murray believed, the legal community had largely failed in its role
as an architect of the public consensus. One cause of this failure
was the rise of industrial capitalism, which led the lawyer to be
seen as a tool of economic interests rather than a public statesman. Another was the rise of sociological jurisprudence, which
severed the ties between legal concepts and the realist epistemology which grounded them. Still a third was the increasing preoccupation of the bar with questions of method and procedure, to
the exclusion of the more basic questions of justice and right. For
all these reasons, Murray believed, the bar had in large part abandoned its guardianship of the public philosophy and lost sight of
its most important societal role.[74]

But such a state of affairs could not continue in the face of
the cultural crisis created by "modernity." Murray argued that
the lawyers of the United States must return to the tradition of
the Revolutionary era and confront the fundamental questions of
public policy; they must retrieve the working language of natural
law and communicate to the people as a whole:

> There is today a general challenge to all ranks and institutions
> of society, that they should rise to the height of the times, lest
> they be overtaken by a flood more disastrous than that from
> which Noah rescued civilization in a primitive wooden boat.
> As it reaches the legal profession this general challenge is an
> invitation to step across the threshold into a new age. . . . The

crucial question is what will be the tenets of the public philosophy in terms of which American society will chart its course? Will they be the ancient principles of truth and justice, of freedom and order, of human rights and responsibilities, that were inherent in the tradition to which our Republic is tributary. Or will command of the new age be taken by some one of the new-found philosophies which are presently at war with the high liberal tradition?[75]

Murray believed that the answer to that question was largely dependent upon the willingness of the legal community to renew the public consensus. Men and women of the law had to interpret the complexities of twentieth century society in terms of the traditional categories of justice and right, and they had to inject the principles of natural law not only into the legal system narrowly defined, but into the broad public philosophy as a whole.

Such a task, Murray believed, could not be accomplished by the legal community acting alone, or even by the legal community acting in concert with the universities. For in both the world of the bar and the world of *academe* the tradition of reason had become so neglected that it had lost much of its vital force and coherence. If the public consensus of the United States was to be renewed according to the principles of natural law, then a third national institution would have to commit itself to the cultural enterprise, an institution which had never abandoned the principles of natural law but had kept them vitally alive during the period of "modernity." In Murray's mind, that institution could be no other than the Catholic community:

> . . . the poignant question is whether and if so how modern men could make vital contact with the lost traditions of civility. In principle we may answer that this vital contact can be made through us, through the Catholic Church, a community within which the tradition is still alive. But the crucial question is "How?" For we may well ask whether the natural law is being communicated by our Catholic colleges or whether it is merely being kept in custody. Custody is not enough. Our great problem is the communication of the public philosophy to the public, which has lost the capacity to believe in the public philosophy.[76]

The Catholic community had for too long sat on the sidelines of the cultural enterprise in the United States; it had operated from a ghetto mentality which was content to maintain the principles of transcendent truth internally, while not engaging in the open and challenging dialogue that was necessary to establish the tradition of reason in the public square.[77] But the Catholic community could afford this luxury no more. It was witnessing an age in which the allegiance of American society to the notions of justice, truth, and freedom was being eviscerated, and only the Catholic community had both the continuity with the tradition of natural law and the vitality necessary to reverse this process.

Murray could not help but savor the irony of this situation. The Catholic community, which had for centuries been suspect in its allegiance to the fundamental principles of American society, which even in the post-war era was labeled "un-American" by Protestant and secularist bigots, this same Catholic community was the dominant social institution that had remained faithful to the American cultural heritage. Looking forward to a day when the ongoing dissolution of the American consensus might be complete, when the American people would completely forsake the transcendent moral identity as a people, Murray wrote:

> If that evil day should come, the results would introduce one more paradox into history. The Catholic community would still be speaking in the ethical and political idiom familiar to them as it was familiar to their fathers, both the Fathers of the Church and the Fathers of the American Republic. The guardianship of the original American consensus, based upon the Western heritage, would have passed to the Catholic community, within which the heritage was elaborated long before America was. And it would be for others, not Catholics, to ask themselves whether they still shared the consensus which first fashioned the American people into a body politic and determined the structure of its fundamental law.[78]

It was clear to Murray that the dawning of this day in America was not too far in the future, and that the Catholic community occupied a strategic position in the fight against the secular concepts of culture. "There falls upon us a major responsibility to assist in the revival, the restatement, the revitalization of the public philosophy of the United States. Upon our success in this task depends, in large part, the future of our Republic and our future within the Republic."[79]

The fulfillment of this responsibility entailed three major tasks for the Catholic community and indeed for all of America's religious communities. The first was to encourage talented religious men and women to enter those professions which had the power to mold public opinion in the United States—journalism, law, medicine, and teaching. By bringing to these fields a religiously-inspired commitment to the order of truth, the dignity of the human person, and the need for just relationships in society, such a corps of committed men and women could truly revitalize the public consensus and reinforce the moral identity of the American people. Secondly, America's religious communities had to form principled, competent, and educated public servants, individuals who could bring the precepts of natural law to the work of government and thus alter the direction which American society was taking in an age of ever-increasing governmental activity. Finally, Murray exhorted the religious communities of America to heal the apostasy of the nation's intellectuals by producing intellectuals who would advance the order of truth by recreating within the academic milieu an understanding of and appreciation for the insights of natural law. "We must find men who will live in the tension between the actualities of secularized intellectual life and the ideals of Christianized intelligence."[80]

These were not tasks that could be accomplished overnight; for the type of cultural renewal which Murray proposed was the work of decades, if not centuries. Murray believed that the United States faced in the spirit of "modernity" the most serious possible challenge to its cultural heritage: the choice between a world devoid of transcendent values and a world where the public recognition of God's existence grounded an order of justice and freedom that truly enhanced the dignity of the human person. America could not choose both worlds, nor could it refuse to make a choice. For as Murray was so fond of saying, "not to choose is to create a vacuum at the heart of society, and nature abhors a vacuum and will fill it with some demonic force."[81]

Murray was not content to tolerate a vacuum at the heart of American culture. His proposals for the renewal of the cultural order in the United States represented a forceful challenge to the nation's religious communities to take up their rightful role of leadership in twentieth century society. Such a leadership would have to respect the religious, social, and intellectual pluralism that was an essential and productive element of American life; but it would also have to anchor that pluralism in the principles of natural law and natural theology. This was the great creative task of the American public theology in the post-war era, a task which Murray labored unceasingly to achieve.

3

RENEWING
THE POLITICAL ORDER

John Courtney Murray was firmly convinced that the primary focus for public theology in the twentieth century lay in the cultural order, that delicate combination of values and beliefs which gives identity and direction to a society. But he was equally convinced that the effort to strengthen the spiritual foundations of American society would falter unless it also reached into the order of government and renewed the political institutions of American life.

In part this concern with the reform of American political institutions arose from Murray's historical analysis of the rise of secularism. In his view much of the damage that secularism had done to Western civilization had been accomplished through the agency of government, and thus it was important to eradicate the secularizing influence of government on society in order to preserve the role of spiritual values in the temporal realm. A second source of Murray's interest in renewing the political order sprang from his work with the National Catholic Welfare Conference, the public policy arm of the American bishops. During the 1940's and 1950's, Murray worked closely with the Conference as an advisor on state aid to Catholic education and on the Church's role in contributing to the formation of public policy. As a result of these experiences, he encountered first-hand the growing belief in certain circles of government that religion had no role in the public sphere, and that the pluralism of American society demanded the exclusion of religious belief from all activities of government. To one who saw the role of religion in public life as not only rightful, but necessary, such an attitude on the part of government clearly called for reform. Finally, Murray viewed the renewal of the political order as a crucial goal of any effective public theology because he recognized that the massive increase in the role of government in American social life in the post-war era had blurred the distinction between state and society and would doom to failure any effort to reclaim the cultural order which did not take account of the role and institutions of government.

For all these reasons, Murray concluded that the effort to achieve justice, freedom, and harmony in American society would have to include a rearticulation of the proper role of government in society and a reexamination of the central institutions of American political life. It was toward these twin ends that Murray devoted much of his time and attention in the 1950's, especially after he was ordered by his superiors in 1954 not to write further on the question of Catholic doctrine on Church and state.[1] If the period of the 1950's constituted Murray's period of exile from the doctrinal debate on religious liberty, it also constituted his emergence as a leading public spokesman for the Church in the United States, a spokesman who presented the principles of Catholic social teaching in a manner which seemed eminently compatible with the American political tradition. To audiences that ranged from the Yale faculty to the Knights of Columbus, from the Center for the Study of Democratic Institutions to the readers of *Life* and *Time* magazines, Murray brought home the same theme: the political institutions of American life were increasingly alienated from their spiritual roots and were becoming enemies to the dignity of the human person rather than supports to that dignity. Unless this process was reversed, Murray told the America of the 1950's, the noble experiment that was American democracy could not hope to survive.

The Nature and Role of Government

In assessing the health of American political institutions in the post-war era, Murray relied principally upon the Thomistic tradition of natural law as a guide to the proper role of the state and government in society. All that has been said in the previous chapter about Murray's application of the fundamental principles of natural law to the order of culture also applies to his use of the natural law tradition to renew the political order. For Murray, this tradition was both experiential and dynamic. It assumed a realist epistemology and a teleological foundation for the human person in all his individual and social relationships. Natural law asserted the existence of God and rooted the dignity of the individual in the sacredness that God had given to him. It was to serve that dignity that government existed. For this reason, natural law grounded both the goals which government should seek to achieve and the method of achieving them.

In part, Murray relied directly upon the works of Thomas in generating his theory of the role of government in society. But to a great extent, his interpretation of the Thomistic tradition was influenced by the efforts which others had made to apply natural law to modern political life. The most important of these was the corpus of social teachings promulgated by Leo XIII. *Rerum Novarum* exercised a critical role in the development of Murray's political thought, and Leo's writings on the nature of politics in *Immortale Dei, Diuturnum,* and *Au Milieu Des Solicitudes* were no less important. In Murray's view, Leo XIII had attempted with great success to begin to interpret the institutions of modern political life in light of the natural law tradition, and if this Pope's writings were often skewed by his antipathy to the excesses of Continental laicism, they nonetheless contained illuminating principles for evaluating any form of governmental activity.[2] The Leonine social corpus was complemented, in Murray's estimation, by the encyclicals and addresses of Pius XII. Murray believed that Pius had retained Leo's central insights into the nature and functions of the state, while transferring the conception of the state from an ethical to a juridical order and thereby eliminating many of the paternalistic overtones that had weakened Leo's analysis.[3] In this way, Pius had formulated a theory of government that preserved the moral richness of the Thomistic idea of politics, while carefully circumscribing the role of the state in a manner which only a post-Nazi era could know was necessary.

In addition to these papal documents, Murray drew fruitfully from the political treatises of three contemporary writers who had sought to present Thomas to modern audiences. The first of

these was Jacques Maritain, whose analysis of the secular crisis in
Europe had been so influential in alerting Murray to the threat
of modern secularism. During the period from 1948 onward,
Maritain and Murray exerted a symbiotic influence on each other's thought. Murray's great skill at defining and clarifying complicated social issues contributed enormously to Maritain's political ideas, while Maritain's rich re-creation of Thomistic
philosophy against the background of modern thought provided
the foundation for Murray's analysis of contemporary political
institutions. Murray considered Maritain's *Man and the State* to be
the deepest and most incisive treatment of political philosophy,
and it would be hard to overestimate the intellectual debt that
Murray owed to this man who shared so much of his passion for
bringing to modern society the insights of medieval faith. In addition to Maritain, two other contemporary political philosophers
were significant in Murray's intellectual development. The first
was Heinrich Rommen, who wrote a massive treatise entitled *The
State in Catholic Thought*. Rommen, like many of the writers who
significantly influenced Murray's notions of state and society, had
been a victim of the Nazi terror, and his interpretation of the
Aristotelian and Thomistic conceptions of politics were markedly
shaded by his distrust of massive government power. A more opti-
mistic assessment of the role of government lay in the work of
Thomas Gilbey. His treatise on politics, entitled *Between Society
and Community*, represented an effort to construct a theory of the
state by looking first at the mediating institutions of society, and
it stressed the idea of "the service character of the state" which
was to figure prominently in Murray's thought.[4]

In recognizing the influence which these authors had on
Murray's delineation of the nature and role of government in
society, it is important to realize that Murray's political treatises
were not merely the amalgamation of a series of borrowed
insights and concepts. On the contrary, Murray added substantially to the Thomistic tradition of politics by reinterpreting the
traditional principles of natural law in the light of twentieth century social and political developments, developments which had
included the rise of totalitarianism, the spread of philosophical
pluralism, and the denial of religious values in the public sphere.
It was in reaction to these manifestations of "modernity" that

Murray significantly modified the traditional Thomistic schema in order to emphasize the limited nature and spiritual roots of government, while simultaneously locating in natural law a basis for the rights of free speech, religious liberty, and democratic process. As a result of these skillful adaptations, Murray has justly been called, in concert with Jacques Maritain, "the major reinterpreter of the Thomist position on politics and the state in the postwar period."[5]

The centerpiece of this reinterpretation was Murray's outline of the primary political principles of natural law as they emerged in light of "modernity." The first of these principles concerned

> the supremacy of law, and of law as reason, not will; with this is connected the idea of the ethical nature and function of the state, and the educative character of its laws as directive of man to "the virtuous life" and not simply protective of particular interests.[6]

This was the principle which Murray believed had been the highest achievement of medieval political thought: the notion that human laws enacted by government should be based not on the relative power of various interest groups in society, nor on a concept akin to Rousseau's "general will," but upon the sacred dignity of the human person rooted in the order of creation. Thus the ethical function of the state, which the French Revolution had falsely taken to include the creation of an all-encompassing ethic for society, instead consisted of being subservient to the order of values that was founded upon the eternal law of God and was discoverable by human reason.

This limitation of the power of the state would be reinforced by the second political principle of natural law, the recognition that

> . . . the source of political authority is in the community. Political society as such is natural and necessary to man, but its form is the product of reason and free choice; no ruler has a right to govern that is inalienable and independent of human agency.[7]

This was the "service character of the state" that Thomas Gilbey had emphasized so strongly in his work. States would differ in their constitutions, but any state which was founded upon principles unacceptable to the community as a whole was politically illegitimate. The notion of consent of the governed was central to Murray's effort to make Thomism understandable to modern American audiences; and his modification of Thomist theory to give greater stress to the active participation of the whole community in governmental decision-making represented a significant example of the dynamism of Murray's natural law framework. Because of this dynamic interpretation of natural law, Murray found no contradiction in arguing that the same theory which had validated the notion of rule by kings in the Middle Ages now demanded democratic decision-making as the norm for contemporary government. The explanation for this evolution lay in the fact that "a new human reality" existed in the modern age, namely the spread of education and new forms of social communications that now made it possible for the people as a whole to take the process of government into their own hands.

If the positive accomplishments of "modernity" made possible a fuller realization of the second political principle of natural law, then the twin dangers of "modernity"—totalitarianism and militant secularism—made imperative Murray's third political principle:

> . . . the authority of the ruler is limited; its scope is only political, and the whole of human life is not absorbed in the polis. The power of the ruler is limited, as it were, from above by the law of justice, from below by systems of private right, and from the sides by the public right of the Church.[8]

This was the core of Murray's vision of politics. Society was prior to the state, and the state was a subsection of wider societal life. While modern political process had attempted to encompass the mediating structures of society, or at least to enfeeble them, natural law demanded that the institutions of family, neighborhoods, and social and economic organizations should remain vital, independent, and secure in their immunity from the control of the state. These mediating institutions were to be the central anchor of a free society, but they were to be complemented by the order of justice. And the order of justice was to be supported by the freedom of the religious communities of the nation, which alone had the power to underscore the inviolability of the *res sacrae* in modern times.

This priority of the rights of society over the rights of the state was also the foundation for the fourth political principle of natural law. It asserted

> . . . the contractual relations between the ruler and the ruled. The latter are not simply material organized for rule by the *rex legibus solutus,* but human agents who agree to be ruled constitutionally, in accordance with law.[9]

This notion of constitutionality was critically important in Murray's conception of politics. And the constitutionality which Murray spoke of for modern times was not the implicit constitutionalism of medieval theory. Rather, it was an explicit compact between those who were to be governed and those who were to govern. Murray believed that the written constitution had been the great genius stroke of American political development, for it made clear that sovereignty resided in the community and could be legitimately ceded to the government only to a limited degree and only with the express consent of the community as a whole. While Murray did not go so far as to say that natural law demanded a written constitution, he was firmly convinced that such an instrument was the clearest and most secure way of incorporating the fourth principle into the workings of government. Just as the increasing literacy and political sophistication of the masses in the twentieth century made it necessary for them to have a greater role in the political process, so too they required that the people as a whole be the agents of government, and that the government never claim power not granted to it.

In order to specify how these fundamental principles could become operative within a political framework, Murray developed a set of working definitions that clarified his distinctions between government, state and society. He had arrived at a rough formulation of these definitions during the 1940's, but it was only in 1951 that they were presented in Murray's thought in a form which they were to retain for the rest of his life. Because of the great attention which Murray gave to refining these definitions, and the importance they took on in his analysis of American political institutions, it is worth quoting them in their entirety.

In keeping with his emphasis upon the priority of society over the state, Murray first defined "civil society" before turning to a consideration of the state:

> Civil society. This is the "great society," whose scope is as broad as civilization itself, of which civil society is at once the product and the vehicle. The term designates the total complex of organized human relationships on the temporal plane, which arise either by necessity of nature or by free choice of will, in view of the cooperative achievement of partial human goods by particular associations or institutions. The internal structure of civil society is based upon the principle of social pluralism, which asserts that there is a variety of distinct individual and social ends, either given in human nature or left to human freedom, which are to be achieved by cooperative association. Each of these ends is the root of a responsibility, and therefore of an original right and function. Hence there arises the principle of the subsidiary function as the first structural principle of society. But the whole society also has the function of preserving and developing itself as a whole. There is a good-of-the-whole, a common good, the social good, pluralist in structure but still somehow one. . . .[10]

Thus the civil society enjoyed a common good which preceded the common good of the state and which was primarily achieved not through the labors of government, but through the action of the mediating institutions of society. It was through the action of society, in all its multi-faceted dimensions, that the cultural enterprise took place, and it was through the action of society that a community came to a sense of peoplehood.

But if the notion of "the people" logically preceded the notion of the state, it also logically entailed it. For there was a need in society to have a legitimate coercive power to serve the common good through the maintenance of the public order, and that function could only be fulfilled by the state.

The state is not the body politic, but that particular subsidiary functional organization of the body politic, whose special function regards the good of the whole. The state is not the person of the ruler; in fact it is not personal at all. It belongs in the order of action rather than in the order of substance. It is a set of institutions combined into a complex agency of social control and public service. It is a rational force employed by the body politic in the service of itself as a body. It is "the power" ordained of God, the author of nature, but deriving from the people. Its functions are not coextensive with the functions of society; they are limited by the fact that it is only one, although the highest, subsidiary function of society. These limitations will vary according to the judgment, will, and capacities of the people, in whom reside primary responsibilities and original rights regarding the organization of their private, domestic, and civil (including economic) life. In accordance with the primary principle of the subsidiary function, the axiom obtains: "As much state as necessary, as much freedom as possible."[11]

Thus in framing his notion of the state, Murray quite explicitly counterpoised freedom against the claims of the state. He was willing to follow the Thomistic and Aristotelian tradition in according to the state a central and wide-ranging function, even going so far as to characterize the state's role as the highest of subsidiary functions, because it concerned the good of the whole people.[12] But he was careful to balance that elevated view of the state with several pointed references to the limits of state power.

Such a careful balance can also be seen in Murray's definition of government.

Government is not the state, any more than government is the law. . . . Moreover, the ruler or rulers are not the government. Government is the ruler-in-relation-to-the-ruled; it is likewise the ruled-in-relation-to-the-ruler. Government gives concrete embodiment to the political relationship implied in the concept of the state. In a general sense, government, like the state, is a natural necessity; but its forms, and the actual content and implications of the political relationship are contingent upon reason and the practical judgments it makes in circumstances. As the notion of the state emphasizes the dynamic structure of the political and legal and administrative institutions whereby society is directed to the common good, so government emphasizes the dynamic action of "the power" on "the people" and "the people" on "the power."[13]

Government was therefore relational in Murray's schema, and the relation which it focused upon was one of power. Power flowed from the community as a whole to the government; and that power was utilized by the government to achieve that part of the common good which lay within the province of the state.

But what was this subsidiary common good? Murray believed that it involved five major objectives. The first, which Murray labeled "the Thomistic end," was domestic tranquility—unity within the body politic. "This I call the juristic end of political society," Murray wrote, "because unity depends chiefly upon law and secondly upon the reasonably stable structure of the forces existent within society."[14] The second end of government was the "Augustinian end," namely, the protection of the moral standards of the community. "This end, which I call the moral end, gives substance to society because it supports all the procedures of law and the total edifice of tranquility that we call peace."[15] Complementing this moral end of political society was Murray's third objective for the state: the end of freedom. "This is the Roman and Germanic idea," Murray wrote. "By freedom (I mean) what Montesquieu meant by it, namely, the empowerment to do what one ought; and secondly, immunity from being constrained to do what one ought not to do."[16] The fourth end of the state Murray dubbed "the Christian end." It obligated the government to seek to attain a fullness of human welfare, that is, "to create public prosperity distributed with proportion in equality until all share in it somehow."[17] Lastly, government was responsible for the common defense of the nation from all external enemies; this was "the power end" of the state.

During the 1950's, Murray referred to these five objectives as the ends of political society. In the mid-1960's, he began to characterize this fivefold schema as "the public order."[18] This shift in terminology reflected Murray's continuing desire to emphasize that the ends of the state were limited in their scope and constituted merely a subset of the common good. "The public good is that limited segment of the common good which is committed to the state to be protected and maintained by the coercive force that is available to the state—the force of law and of administrative or police action."[19] Summing up his theories of society and the state, Murray wrote, "In general, 'society' signifies an area of freedom, personal and corporate, whereas 'state' signifies the area in which the public powers may legitimately apply their coercive powers. To deny the distinction is to espouse the notion of government as totalitarian."[20]

Elaborations on the Concept of the Public Order

Murray recognized that any substantial and useful theory of politics in the modern era would have to answer the central question of twentieth century political life: What is the precise scope of the public order? The growth of government was not merely a component of totalitarianism; it was a fact of life in every form of political society. Moreover, Murray recognized, the growth of government was not axiomatically bad; in many cases it reflected the need to meet legitimate societal needs in an increasingly complex world. For this reason, Murray felt the need to refine his notion of the fivefold ends of political society, in order to provide more concrete methods for distinguishing between increased roles for governmental action which truly served the common good, and dangerous encroachments of government power into realms that should be reserved for the mediating institutions of "the great society." This process of refinement did not take place all at once, but came in several stages, as Murray confronted specific problems of public policy and tried to address them.

During the 1950's, Murray became embroiled in a controversy over the question of censorship in America, a controversy in which he angered not only those who were totally opposed to any limitations upon the publication of pornographic materials, but also the leaders of the National Catholic Welfare Conference, who had endorsed a rather stringent program of government limits upon publication.[21] In the course of this debate, Murray came to recognize the need to define much more clearly the second end of political society, namely "the defense of the moral standards

of the community." Murray himself recognized that such a formulation could be interpreted to include the most extensive possible assertions of governmental authority, and thus he was
emphatic in stating that the aim of government could not extend
beyond the maintenance of moral standards absolutely required
for the workings of society:

> . . . the moral aspirations of law are minimal. Law seeks to
> establish and maintain only that minimum of actualized
> morality that is necessary for the healthy functioning of the
> social order. It does not look to what is morally desirable, or
> attempt to remove every moral taint from the atmosphere of
> society. It enforces only what is minimally acceptable, and in
> this sense socially necessary.[22]

Law, in Murray's view, had to be rooted in morality. But its aims
were not to generate a truly moral society; rather, they consisted
of establishing a threshold of moral standards in society. The criterion for determining that threshold was not "What is possible?"
but "What is prudent?" In order to emphasize this point, Murray
suggested that the following questions be asked about the legitimacy of any law which is proposed to enforce public morality.

> . . . will the ban be obeyed, at least by the generality? Is it
> enforceable against the disobedient? Is it prudent to under-
> take the enforcement of this or that ban, in view of the pos-
> sibility of harmful effects in other areas of social life? Is the
> instrumentality of coercive law a good means for the eradi-
> cation of this or that social vice? And, since a means is not a
> good means if it fails to work in most cases, what are the les-
> sons of experience in the matter?[23]

Even if these questions could be answered in the affirmative,
Murray stressed, any effort to utilize the coercive power of law to
enforce moral standards should always keep in mind the primary
political principle of natural law, that "the more important forces
that make for social order rise from the depths of the free human
spirit—the forces of civic virtue, which give birth to a love of the
common good, the forces of moral virtue, which instill a spirit of

social justice and charity into all human associations, and above all the forces of religious faith. . . ."[24]

In emphasizing that the moral functions of government were quite limited in scope, Murray was in no way denying the ethical nature and role of the state. For while he endorsed Pius XII's shift from a primarily ethical to a primarily juridical notion of the state, Murray believed that Leo XIII had been correct in arguing that every government is forced to adopt some fundamental stance toward the moral heritage of the community; either its actions will enhance that moral heritage, or they will challenge it.

> It follows therefore that there can be no such thing as governmental neutrality in questions concerning the moral bases of society. Such neutrality would, as I have just said, be as impossible as it would be immoral. The official attitude in such questions must be partisan; government must take a side. Concretely, it must positively favor the human heritage against those who would dissipate it by the corrosion of doubt, denial, or cynicism. This is its obvious duty to the society of which it is the agent; this, at the very least, is a matter of vital political self-interest.[25]

To deny this reality, Murray believed, was to posit an ahistorical concept of government. This was precisely what the movement of Continental laicism had done: in the guise of impartiality, it had cut away the religious underpinnings of European culture and set the *res sacrae* adrift from their theoretical moorings. And in the process, it had eroded moral standards throughout society and unleashed the demonic scourge of modern totalitarianism. For Murray, the lesson was clear: "government is inescapably on the side either of good or of evil. It cannot evade the law of all human action; for it is itself a manner of human action."[26]

A second major specification of the limits of "the public order" can be seen in Murray's writings upon the economic role of the government in society. As has been mentioned earlier, economics was one area which Murray shied away from in his writings and speeches. He recognized that the modern study of economics was an increasingly complex field in which he had little expertise, and so he was loath to venture into the thickets of substantive economic analysis.[27] Yet he also recognized that the expansion of government in the twentieth century consisted in large part of increased intervention in the economy, and so he formulated a series of guidelines with which to evaluate proposals for new economic activities on the part of the state.

The central themes of Murray's analysis of the economic function of the state sprang from his application of *Rerum Novarum* to the situation of post-war economic life. Murray argued that in his path-breaking encyclical on justice and the industrial order, Leo XIII had outlined four basic principles for government activity in the economic sphere. The first of these principles assigned to government a concern for the general prosperity of society; the institutions of the state were obligated to enhance the economic well-being both of individuals and the community as a whole.[28] Clearly, Murray did not intend this to signify that the state enjoyed the primary responsibility for the creation of general prosperity, but he did believe that the "general providence" of the government toward the economic well-being of its people was the essential premise for any governmental action in the economic sphere. This was underscored by the second principle of Murray's interpretation of *Rerum Novarum,* the assertion that "the essential action required of government . . . is an action in favor of the free associations within the commonwealth upon which, according to the principles of right social order, there falls in the first instance the responsibility for promoting the particular social goods which integrate the common good. . . ."[29] Having reiterated the primacy of mediating institutions in promoting the prosperity of society, Murray outlined his third principle derived from *Rerum Novarum.* Here he quotes Leo XIII directly: "If therefore any injury has been done, or threatens to be done to the interests of the community—the kind of injury which cannot otherwise be repaired or prevented—it is necessary for public authority to intervene."[30] The direct action of government in such cases was to be limited by the specific evil it was directed to remedy and could extend no farther. This severe stricture on the role of the state was mitigated, however, by Murray's fourth principle of *Rerum Novarum:* "the special duty of government to come to the aid of 'the unhappy multitude, which has no security through resources of its own.'"[31]

Murray believed that through these principles Leo XIII had drawn a careful balance between state interventionism and the state neutrality of liberal economics. The encyclical, in concert with the modifications proposed by *Quadragesimo Anno,* carefully prescribed the limits to the activity of government. At the same time, Leo XIII had "boldly taken from the enemy the truth that he had—the principle that government, under the conditions of modern society, must take an active role in economic life."[32] The reasons for this change were manifest:

> Industrialism had wrought a progressive depersonalization of economic life. And the impersonality of the employer-employee relationship had in turn bred moral irresponsibility. A new "master" had appeared, the corporation. . . . The private conscience had ceased to be an effective means of social control. Therefore the only alternative to the tyranny of socialism or the anarchy of economic liberalism was the growth of the public conscience and its expression through the medium of law and governmental act—a medium whose impersonality matched the impersonality of the economic life into which it was thrust as a principle of order.[33]

Thus just as the creation of a new "human reality" in the form of widespread literacy had called for a change in the application of the principles of natural law to the constitutional order, so too a new "human reality" in the form of depersonalized economic relations called for a change in the application of natural law to the economic order. And a critical factor in determining the scope of government action lay in the needs of Leo's "unhappy multitude," the poor of the world.

Murray recognized that changes in the economic structure of society since the time of Leo XIII had rendered some of *Rerum Novarum*'s analysis anachronistic—the encyclical's failure to address issues of fiscal and monetary policy and to answer questions raised by the growth of general welfare policies were two such areas. But Murray believed that governmental economic activity should continue to be defined as a measured response to grave social evils which could not be obviated by other means. "The fact that such social evils exist on a fairly large scale today should not be seen as invalidating this approach."[34] For to abandon this principle was to abandon the third political precept of natural law: the Christian concept that the state is a set of limited ends which do not engulf the great society.[35] At the same time, not to recognize the new and legitimate demands for government intervention brought on by modern and depersonalized economic processes was to subscribe to the liberal economic rigidity that both Leo XIII and Pius XII had condemned. The only course compatible with the principles of natural law, Murray concluded, lay in a careful case-by-case analysis, retaining a delicate balance between the need for limited government and the human suffering that cried out to be remedied. In seeking such a balance, it would be necessary to forge creative new solutions to the problems proposed by modern economic life; such institutions as workers' cooperatives and labor-industry councils could be opportunities to coordinate the enormous institutions of industrialization without the direct supervision of government.[36] Balance and creativity: these were the necessary tools for defining the economic dimension of "the public order" in the present age.

Religion and the State

One further element in Murray's conception of the role of the state in society needs further elaboration before it is possible to turn to his critique of American politics, and that is the body of thought which Murray developed concerning the relationship between religion and the state. Indeed, Murray's work on the issue of Church-state relations remains the most celebrated facet of his life's work, for it provided much of the ground-work for the monumental shift in Catholic doctrine which occurred with the promulgation of *Dignitatis Humanae* in 1965. It is in this area of Church-state relations that Murray's thought shows the most development during the period from 1940 to his death in 1967, but in keeping with the focus of this work the stress here will be given not to the process of development, but rather to Murray's mature thought on this question as it affected his critique of the American political system.

In Murray's view, the primary right which religion in general and religious bodies in particular legitimately demanded from the state was the right of freedom—or, as Murray was so fond of putting it, the right of immunity from the power of the state. In its first instance, this immunity was the demand of the individual person, secure in his human rights, for freedom from coercion in the religious sphere:

> (This claim to immunity) is valid not only in its objective foundation, which is man's native dignity, but also in the crucial instance, in the citizen's confrontation with the authority that has charge of the juridical order. If there be an authority that can possibly enter a counterclaim to the claim of the human person to immunity from coercion in matters religious, this authority could only be government, which is responsible for the establishment and maintenance of the juridical order of society. However, the moral claim or right of the human person is original, as original as the human person itself, which is the foundation, the end, and the subject of the whole juridical order. . . . Therefore, the basic exigence of the human person is immunity from coercion, and the human rights that spring from it are in possession. Government must accept the burden of proving that it has the right to bring coercion to bear. This, however, it cannot do, except when its own fundamental responsibility becomes controlling—in the case of the violation of the public order; a contravention of the necessary conditions of social coexistence; or a public offense that imperils the pillars of society. . . .[37]

Thus Murray did not see the individual's claim of immunity as totally inviolable; the state could override this claim in cases where the public order was truly in jeopardy. But the claim of immunity in the religious sphere was so strong that the state had to present overwhelming evidence that society was truly at risk before it could interfere with a person's religious beliefs or practices.

Moreover, the claim of freedom from the power of the state did not belong merely to individuals, but extended to religious communities in their corporate identities. Again, it was framed within the concept of immunity.

> As asserted in the interpersonal order of human rights, the freedom of the Church, whether as a community or as an

authority, is and can only be negative in its content; it is a freedom "from" any manner of coercive constraint imposed by any secular power. As further guaranteed in the constitutional order of civil rights, the freedom of the Church consequently appears as an immunity.[38]

This was the great issue which the Church had sought to vindicate since the time of Gelasius: the conviction that the power of the state should not extend to the sphere of religious belief and practice, and that religious communities, not the state, had the responsibility for making society religious. "Government does not stand in the service of religious truth, as an instrument for its defense or its propagation . . . the duty of service (to religion) is discharged by service rendered to the freedom of religion in society."[39]

In arguing for the immunity of religious practice from the power of the state, Murray was saying little that would unsettle modern secularist thinkers. Implicit in Murray's approach to religion, however, was the idea that the state does have an interest in promoting the religious health of society. And this is where Murray's conception of the role of the state crashed headlong into the heart of secularist doctrine. For Murray was convinced that the flourishing of religion was a fundamental part of the common good of society. "The values of religious experience, personal and communal . . . are not simply transcendental," Murray wrote in 1967, "they also affect the substance and quality of human life in the civil community. (Thus) the duty of government to the common good in the fullness of its realization necessarily includes a duty to religion in society—the duty of recognition and favor. No legal transcription of this duty is suggested; only the principle itself is affirmed."[40]

Murray may have argued that including religious vigor among the elements of the common good of society did not suggest any legal transcription of the duties of the state, but both Murray and the secularists whom he opposed recognized that such an interpretation of the common good would generate a significantly more positive stance toward religion in general on the part of the state. And in an age when the state's role was dramatically increasing, the stance of the state toward religion in general was critically important. It was for this reason that Murray pressed home again and again his argument that religious values constitute an essential part of the common good of society, and that in denying this truth modern secularism cast itself as an enemy to society:

> ... the ancient tradition which regarded the atheist as the enemy of ordered society had not been evacuated of all truth. . . . The Christian must regard militant laicism or secularism as inimical to the orderly progress of society toward justice and freedom. In particular, its dogma of absolute separation of church and state is unacceptable, even on the grounds of the common good of society. The principle of religious freedom does indeed demand a certain separation of church and state, in the sense that religious affairs are removed from the competence of the state. Similarly, the true secularity of society is to be recognized, as *Gaudium et Spes* recognizes it, in the sense that the "good of society" is to be regarded as an end in itself. . . . On the other hand, no Christian can admit what the Council refused to admit, namely that secular government may maintain a neutrality of indifference toward religion. . . .[41]

But this was precisely what the secularist drift was forcing Christians to admit in American society. Just as Continental laicism had enticed progressive believers to endorse the supposed neutrality of the state, only to see that neutrality used to undermine religion, so too modern secularists were urging believers to endorse a total separation of Church and state in the twentieth century. And the results of both these movements would be the same: the destruction of the religious vitality which underlay the *res sacrae* in society. It was precisely in order to avoid such an outcome that Murray invoked the same principle which he had utilized in treating the role of the state toward fundamental moral norms: the state must make a choice; not to choose is to opt for a vacuum of values. When faced with a choice between promoting religious aridity and religious vitality, the state must take a fundamental stance in favor of the latter, so that, in the words of the Council, "society itself may enjoy the benefits of justice and peace which flow from the fidelity of men toward God and toward his holy will."[42]

But addressing the question of the state's responsibilities toward individual believers and religious communities was only one-half of the issue raised by the interaction of Church and state. Equally important was the question of the legitimate role of religious values in influencing the activities of the state. Murray believed that religion had an irreplaceable role in the formulation of public policy. Only religious belief could anchor the identity of the state in an order of justice which was deeper than the passions of the people or the whims of the rulers. Only religious values could provide a full-blown theory of the dignity of the human person, which was the sole legitimate end of the state. And only religious communities had the ethical power to awaken a moral consensus in the people of the nation and to focus that consensus again and again on the public issues which come to the fore of political life. Thus Murray maintained from his first published piece to his last that religious values were essential to the establishment of sound public policy and to the realization of the limited temporal end which was entrusted to the state.

But anxious as Murray was to see religious values involved in the formation of public policy, he was just as anxious to insure that theology not rigidly control political policy. For too intimate a bond between religious beliefs and the actions of the state would lead to "the peril of the corruption of both—the corruption of religion and the corruption of the state."[43] The end of the state was markedly different from the total end of the human person, and any effort to mix these two perspectives indiscriminately could only produce poor public policy and great hostility in a religiously pluralistic society. The proper path lay in the mediation of religious truth by the public philosophy of the natural law tradition:

> The Catholic assumes that "religion," for all its indispensability as the basic energy of civilization, is not a force directive of public affairs, except in so far as its truths and imperatives are transmitted to society and to the state through the medium of the public philosophy that has been elaborated by human reason over centuries of reflection and experience.[44]

Herein lay the answer to the proper role of religious values in guiding the actions of the state: they must give spiritual energy to the actions of government; they must give a moral grounding to the actions of government; but they must never be used to determine public policy in a manner which violates the limited nature of the state as defined by the principles of natural law. Reason, not the biblical ethic or any other specific religious concept, was to be the force directing public affairs in the just state, according to Murray.[45] And reason, which was deep enough to grasp the existence of God's order of justice, yet broad enough to be intelligible to all sensible men and women, was fully capable of guiding the actions of the state toward freedom, justice, and truth.

The American Political Tradition

John Courtney Murray did not set out to formulate a comprehensive theory of the state. Indeed, Murray never brought together all of his writings on the nature of the state in any one article; one must pore through his life's work, both published and unpublished, in order to put together the elements which comprised Murray's theory of politics. The reason for this is that Murray did not see his theory of the state as an end in itself. Rather he saw it as an instrument with which to clarify the two major issues which preoccupied him for over forty years—the question of religious liberty and the effort to construct a public theology for contemporary America. In the course of addressing both of these issues Murray utilized his theory of the state repeatedly to assess the American political tradition in light of Catholic teaching, and his novel interpretation of American politics still stands as a compelling outline of the political experience of the American people.[46]

The most striking element in Murray's description of American politics was that he not only found it to be consonant with Catholic theology, but also found it to be a product of Catholic theology.

> In the Constitutional period of American history, the prevailing view was there are certain principles of right and justice which, by reason of their intrinsic excellence, ought to govern the action of men in society; that these principles are prior in

origin and dignity to all human enactments; that they are
independent of the human legislative will, and binding upon
it; that they are as eternal and immutable as the order of reason itself, because like it, they have their source in the Eternal
Reason of God; that in relation to such principles human laws
are merely a record or a transcript, and that their enactment
is not an act of will or power, but one of discovery and
declaration.[47]

One can be forgiven for wondering if these words were meant as
a description of views of the Founding Fathers, or as a description of the principles of natural law. But the parallels between the
two were not accidental in Murray's eyes. For it was his belief that
the best paradigm for understanding the constitutional tradition
in the United States lay not in the thought of John Locke or the
Enlightenment, nor in the economic analysis of Charles Beard,
nor in the sociological notions of jurisprudence propounded by
Oliver Wendell Holmes, but in the tradition of natural law as it
had been developed and propounded within the Catholic
Church.

Such a proposition was not as difficult to defend as one
might think. True, the United States was a Protestant nation at
the time of its founding, and the framers of the Constitution
would never have looked at their work as an outgrowth of Catholic theology. But during the 1940's a series of scholars led by
Clinton Rossiter had reevaluated the fundamental precepts that
underlay the American political tradition, and they had concluded that these precepts could be most fruitfully viewed not as
extensions of Enlightenment thought, but as part of the tradition
of natural law.

In basing their final campaign of resistance to imperial power
on "the supreme and uncontrollable laws of nature," the
Americans stood firm in one of their greatest traditions. . . .
The mind of God as read by history, the plan of nature as
analyzed by right reason, and the history of mankind as interpreted by the scholars of the nation all proclaimed the reality
of moral limits on political power.[48]

In Murray's eyes, the historical work done by Rossiter and his
colleagues confirmed what the Catholic community had always

known about the American constitutional tradition: that it was consonant with Catholic social teaching precisely because it sprang from the same epistemological and historical roots, and because it endorsed the tradition of reason as the basis for all political activity.[49]

The reason for this happy circumstance, according to Murray, lay in the nature and timing of the Revolution which had established and formed the American political tradition. The founding of the United States took place before the liberal tradition of Western thought had been secularized by the Revolutionary messianism of 1789. The great medieval principles of government, as they had been enshrined in the English tradition of common law, were the principles of government upon which the Founding Fathers had been raised. And because the break of the colonies from England was a limited severing of political ties, rather than a comprehensive social revolution, the great liberal tradition of political and social thought was not overturned in 1776. "By reason of this fact, the American revolution, quite unlike its French counterpart, was less a revolution than a conservation. It conserved, by giving newly vital form to, the liberal tradition of politics, whose ruin in Continental Europe was about to be consummated by the first great modern essay in totalitarianism."[50]

Murray believed that one could see this fundamental distinction between the American and Jacobin traditions in the fact that American politics saw the created order of God, rather than the unrestrained will of the people, as the foundation for political life:

It may be remarked here that the famous American phrase "We, the People . . ." is the very negation of Jacobinism. The American concept of "government by the people" does not attribute to the people the divinity implied in the Revolutionary idea of "the sovereignty of the people"; it simply embodies the ancient principle of consent in a developed and still recognizably Christian sense. The American system neither supposes nor effects an exile of God from society. Finally, the state itself, in its distinction from society, rests on no pretense that even political life can be organized "without any regard

for God or for the order established by Him." On the contrary, the Constitution of the U.S. has to be read in the light
of the Declaration of Independence, in which there is explicit
recognition of God and of an order established by Him—the
order of human rights, which is part of the universal moral
order to whose imperatives the political order must be
obedient.[51]

It was the great good fortune of the United States that the most
corrupting elements of secularism had never entered the mainstream of American politics. The U.S. had known little of the messianic ideology of the Jacobin tradition. It had escaped the
upheavals wrought by Continental laicism. America had been
spared the brutal totalitarianism of the twentieth century, and the
banishment of God from the public square which had made that
totalitarianism possible. From its founding in 1776 to the end of
World War II, the United States had preserved a vibrant and balanced political tradition because it never lost sight of the natural
law principles which lay at its base.

As a result, Murray believed, one could find in the political
dimension of the American consensus all of the fundamental precepts which comprised the Thomistic theory of the state. Chief
among these was the distinction between the state and society,
and the recognition that the state was comprised of a series of
limited ends designed to serve the wider good of society:

The American people have repudiated the Continental concept of the omnicompetent society-state. The consequence is
that the state remains interior to society, not outside of it, as
it were, and surrounding it. The state is an aspect of the life
of society—a pervasive aspect (as modern law is pervasive) but
not an all-embracing or omnicompetent aspect. The state
stands in the service of society and is subordinate to its purpose. It is limited even in its office of ministry—limited by a
whole structure of personal and social rights not of its creation, and limited too by the principle of consent. The state is
not primatial; society possesses the primacy over the state.
And in the sense that the spiritual is located in society, not in
the state, the principle of the primacy of the spiritual over the
political holds sway. Moreover, the channels for the enforce-

ment of this primacy exist in the form of popular institutions
of rule, through which the conscience of society makes itself
the norm for the action of the state.[52]

In Murray's mind there could be no political proposition more
antithetical to the American tradition than the idea that the state
defined its own scope and its own morality. The heart of America's success in maintaining a healthy society was in its adherence
to the medieval principle of "The Great Society" which proclaimed that government was meant to serve, not to dominate.

But how was this over-arching principle to be maintained in
the actions of government? Through the power of the Constitution, according to Murray. Indeed, it is difficult to overestimate
Murray's respect for the U.S. Constitution as a political instrument. For he saw the Constitution not merely as a document
which apportioned the powers of government in the American
system. It was also the living receptacle of the political faith of the
American people, a receptacle which communicated to each new
generation the fundamental truths of natural law:

> Three things about the American Constitution, in its original
> form of 1787 and its subsequent development through
> amendment and judicial decision, have made it the object of
> reverence, even to the point of worship, among the American
> people. First, it is regarded as a document that gives expres-
> sion to the great common principles of freedom, equality, and
> justice which are the moral heritage of mankind, precepts of
> that higher law under which government must stand, because
> it is the law of God, declared through nature and reason. Sec-
> ond, the Constitution was the work of wise men, whose wis-
> dom has been tested by time and proved true. Veneration of
> the "Founding Fathers" is bound up with veneration of the
> Constitution whose framework they devised with such wisdom
> as to make it a genuinely living law, adaptable to the lessons
> of a later experience.[53]

In short, the U.S. Constitution, especially when read in conjunc-
tion with the Declaration of Independence, reflected all of the
primary principles of natural law contained in Murray's theory of
the state. It clearly rooted human law in the created order of jus-

tice. It proclaimed that political authority sprang from the action of the community, and that the state must serve the wider good of society. Finally, the Constitution presented the fivefold aim of the state within a framework tight enough to avoid the totalitarian tendencies of modern life, yet dynamic enough to bring the processes of government to bear upon the new challenges generated by twentieth century society.

One could discern in the Bill of Rights this same concern for Christian principles of politics, according to Murray. For the first ten amendments to the Constitution represented a clear limitation upon the extent to which the power of government could intrude into the lives of its citizens. Like Murray's concept of "the public order," the Bill of Rights stated forthrightly that the moral aspirations of law are minimal, and that freedom rather than coercion should be the dominant theme of societal life. Equally important, in Murray's view, was the notion that the liberties enumerated in the Bill of Rights were not derived from abstract and individualistic reasoning, as the French Declaration on "The Rights of Man and the Citizen" had been. On the contrary, they sprang from a social conception of the human person that reflected both the Thomistic tradition and the notion of *res sacrae:*

> The American Bill of Rights is not a piece of rationalist theory; it is the product of Christian history. Behind it one can see, not the philosophy of the Enlightenment, but the faith of Christianity. The "man" to whom America extends a Bill of Rights is, whether he knows it or not, the Christian man.[54]

And only "the Christian man" could ever be secure in his liberties because they rested not upon a piece of parchment, nor even upon a consensus among the American people, but upon an order of values which would never fall prey to the tides of passion, or fanaticism, or intolerance.

But if Murray saw in the Bill of Rights as a whole a brilliant reflection of the Christian conception of politics, it was the First Amendment which represented to him the centerpiece of the American political tradition.[55] The Founding Fathers, in his view, sought not the religious sterility fashioned by the Jacobin government, but the religious flourishing that was necessary for the maintenance of social virtue. And the political heritage of the United States had always borne witness to the fact that only values rooted in religious faith had the power to endure the challenges which come to any sovereign people. "Virtue must have its roots in religion," he wrote in 1956, "not in some Comtean 'religion of humanity,' but in that basic moral virtue whose two acts are, first, an adoring, thankful prayer to the God who is Creator and Lord of human life, and second, a humble devotion to the imperatives of His divine will. This is the American Proposition."[56]

But how could one foster such a flourishing of religion in a nation as diverse as the United States? In Murray's view, the First Amendment did so by recognizing three realities. The first was the immunity of the conscience of the individual from the coercive power of the state. The second was the religious plurality of America and the injury which would accrue to the peace of society from any effort to impose religious orthodoxy. The third was the limited end of the state which did not extend to matters of theological disagreement.

> The state is not a theologian, a prophet of the way to eternal salvation; in Madison's phrase, it is "not a competent judge of religious truths," able to use its authority to enforce their acceptance. Rather, the American state is essentially a layman, who in matters of religion accepts the authority inherent in the consciences of the human persons who are its citizens, and is obedient to their exigencies, insofar as these do not conflict with the public order.[57]

In recognizing these truths, the First Amendment rendered to American society the primary service toward religion which Murray called for in his theory of the state: namely, the enhancement of religious freedom and the clear recognition of the state's inability to intrude upon religious conflicts.

But in the very act of declaring its incompetence regarding religious divisions, the First Amendment made clear its fundamental divergence from the supposed neutrality of Continental laicism. For whereas Continental liberalism saw "freedom of religion" as "freedom from religion," the First Amendment saw just the opposite. "It has meant the freedom of religion to make society religious, by all its inherent resources of persuasiveness. Americans have recognized that the spiritual and moral enterprise which is democracy cannot succeed unless the churches themselves are engaged in it, in their own way. . . . To the same end, a general 'encouragement of religion' is in the best traditions of American government.''[58] In short, as Murray's theory of the state demanded, the U.S. Constitution declared its incompetence to interfere in religious questions, while simultaneously professing a general regard for religion as part of the common good of society. "It does not envisage an evacuation of the Christian substance of society; it simply imposes restrictions on the legal activity of the state.''[59]

When one stands back and examines Murray's outline of the political heritage of the United States, what emerges is not a comprehensive portrait of American politics, but a consciously selective one. How, then, is one to understand Murray's conception of the American political tradition, or, as he preferred to call it, the American Proposition? By understanding first and foremost that Murray saw the American political tradition as an ideal as much as a reality. Certainly he believed that at the founding of the Republic, and for much of its history, the principles of natural law had been the primary foundation for American politics. And he would have been the first to reject the idea that any ideal of government which is divorced from realities of political life could assist a nation in its search for the common good. But in the final analysis, Murray's conception of the American political tradition represents not a complete portrait of American political history, but a distillation of the noblest aspirations of that history. For Murray, the American Proposition constituted a great experiment in self-government, an experiment which had brought new hope to the world. "The Great Experiment was a Great Hope precisely because it was an effort to set at the center of organized social life the idea of man in his sacredness, in his panoply of human rights, with his endowment of spiritual freedom, as a being created by God, who must make his own creations serve purposes defined by God.''[60]

By thus portraying the American political tradition as normative rather than descriptive, Murray invested it with the same power in the political order which his concept of the public consensus had in the cultural order: the power to challenge the American people to reverse ominous trends which secularism and the spirit of "modernity" had wrought in American life. That these trends existed he had no doubt.

> ... today as we view the status of the Great Experiment, we may well wonder whether the tragic historical flaw which weighs upon human achievements is now beginning to operate upon this one. Is democracy, the depository of man's hopes for freedom, destined to become simply a new grave for the ancient inspiration, once more foiled, frustrated, slain?[61]

Murray's answer was an unequivocal "no." And it was a "no" that was rooted in the belief that the noblest ideals of the American political tradition, so visibly reflective of the principles of natural law, must once again be mobilized to reform the political life of the United States. The American Proposition was not merely a tradition which should be reverenced; it was also the answer to the most momentous and complicated political problems facing the American people in the post-war era.

The Idolization of Democracy

The first area of American politics which needed reform in the post-war era, according to Murray, was the notion of democracy itself. Democracy was the very essence of the American Proposition; it had undergirded the efforts of the Founding Fathers to establish a new nation, and it was the guiding principle which Americans had always believed marked their destiny as a people. But while Murray fully shared the American attachment to democratic process, and indeed argued that democracy was a firm mandate of natural law in an age of widespread literacy and education, he was convinced that the democratic idea was being corrupted in twentieth century America. "Democracy was conceived to be man's servant; but now it is becoming his idol. And we know that it is the fate of those who worship idols that they should be enslaved to what they worship. Democracy, once a political and social idea, now pretends to be a religion."[62]

The first element in this corruption of the democratic ideal concerned the growing tendency of Americans to define democracy in purely procedural terms, rather than as a full-bodied theory of human and political rights. Increasingly, Murray believed, Americans evaluated their political processes on the degree to which they adhered slavishly to democratic procedures, rather than on the just outcomes which they produced. "I should say that I by no means deprecate the value of procedures," Murray wrote. "But it still remains true that to reduce the entire substance of democracy to a matter of the method of doing things, independently of any judgment on the rightness or value of what is done, is to abandon the public philosophy and the political tradition which launched our Republic."[63] Moreover, in Murray's view, it was to falsify the true meaning of democracy itself:

> I take it that the political substance of democracy consists in the admission of an order of rights antecedent to the state, the political form of society. These are the rights of the person, the family, the church, the associations men freely form for economic, cultural, social and religious ends. In the admission of this prior order of rights—inviolable as well by democratic majorities as well as by absolute monarchs—consists the service-character of the democratic state. And this service-character is still further reinforced by the affirmation, implicit in the admission of the order of human rights, of another order of right also antecedent to the state and regulative of its public action as a state; I mean the order of justice.[64]

Murray believed that the American people had, to a great extent, lost sight of this fuller understanding of democracy, and were substituting for it a narrow proceduralism which evaluated political actions not upon the basis of right and wrong, but upon the momentary wishes of the majority. This narrow interpretation of democracy held that

> politics is worked out by the community by the democratic process of free discussion and free choice of the individual as individual. This is proclaimed as the American way. Law is not the mind of the Law-maker, but the will of the people in terms

of the majority. This will of the majority is law in as far as the community can enforce it. It has different meanings at different times, relative to the concrete period. There is no relation to any such abstraction as the natural or divine law.[65]

Murray's disdain for such a way of thinking can be gauged by the fact that he called such a theory of democracy "totalitarian democracy," and he saw it as the modern day equivalent of the political monism which had led to the degradation of the *res sacrae hominis* throughout the history of Western civilization.[66]

Murray believed that it was no accident that this view of democracy was becoming dominant in the United States just as secularism was on the rise. For he saw the idolization of democracy as one more manifestation of secularist influence in American society. It was the political dimension of the secularist assertion that the human person was self-sufficient, his own creator and ruler and judge.

> Consciously and unconsciously democracy is being transformed into the political and social organization of a great error, whose source is in the pagan darkness that always lingers, never fully clarified, in the mind of man. I mean the ancient idolatrous error of the self-sufficient man, who regards himself as sole architect of his own freedom, single author of the values that govern his life, ultimate judge of right and wrong, true and false.[67]

This great error was none other than the denial of God's crucial role in the political process, as the author of the *res sacrae* which could be the only anchor for a true democratic society. The propagation of this error was a fundamental apostasy from the American political tradition; it represented the divinization of a political system which could only end in servitude for the human person, rather than freedom.[68]

But this apostasy represented not only a threat in the political sphere. It constituted, in Murray's view, a threat to the entire social and cultural order of American society. For a central corollary of the new democratic ideology was the conviction that "the democratic process as such is somehow valid, universally valid and singly valid in the determination of all matters both of truth and of value. . . ."[69] Democratic process was to be utilized not only in strictly political questions, but in the determination of all issues of import in every institution of society. To Murray, this was nothing less than political monism in a new garb:

> What is urged is a monism, not so much of the political order itself, as of a political technique. This proposition is that all the issues of human life—intellectual, religious, and moral issues, as well as formally political issues—are to be regarded as, or resolved into, political issues and are to be settled by the single omnicompetent political technique of majority vote. On the surface, the monism is one of process; Madison's "republican principle" affords the Final Grounds for the Last Say on All Human Questions. But the underlying idea is a monism of power: "One there is whereby this world is ruled—the power in the people, expressing itself in the preference of a majority; and beyond or beside or above this power there is no other."[70]

This novel monism, so alluring in its regard for the democratic spirit of "modernity," posed an overwhelming threat to American society and culture, in Murray's view. It was the root of the ethical relativism that was increasingly dominant in the intellectual life of the nation, and it threatened to undermine the legitimacy of every social, religious, and cultural institution which did not accept the democratic process as its basic organizing principle.

Murray believed that this extension of democratic monism to the cultural sphere posed two specific threats which had to be met directly and forcefully by religious men and women. The first threat was to the legitimacy of religious institutions; for the tenets of totalitarian democracy struck at the very heart of the ecclesial self-understanding of non-democratic institutions such as Catholicism. "The dogmatic ideology of democracy says it is implicit that Catholicism is authoritarian because it is hierarchical. There is no place for it in democracy. All manners of human relationships are to be organized on democratic lines. The claim today is that men freely come together to form a Church, as any society. This assumption is also dogmatic, that is, not proven and not provable."[71] Murray disputed the notion that the Church was a voluntary organization which should be run on democratic lines. He disputed even more the claim that all churches should be democratic in order for them to be considered truly "American." And he disputed most of all the intrusion of procedural democratic monism into the religious sphere, for this intrusion represented a dangerous confusion of the temporal order with the spiritual order, a confusion of the order of politics with the order of truth.

But the threat of democratic proceduralism to the cultural order was not limited to religious bodies; it also endangered the whole order of morality in society. Murray was deeply concerned about the growing tendency in American society to equate legality with morality, and thus to lose all sight of the distinction between private and public morality.

> Unless this distinction, like that between morality and law, is grasped, the result is a fiasco of all morality. From the foolish position that all sins ought to be made crimes, it is only a step to the knavish position that, since certain acts . . . are obviously not crimes, they are not even sins.[72]

Such a "knavish" position was in sharp contrast to the more subtle relationship between morality and law which characterized Murray's own theory of the state. For Murray was in many ways a minimalist in his expectations of law. He saw it as protecting the public order and not as a moral blueprint for society. American society had also historically been minimalist in its expectations of law. But Murray discerned in post-war America a growing belief that law *did* represent a moral blueprint for society, that public morality was coextensive with legal enactments, and that even private morality must be judged by its accordance with current legislation. In Murray's mind, this represented a totalitarian notion of democracy and government, and a betrayal of the divinely instituted order of values which had guided the United States since its inception. If such a trend were to continue unabated, Murray believed, the moral health of the United States would be irredeemably damaged; for while a society could flourish when its expectations of law were minimal, it could not flourish when its expectations of morality were minimal.

Thus in Murray's eyes the idolization of democracy represented an insidious trend in twentieth century America. The fundamental insight of the Founding Fathers—that just laws can best be attained through democratic procedures—had been turned on its head, leading to the belief that democratic procedures were the measure of, and not the means to, justice in law. The first principle of the American Constitution—that the political sphere is limited in scope—had been evacuated of all substance, as both religious and moral truths came to be evaluated on the basis of their adherence to democratic processes. Murray was far from despairing of the democratic impulse; he still saw it as the great hope of humankind in the twentieth century. But he was convinced that it would continue to be a hope and not a threat to humankind only if it were confined to the political sphere and not regarded as a foundational principle for the entire cultural order. "If you make a divinity of a political and social system," Murray wrote, "you become its creature; you risk becoming a political and social slave."[73] It was Murray's goal that no such slavery would be the legacy of twentieth century America.

A Wall of Separation

The growing idolization of democracy was a serious threat to American society in Murray's view, but it was merely one manifestation of a much larger danger to the United States: the progressive secularization of the nations's political institutions. Murray firmly believed that the greatest service which government could render to religion was the provision of an atmosphere of freedom. But he recognized that in the twentieth century, which was witnessing an ever-expanding role for government, the critical question would be whether that freedom was to be based on a recognition that religion forms part of the public good, or on a dogmatic assertion that government should have no contact with anything religious:

> Woodrow Wilson in *The New Freedom* showed how exclusive insistence on freedom as sheer immunity from governmental power opens the way to the tyrannies of other powers, not governmental, that gain control of governmental processes. The lesson has been heeded in the economic field; it needs to

be hearkened to in the religious and educational fields. Join
a rigidly negative concept of religious freedom, as sheer
immunity from coercion by governmental power, to a rigidly
absolute, end-in-itself concept of separation of church and
state, as meaning absolutely no aid to religions by government, and you have opened the way to the subtle tyrannies of
irreligion, secularist ideologies, false political and educational
philosophies, and the dangerous myth of "democracy as a
religion." Such a development is utterly foreign to the letter,
spirit, and intent of the First Amendment, and will be consequently disastrous to American society.[74]

Yet disastrous as the development was, and contrary to the spirit
of the First Amendment as it might have been, it seemed unde-
niable that the twentieth century had witnessed a growing consensus within the United States that there should be a clear wall
of separation between government and religion, and that government's concern for the flourishing of religious life in the nation
was to be a thing of the past.

The primary vehicle for this secularization of American political institutions was the United States Supreme Court, in Murray's view. In the cases of Everson versus the Board of Education
(1947) and McCollum versus the Board of Education (1948), the
Court had endorsed the concept of a "wall of separation"
between Church and state, thus giving rise "to the decided
impression that the state . . . is now neutral *against* religious
belief."[75] According to the principles advanced by the Court in
these two cases, government could not touch religious belief or
practice in any way which might be seen as support for religious
purposes. Murray believed that such reasoning turned the First
Amendment on its head and wholeheartedly embraced the core
of the secularist agenda: "In the name of freedom of religion it
decrees that the relations of government to religion are to be controlled by the fundamental tenet of secularism—the social irrelevance of religion, its exclusion from the secular affairs of the
City and its educational system, its relegation to the private forum
of conscience or at best to the hushed confines of the sacristy."[76]

Murray saw such a view as a direct repudiation of the American Constitutional tradition. The goals of the First Amendment
had been to safeguard the full and free exercise of religion by

preventing the government from favoring any single religion over another. Thus the restrictions on government activity which the First Amendment had erected were instrumental to the free flourishing of religion; in no way were they reflective of a hostility to religion.

> The whole intent of the First Amendment was to protect, not to injure, the interests of religion in American society. Here there enters with its full force the fact also adverted to by the Court in the earlier Zorach case, "We are religious people whose institutions presuppose a Supreme Being." Lincoln put it more briefly in his famous phrase "This nation under God." In America the separation of government and religion . . . does not mean that government is hostile or even indifferent to the things of God. On the contrary, the tradition in America has been . . . that government respects the religious nature of the people and accommodates the public service to their spiritual needs.[77]

Murray may have believed that this had been the tradition in America for most of its history, but he clearly recognized that the new absolutism with which the Supreme Court was interpreting the separation of Church and state would produce a new tradition in which government's total exclusion of religious life from its purview would signal hostility, and not support for religious belief.

The primary example of this hostility, in Murray's view, lay in the sphere of education. For in the total exclusion of religious schools from any public aid whatsoever, one could discern the ultimate consequences of the absolutization of the separation between Church and state. The individual who sought an education for his child which included religious values was to be denied any public support, while the individual who did not demand that religion be part of the educational curriculum for his child was to be wholly supported. The school which brought any mention of God into the classroom was to be penalized, while the school which taught its students about a world where God did not exist was to be rewarded. Murray viewed such a situation with alarm, and he labeled it "the subsidization of secularism, as the one national religion and culture, whose agent of propagation is the secularized public school."[78]

Murray clearly recognized that the issue of government aid to religious schools, and the overall question of government's stance toward religion, were intricate problems. But he did not believe that they reduced to a choice between either the excessive entanglement of Church and state or the total exclusion of religious practices from the purview of the state. Rather, Murray suggested that the solution to this vexing issue could be found in the traditional American principle of accommodation.

> (The principle of accommodation) is simply an extension of the more general principle of the service-character of American government. . . . It has never been the tradition in America for government in any of its agencies to regard the spiritual and religious needs of the people as being entirely outside the scope of its active concern. On the contrary, instances of government accommodating its public service to these needs are deeply embedded in our constitutional tradition.[79]

Hence the essence of the principle of accommodation was that at times government aid to religion represented a legitimate accommodation of the public service to the spiritual needs of the people. Chaplaincies in the armed forces and non-taxation of religious property were merely two examples of how this principle had operated in American history. The two criteria which indicated whether the principle of accommodation should be invoked in a given case were these: first, that accommodation should not infringe upon, but should support, the free exercise of religion; and second, that the government's responsibility for the general activity under discussion (e.g., education or the care for the needs of military personnel) should be clear.[80] By using this principle, Murray believed, it would be possible to be faithful to the tenets of the First Amendment in an age of ever-increasing government; for in this way both the flourishing of religion and the exclusion of the state from interference in religious affairs would be served.

But Murray saw that even if the question of government assistance could be solved to the satisfaction of all, there would still remain a very troubling trend in American public policy: the growing tendency to exclude all beliefs based on religious sentiment from the nation's political discourse. "There is the gulf of an idea rising in the United States," he wrote. "This idea proclaims that a man whose conscience acknowledges as the rule of its formation the spiritual authority of the Church is somehow not a free man and should not be admitted to the full stature of a free society. . . . I think that this idea contains an intolerable inquisitory principle. By what right does government, or society for that matter, inquire into the means whereby my conscience is formed?"[81] Yet Murray believed this was precisely what society was inquiring into, as the opinions of men like Paul Blanshard gained greater currency. Once again, the First Amendment was being turned on its head, as the words which were written to safeguard the flourishing of strong religious belief were now used to delegitimize the political opinions of all those who held such beliefs. And the Constitutional tradition which had been based upon God's order of justice was now being interpreted to mean that organized belief in God should have no role in forming the public policy which seeks after justice. Murray recognized both of these developments for what they were: a renunciation of the American political tradition and a clear violation of the principles of sound public philosophy. But he also recognized that both of these beliefs were gaining ground in American society, and that if they were to be combatted effectively, it would be necessary for the believing people of the United States to organize a response which was clear, reasoned, and forceful. It was in order to organize such a response that Murray turned once again to the religious communities of America.

Renewing the Politcal Order

The crisis in the political order which Murray had outlined was clear and vivid; if the ominous trends which he discerned in American politics were often subtle in their workings, they were nonetheless dangerous in the threat which they posed to the future well-being of the nation. At its heart, this crisis was one of apostasy, in the fullest sense of that word. It was an apostasy from a rich political tradition that had found its roots in the principles of natural law. It was apostasy from the liberal values of the West, which limited the role and nature of the state and protected the *res sacrae* of the human person. And it was an apostasy from the religiously-founded conception of politics because it was an apostasy from the belief in God himself:

> Contemporary democratic ideology . . . does not deny God. But it surely ignores him. Surely this ignorance is being installed at the center of the democratic idea, as a fatal corruption. Ignorance of God has acquired status in public law; it is woven into the national mores; it is socially accredited in institutions. The man ignorant of God has become a social type; and his ignorance is socially transmitted by a multitude of social mechanisms; not least perhaps by the central institution of public education. The democracy which owed its origins to spiritual insight now trusts its future to spiritual ignorance. . . . How shall the freedom of the spirit be born of spiritual ignorance? How shall the Great Hope not turn into a great deception, if it is divorced from its dynamic inspiration?[82]

How indeed? The answer was to be found in the religious communities which had retained their fidelity to the spiritual foundations of American society and which could rearticulate them in the twentieth century.

4

RECONSTRUCTING
THE INTERNATIONAL ORDER

If John Courtney Murray had been writing in the period after World War I, perhaps he would have confined his public theology solely to the cultural and the political orders. But the fact was that Murray did not write for the inter-war period. His prescriptions for the renewal of American society were forged in the period 1940–1967, and as a consequence they sought not only a reform of America's domestic structures, but also a clarification of America's participation in the international order. The years immediately following World War II witnessed an almost total reversal of America's vision of itself as an actor on the world stage. The nation which for nearly two centuries had treasured its remoteness from the conflicts of Europe now realized that its immense military and economic power could not help but have a critical impact on the shape of the international order. The U.S. could no longer afford to consider foreign policy a secondary concern. As a consequence, Murray subjected the central tenets of American foreign policy to a searching analysis, in order to insure that the religious and moral bases for that policy would be vibrant, strong, and clear. His trenchant critique of American policies and his constant recourse to first principles in the evaluation of foreign policy issues constitute a vigorous effort to reconstruct the international order in the post-war era, not in an American image, but in a moral image.

Murray's entry into the field of international relations was occasioned by the same series of papal pronouncements which had first alerted him to the nature of the secular crisis—the encyclicals, allocutions, and decrees of Pope Pius XII during the wartime and post-war period. It was clear to Pius, the veteran diplomat, that the Old World was passing away in the ruins of London and Dresden and Hiroshima, and that the moral order which had characterized international discourse since the time of Napoleon was to be no more:

> We have to face today a fact of fundamental importance. Out of the passionate strife of the parties concerning peace and war aims, a common opinion emerges. It is that all Europe, as well as the separate nations, are in such a process of transformation that the beginning of a new period is clearly recognizable. . . . It is true that opinions and aims diverge; yet they agree in their will to establish a new order, and in their conviction that a return to the old order is neither possible nor desirable.[1]

Such a time of transition could be a period of tremendous promise, or it could be a period of moral apostasy and decline; but there was no avoiding the fact that a transition of major proportions was indeed occurring in the international realm, and that a new order was truly being established. It was Pius' genius to perceive that the fundamental question in the construction of the post-war world was not one of power, or diplomacy, or ideology, but rather the question of whether or not the new world order would be built upon a sound moral foundation. And it was Pius' legacy that he outlined for the world what form such an order should take: "(We must seek) a new order . . . founded on that immovable and unshakable rock, the moral law, which the Creator Himself manifested in a natural order, and which He has engraved with indelible characters on the hearts of men."[2]

Murray saw in Pius' call for such a new world order a sacred mission which the United States was called to embrace in a special way. For this reason, beginning in 1944, Murray undertook to bring to the religious men and women of the U.S. a new understanding of their role in the world and of the principles which their faith called them to live by in contributing to the formation of the nation's foreign policy. In Murray's view, there were four such principles:

1.) a religious conviction as to the sovereignty of God over nations as well as over individuals; 2.) a right conscience as to the essential demands of the moral law in social life; 3.) a religious respect for human dignity in oneself and in others—the dignity with which man is invested inasmuch as he is the image of God; and 4.) a religious conviction as to the essential unity of the human race. In terms of these four principles the natural order of justice between men and nations is set up, made obligatory, and sanctioned.[3]

It was Murray's belief that in order for America's foreign policies in the post-war era to be truly conducive to a just world order, these principles would have to be alive and active not only within the policy-making community, but within the nation as a whole. For as the mass-based movements of Nazism and fascism had pointed out all too clearly, foreign policy agendas in the twentieth century could be set not only by the traditional elites, but by the masses as well. It was Murray's dream that the people as a whole in the United States would indeed set the foreign policy agenda for their nation in the post-war era, and that that agenda would be characterized by fraternal solidarity, a dedication to peace, and equal regard for the strong and the weak of this world.

In embarking upon this effort, Murray clearly recognized that the traditions both of the American people as a whole and of the Catholic community in particular did not augur well for a just and internationalist foreign policy based upon the will of the people.

There is an immense work to be done toward the education of the public conscience in the United States. . . . (In fact) we have not yet been able to draw considerable sections of our Catholic citizens away from several conceptions fundamentally opposed to our own high Catholic thought—away, for instance, from adherence to outworn concepts of unlimited national sovereignty, national isolationism, economic individualism, interracial prejudice.[4]

Moreover, in addressing the questions posed by America's new status in the world, there was no national tradition to guide the people of the United States. There was no "American Consensus," as there had been in the cultural order; no "American Proposition," as there had been in the political order. For too long the United States had been an isolationist nation, afraid of being entangled in the conflicts of the Old World. Now it would have to generate an entirely new outlook on questions of international relations, an outlook based on America's predominance in world affairs, rather than on provincialism and isolation. "We must not go back to the pacifist isolationism of the decades following the First World War—nor go on to the imperialist isolationism that may present itself as our future temptation."[5] It was Murray's goal to insure that the United States would avoid both isolationism and imperialism by vigorously bringing to the debate on U.S. foreign policy a religiously-informed concern for justice in the international order. "Our task is to give our national aims a genuinely Christian definition, and strenuously to see to their embodiment in the social structure of national and international life."[6] It was a task which was to go largely unfulfilled in Murray's lifetime, but in the process of advancing it Murray clarified not only which questions represented the most important ones for American foreign policy, but also how they should be addressed.

A Question of Morality

Murray believed that the premier question of American foreign policy concerned the relationship which should exist between morality and international relations. And during the time in which he was writing, most of the leading figures in the field of international relations would have agreed with him. In the wake of World War II, political scientists in the West reexamined the series of events which had led to the outbreak of war in 1939, and most of them concluded that the remilitarization of Germany and the attack upon Poland could be attributed in large part to one thing: the utopian view of foreign policy that was epitomized by the views of Woodrow Wilson and Neville Chamberlain. It was utopianism which had led the leading nations of the world in the inter-war period to assume that the power of suasion could deter aggression. It was utopianism which held out the view that there was a harmony of interests among nations and that the interests of all nations could be accommodated peacefully. And it was utopianism which led Britain and France to mistake the remilitarization of Nazi Germany as no more than an effort to redress legitimate grievances left over from the Versailles Peace Conference.[7] In the fledgling science of international relations, there was an emerging consensus that the relationship of morality and foreign policy was indeed the central question, and that the answer to that question lay not in the utopian thought which characterized the views of Wilson and Chamberlain, but in a new brand of foreign policy thinking which went under the heading of "realism."

The most articulate and influential exponent of "realism" in the American setting was Hans Morgenthau, whose brilliant treatise on *Politics Among Nations* revolutionized both the study and formulation of foreign policy in the United States. The essential precepts of realism, according to Morgenthau, were simple: 1. international relations are governed by objective laws that are rooted in human nature; 2. the central law of international relations dictates that policymakers think and act solely according to their national interests defined in terms of power; 3. ethics in international relations judges by political consequences alone; neither intentions nor universal moral norms are admissible.[8] In Morgenthau's view, what was usually termed morality in the international arena was either a fiction or foolishness. It was a fiction when a nation professed to take actions out of moral considerations, since closer inspection would almost always reveal that power considerations were at the heart of the nation's choice. And it was foolishness in those rare instances when moral considerations truly did influence foreign policy, since any moral action was doomed to failure in a world where no true community of nations actually existed. The realist worldview was a complete repudiation of both Wilsonian idealism and the use of moral norms as a foundation for international relations. It answered the question of the role of morality in foreign policy by asserting the autonomy of international relations and embracing an ethic whose only measure was the achievement of power.

It might seem that such an approach to international relations was utterly amoral in its roots, and that it would have little appeal to a nation which had always prided itself on its moral uprightness. But in fact "realism" sprang not from a rejection of the moral nature of the human person, but from the profoundly moral, yet equally pessimistic, assessment of society which was contained in the works of Reinhold Niebuhr. Niebuhr pointed to "the sinful character of social man" as the basic datum of international life. While the application of love on an interpersonal level could heal the sinfulness which corrupted the human person, there was no way of applying this individualistic love on the international plane; and thus in the relations among nations the only sensible dictum required the "balancing of power with power" at every turn.[9] Love may have been the preeminent virtue in Niebuhr's theology, but in a world where love was impotent to change structures, prudence would have to triumph over charity in international relations, and the search for power and security over the search for justice.

Murray believed that the "realist" critique of Wilsonian idealism had legitimately challenged a moralistic strain which had characterized American foreign policy for much of its history. For too long, he argued, Americans had approached foreign policy questions with a moral simplism which confused individual ethics with societal ethics, and which failed to recognize the dilemmas raised by the institutionalization of human action. "(This morality) did not go beyond the false notion that society is simply the sum of the individuals living in it, and that public morality is no more than the sum of private moralities."[10] As a consequence, this older American moralism had no capacity to face the complexities of modern international life and to differentiate between those choices which would advance the well-being of the international order and those which would bring catastrophe. All that this older moralism could do was to cite facile absolutist slogans in the manner of John Foster Dulles, and then to act as if the world were the individual writ large. In Murray's view, realism had skillfully pointed to the weaknesses of such an approach in a world of ever-growing complexities, and for this reason it had legitimately displaced the Wilsonian tradition as the central theoretical core of American foreign policy.

But if Murray agreed with realism's critique of the older American moralism, he categorically rejected the alternative moral stance which Morgenthau and Niebuhr had outlined. In its reaction against the absolutism of the old utopian morality, realism had moved toward a situationalism in which all principle became lost among the contingencies and complexities of modern life. In its reaction against the simplism of the Wilsonians, realism saw all moral questions as so complicated by structural sin that truly moral action was reduced to serving the national interest. And in reaction to the self-righteousness of the older moralism, realism asserted that "to act is to sin, to accept responsibility is to incur guilt, to live at all is to stand under the judgment of God, which is uniformly adverse, since every act of moral judgment is vitiated by some hidden fallacy, and every use of human freedom is inevitably an exercise in pride."[11] The "morality" which realism proposed was not a morality at all, in Murray's view, for it failed to recognize that despite the limitations upon human action in the international arena, there was a clear set of principles and standards to which all human action was bound. And those principles and standards were far broader and deeper than mere efficiency in the quest for power.

Power. Murray believed that this was the central issue which had led both the idealists and the realists astray. The older American moralism had seen power as evil and corrupting, and had believed that America's innocence could best be preserved by remaining isolated from the power-conflicts of Europe. The realists also believed that power was corrupting, but asserted that the quest for power is unavoidable for a nation; hence no innocence was possible in a realist world. For Murray, both utopianism and realism ultimately foundered as moral guideposts for American foreign policy because neither could adequately answer the pre-eminent moral question for the United States in the post-war age: "In what moral terms is America to justify itself in its possession of power; and in what terms is America to justify itself to the world for its uses of its power?"[12]

Murray's answer to this question was to be found in a moral tradition which did not see the use of power as intrinsically corrupting, which did not confuse the collective and individual realms of morality, and which did not partake in either the absolutism of the idealists or the situationalism of the realists. That tradition could be none other than that of natural law.

The tradition of reason was able to solve the dilemmas left unanswered by both realism and idealism, according to Murray, because natural law bridged the gulf between individual and collective moralities by clearly differentiating between the moral nature of the individual person and the moral nature of the state.

> Society and the state are understood to be natural institutions with their relatively autonomous ends, or purposes, which are predesigned in broad outline in the social and political nature of man, as understood in its concrete completeness through reflection and historical experience. These purposes are public, not private. They are therefore strictly limited. . . . The obligatory public purposes of society and the state impose upon these institutions a special set of obligations which, again by nature, are not coextensive with the wider and higher range of obligations that rest upon the human person. In a word, the imperatives of political and social morality derive from the inherent order of political and social reality itself, as the architectonic moral reason conceives this necessary order in the light of the five-fold structure of obligatory political ends—justice, freedom, security, the general welfare, and civil unity or peace.[13]

In natural law, the ends of the state and society in international intercourse determine the moral obligations imposed upon them. Thus the confusion of individual and collective morality which characterized the idealism of Wilson and Dulles was poor moral reasoning.[14] For it constituted a refusal to acknowledge that the moral demands placed upon the state are more limited than those placed upon the individual. Equally, the moral reductionism which characterized realism was poor moral reasoning. For it refused to acknowledge that the moral demands placed upon states, while less stringent than the demands placed upon individuals, did not reduce merely to prudence in the search for power. Rather, they consisted of the obligations imposed by the fivefold ends of the state in a given historical situation.

In clarifying the moral ends of the state in the international sphere, natural law also clarified the role of power in foreign policy. Murray saw two forms which military power could take in international relations. The first he defined as force, i.e. "the measure of power necessary and sufficient to uphold the valid purposes both of law and of politics." The second he termed violence, i.e. "that use of power which destroys the order both of law and politics."[15] In Murray's view, the distinction between these two forms of power was a teleological one based upon the ends of the state; power was in itself a morally neutral term, which could be used for good or ill. The criterion which determined whether a particular use of military power was one of force or violence was clear in principle, if often difficult to determine concretely: Does the utilization of power in this case serve the five-fold ends of the state in relation to the international community?

The issue of the moral obligations of the state and the just use of power in international life constituted the two central questions regarding morality and foreign policy in the post-war world. But they pointed to a more immediate issue raised by America's rise to dominance in the 1940's: How could the United States pursue a foreign policy which was ethically correct, but which reflected America's status as the great power of the Western world? Murray's answer was clear and penetrating:

> One thing is clear. The real issue does not concern the moral quality of this or that element of American foreign policy. The real issue concerns the nature of morality itself, the determinants of moral action, the structure of the moral act, and the general style of moral argument. One cannot argue moral issues until they are stated, but what are the terms of statement of the moral issues involved in foreign policy? One cannot come to practical solutions until one has first formulated the relevant principles and also analyzed the factual situation in which the principled solution is to be practiced. . . .[16]

It was toward these two tasks of formulating the relevant principles and analyzing the factual situations of the post-war world that Murray directed his efforts in the international order. Rejecting the moral simplism of the utopians and the moral ambiguousness of the realists, Murray evaluated each of the major challenges facing post-war America in light of the tradition of reason; and his resulting prescriptions for the formulation of United States foreign policy consistently reflected both the need for first principles and the complexities of the nuclear age.

In Search of an International Community

The first issue which Murray analyzed according to the principles of natural law was the very issue which had led the realists to embrace the concept of power politics: the question of whether or not there was a genuine international community in the post-war world. It was the conviction of Morgenthau and Niebuhr that morality could not be effective in international relations precisely because there was no international community strong enough to demand and receive the allegiance of the various nations and citizens of the world. In Morgenthau's view, morality would always fail in foreign relations "because 1.) the principle of equality between members of the community is not applied, and is indeed not easily applicable, in the world community; and 2.) the principle that the good of the whole takes precedence over the good of the part, which is a postulate of any fully integrated community, is not generally accepted."[17] Until a true community of nations did evolve, the realists argued, it was useless to speak of an international morality or even of a morality which nations should follow in their foreign policies.

Murray recognized that the realists' point was a valid one; it was difficult to speak of international morality, especially in terms of natural law, unless there was a genuine international community upon which moral claims could be made and moral precepts based. Moreover, the existence of a true international community was a persistent and necessary presumption of Catholic social teaching; indeed it formed the heart of Pius XII's declarations on the need for a moral world order in the post-war era. But in Murray's view the existence of an international community went beyond even this. It represented more than merely a refutation of the realist worldview or a pre-requisite for the realization of Catholic social teaching. It was, in itself, a theological assertion of great richness, "the reflection on the secular-political plant of a central article of Catholic belief—the religious doctrine of the supranational spiritual unity of mankind."[18]

For all these reasons, Murray decided to confront the realist challenge head-on and to demonstrate that an international community did exist in the post-war era, if only in inchoate form. Murray argued that it was wrong to look only at the relationships among nation-states in asking whether or not an international community exists; one had also to look at the myriad of less formal social, economic, and cultural relationships which bound the peoples of the world together ever more progressively as the twentieth century progressed. And if one did look at the world in this way, the existence of a true international community would gradually become apparent.

> Properly speaking, nations did not create the dynamic system of relationships which is the international community solely by sovereign acts of their national wills. This community has gradually come into being by a natural process, by the operation of a law resident in the very being of national states and manifested by the historical development of their organic independence. I mean the natural law of human sociability, which expressed itself as well on the international plane as on the domestic and national planes.[19]

By the middle part of the twentieth century, the law of human sociability was manifesting itself in worldwide communications networks, systems of banking and commerce which spanned the globe, and a growth in international travel which broke down the barriers of cultural isolation. As a consequence, the bonds of an international community were gradually being formed, a community with its own identity and ends.

In arguing for the existence of a true international community, Murray forthrightly acknowledged that this community was only an incipient one, that it did not constitute a mature and cohesive social body. He recognized that the international community had no clear juridical form, that it had no consensus which underlay it, and, most importantly of all, that the nations of the world did not acknowledge by their actions the existence of an international community which limited their sovereignty in any meaningful way.[20] At the same time, Murray pointed repeatedly to the less formal, but more important ties which were increasingly binding societies together; the world was becoming interdependent in almost every area of human endeavor, and if the nations of the world did not recognize the emergence of this international community, their citizens would surely suffer.

"Nations were sociable before they agreed to associate. They are, by nature, brothers and sisters, members of a family, dependent on one another, destined to aid one another. They may refuse the obligations of family life; but they do not cease to be a family—they merely become an unhappy family."[21]

It was to prevent the international community from becoming an unhappy family in the post-war era that Murray pressed repeatedly for the juridical organization of the nations of the world.

> The international community has historically emerged as a natural society (a society which exists by the laws of man's social nature), with its own proper good. The law of nature, therefore, demands that this society be organized in a properly human way for the prosecution of its common good. This properly human mode of social organization is juridical organization—a rational system for the control of possibly conflicting freedoms through juridical institutions. Upon the free will of men and nations, therefore, devolves an obligation from natural moral law to establish such institutions.[22]

Because the international community had evolved to such a degree that it represented an independent human society with its own ends, natural law demanded that this community should be organized in order that these ends could be attained. One had only to look at the manifold ways in which the ends of international society were frustrated by a lack of organization—through national rivalries, trade disputes, and outbreaks of war, to name just a few examples—in order to grasp the potential which a vibrant and cohesive juridical international community would have for enhancing human well-being. For this reason, according to Murray, the erection of such an organization was not merely an option for the human race; it was an imperative of moral law.

In calling for the organization of the international community, Murray did not seek the creation of a world state which would crush the legitimate independent sovereignties of existing nation states. In his view, such an approach would lead to precisely the type of totalitarianism which religious men and women should be fighting.

> Such a political conception is unrealizable . . . it looks, in fact,
> like a projection on the international plane of the individu-
> alistic liberal illusion that has contributed to the wreck of
> national society itself. This individualistic illusion would deny
> that there are any institutions that mediate between the iso-
> lated individual and the World State; it would deny the right
> to prosecute by institutional, organized action the interme-
> diate special goods of particular groups—Labor, Industry,
> the Church, particular sovereign States.[23]

A truly just world order would recognize the legitimate role of
both national sovereignties and all subsidiary institutions, while
simultaneously erecting an international organization whose only
function and jurisdiction would be to meet those human needs
which the national sovereignties and subsidiary institutions could
not meet. In essence, Murray believed, there were two such functions: 1. the creation of moral and legal standards to guide
nations in their relations with one another; 2. the use of coercive
power to defend the juridical order when nations violated these
moral and legal standards.[24] Murray argued that the moral law
itself could be no more specific than this in its demands for a
juridical world organization; it could not specify the form of
political organization, the exact manner in which coercion should
be employed by the world body, nor the details of the legal prescriptions which a world body would enact. What the moral law
could and did do in the twentieth century was to demand forthrightly that citizens encourage the gradual and progressive constitution of the international community. To take refuge in the
seeming inevitability of unlimited national sovereignties was an
act not only of political ignorance, but also of moral ignorance.[25]

Murray recognized that the moral imperative for the juridical organization of the international community did not seem
clear to all of his countrymen, or even to the majority of Catholics
in the United States.

> A puzzling phenomenon in America is the hostility of many
> Catholics, and the indifference of many more, to the idea of
> an organized international community. More is involved than
> rational patient criticism of the institutions that presently
> embody the idea—the U.N. and its many agencies. Criticism

of this kind is altogether proper. The puzzling thing is the opposition to the international idea itself. Even more puzzling is the passion that not seldom seems to animate this opposition. It seems to be supposed that the international idea came from the "liberals," or even from the Communists; that Catholics must therefore combat it as they combat secularist liberalism and atheistic communism.[26]

Murray wished to make clear that this "international idea" came from neither the "liberals" nor the communists, but from the clear precepts of natural law as applied to the current world situation. It was the duty of religious men and women to work for the realization of this juridical organization. It was their duty as citizens of the United States and as members of the international community which was emerging more clearly in the world with each passing year.

Murray was never a utopian. As the 1960's dawned, and as the limitations and defects of the United Nations became ever clearer, he did not adopt a dogmatically defensive attitude toward the U.N. Instead, he readily admitted both the mistakes which the fledgling organization had made and the enduring lack of an international consensus regarding the proper role which the United Nations should play. At the same time, he never wavered in his dedication to the principle that an international community had indeed been created by the interdependence of twentieth century life, and that the moral law demanded a world body capable of advancing the common good of that international community. He found solace in the call of *Pacem in Terris* for a truly effective international public authority, an authority which would "be set up by common accord and not imposed by force."[27] He found hope in the tremendously positive response which John XXIII's encyclical on peace received from national leaders around the globe. And he found collaborators in a new generation of Americans who had been raised, not in an era of isolationism and security, but in an era of interdependence and nuclear insecurity. In his first article on the need for a juridical international organization, written in 1944, Murray had stated:

> There are only two ways to world peace. The first—the system of power—has not worked. The second—the system of jurid-

ical organization—has not been tried. If we do not make it work, we must resign ourselves to the barbarism of a Third World War. It must be made to work. The system must be organized as soon as possible. It will not be at once ideally perfect. But the machinery must be kept going, no matter how it creaks and groans; and we must improve it in the light of experience. . . . World order is a demand of moral law; and we are bound to do what is possible at the moment however remote the ideal may be.[28]

By the time of his death, Murray's optimism about the possibilities for accomplishing this objective might well have been diminished, but his zeal for establishing a truly just and juridically organized world order had diminished not at all.

A Spiritual Menace

At the end of World War II, Murray had hoped that the next twenty years would be characterized by a universal effort to build a moral world order and a juridically organized international community. Instead, the post-war period was to be characterized by a conflict which excluded that formation of an effective world organization and threatened the planet with nuclear holocaust: the conflict between the United States and the Soviet Union. Communism, in Murray's view, represented the most demonic threat to human values which the world had ever known, surpassing even the horrors of Nazism. It constituted "the central crisis of history,"[29] because it created a great divide throughout the world between the liberal values of the West and the totalitarian and atheistic worldview of modernity.

> Essentially, it came out of the East, as a conscious apostasy from the West. It may indeed be said that Jacobinism was its forerunner; but Jacobinism was itself an apostasy from the liberal tradition of the West, as well as from Christianity, by its central tenet that there are no bounds to the juridical omnipotence of government, since the power of the state is not under the law, much less under God. In any case, communism has assumed the task at which Jacobinism failed—that of putting an end to the history of the West. Communism has undertaken to inaugurate a new history, the so-called

> Third Epoch, that will abolish and supplant what we called the
> two Western epochs, feudalism and capitalism.[30]

An important element of this threat lay, of course, in the military
power of the Soviet Union as the central "missionary" agent of
world communism. But the more important threat of communism in the twentieth century, according to Murray, lay in the
spiritual menace which Marxist doctrine posed to the West. The
great crisis of history revolved not so much around the question
of who would be able to garner the greatest military forces in the
world, but rather around the question of which side would be
able to garner the greatest spiritual resources for what was essentially a war of ideology and vitality.

    One of the elements of the cold war which bothered Murray
was the fact that the West had been slow to awake to the spiritual
challenge of communism and even slower in formulating a
response to it:

> Communist doctrine is an affront to the Western tradition of
> reason; and the manner of empire that it sustains is a further
> affront to the liberal tradition of politics and law that was
> born of the Western tradition of reason. The further fact is
> that the West was so late in feeling the affront and still seems
> largely impotent to deliver against it an effective doctrinal
> answer, in a moment when a doctrinal answer is of the highest
> practical importance, not only to the East that will hear it, but
> to the West that will utter it—immediately, to itself. Professor
> Toynbee may, in fact, be right, in saying that the West now
> identifies itself with technology, as its cult and its sole export.
> If this be true, this failure of understanding, leading to a
> denial, more or less explicit, of the Western tradition by the
> West itself, would be the fateful "internal contradiction" that
> might lead to downfall. Ironically, Marx never saw this form
> of "internal contradiction," although it is the greatest weak-
> ness in the camp that he opposed.[31]

The essential challenge to the West was not one of arms; it was
one of the spirit. The demonic element of communist doctrine
was its total denial of the *res sacrae* in every facet of human life—
religious, social, economic, and cultural. Yet in spite of this

demonic attack upon the core of the human spirit, communist doctrine held a certain allure for the peoples of the twentieth century. It spoke of equality in an age where the equal status of all persons was gradually becoming accepted. It spoke of "the rule of the people" in an age when the democratic idea was being extended to the former colonial nations of the West. It spoke of eliminating poverty to a world where grinding poverty was a daily way of life, for many, if not most. And it spoke of all of these things with a vitality that contrasted sharply with the flaccid ideologies of the West. For all of these reasons, Murray argued forcefully that the communist threat should not primarily be seen as one of military conquest, or of espionage, but as one of intellectual combat. "It is on this plane—the plane of intellectual combat—that the conflict very largely lies, and I'm inclined to think that we've woefully neglected it here."[32]

What was needed, according to Murray, was a spiritual unity in the United States which would act as a counterpoise to the threat of communist doctrine. During the 1950's, the U.S. achieved such a unity, but it was a negative and empty unity which Murray would have no part of:

> The danger is that this country may be driven into a unity based simply on negation, on anti-communism, and the danger of this is greater in proportion as the opposition to communism is more passionate and less intelligent. This would be a shame, because such unity would be one born of fear, one born of a sense of menace. It is good indeed to know what we are against, but it is far more important to know what we are for.[33]

To know what we are for. This was the central task for the United States in the international arena: not to fight communism, but to promote a world order which enhanced the *res sacrae hominis*. The intellectual combat which the cold war had produced concerned two differing visions of the world; the United States would be victorious in advancing its own vision of the world only if that vision had some clarity, and only if it was grounded in moral principles strong enough to elicit the support not only of the American people, but also of the other peoples of the world.

Thus Murray turned to the American people in the 1960's and asked very forthrightly:

> What kind of order in the world do you want? What are its premises and its principles? What is to be the form of its institutions—political, legal, economic? How do you propose to help this disorganized world? Or do you not propose to help? Or do you perhaps think an order of peace, freedom, justice, and prosperity will come about in the world simply by accident, or by sheer undirected technological progress, or by the power of prayer, or by what? Order is, by definition, the work of the wise man: *sapientis est ordinare*. It is the work of men and peoples who are able to say: there are truths and we hold them. Hence the disordered state of the world itself puts to America the question: What are your truths?[34]

This was the central question to be addressed to the American people regarding the nature of their foreign policy: What are your truths? What are the truths of the moral order which guide your decisions? What are the truths which your power throughout the world advances? What are the truths which you put forth to combat the spiritual challenge of communist doctrine?

Actually, in his very phrasing of the questions which he put to the American people, Murray had signaled his own answer to central questions of American foreign policy. For in pointing to the values of peace, freedom, justice, and prosperity, he hearkened back to the fivefold ends of political society which had undergirded his analysis of America's domestic politics. It was precisely these fivefold ends, Murray argued, which should guide American foreign policy in both its formulation and its execution.

> We have to project the notion of peace into a world that is divided and disordered and belligerent and unable to contain the pluralisms that exist within it and combine them into an order of peace. We have to project the notion of justice into a world of unjust injustice and manifold inequalities. We have to project the notion of freedom into a world that is the scene of multiple enslavements. We have to project the notion of welfare into a world of misery. We have to project a notion of power into a world that is all too prone toward the uses of

force and violence in pursuit of political aid. Now I am sug-
gesting that these five ends taken singly and in combination
afford the basic criterion of all our foreign policy and action.
They enable us to discern in general when policy erection is
bad, and since they are not arbitrary ends but inherent in the
existential ends of human society, they give us the norms of
judgment of alien systems and tell us therefore what we must
in principle oppose as well as what we must in principle
promote.[35]

Using these fivefold ends of political society, Murray was able to
construct a full-blown theory of American foreign policy which
was capable of clearly distinguishing the vision of the United
States from the vision of the Soviet Union. And such a foreign
policy would not be characterized by the negativity which had typ-
ified much of American foreign policy during the cold war,
whereby the need for the "containment" of communism automatically saw any enemy of communism as a friend of the United
States. No, the foreign policy which Murray proposed was an eminently positive one, which challenged communism in the confidence that the West could indeed bring greater freedom, peace,
justice, prosperity, and security to the world. In terms of such a
positive U.S. foreign policy, the criterion determining America's
friends would be the willingness of other nations to provide their
citizens with the fivefold ends; and the criterion for determining
all of America's interventions on the world stage would be: How
do they serve the ends of political and human society in the
world?

In setting forth the fivefold ends of political society as the
foundation for American foreign policy, Murray recognized that
he might be accused of the same sort of naive idealism which the
"realists" had criticized in the policies of Wilson and Chamberlain. Thus he reiterated his position that the moral imperatives of
natural law are not in any sense divorced from reality; on the contrary they are both formulated and applied with the explicit recognition that reality and structural constraints must be fully taken
into account in developing any sound foreign policy:

> We have to grasp the relation between reality and morality,
> between the ideal and the given. We have to recognize, for

instance, that a policy that is economically unsound cannot be morally good, and recognize that a policy that makes no military sense doesn't make any moral sense either. And we have to realize that it is not morally right to try to do by law what law in its nature cannot do. We have to recognize that fiscal stupidity cannot be justified by moral idealism. In other words, we have to have a sagacious respect for the real in all its forms. . . .[36]

This was the true realism—not the reduction of all morality in international affairs to the pursuit of national power interests, but rather the pursuit of the international common good taken with full regard for the restrictions which reality imposes on the ability to achieve that common good.

In Murray's view, the three areas in which the international common good was most at issue in the post-war world were the revolt of humankind against economic misery, the demand of the peoples of the world for the right to participate in the political process, and the campaign to make citizens secure and inviolate in their human rights of religion, speech, and association. Murray recognized that at times there had to be a trade-off in the attainment of these ends, between the accomplishment of political freedom and the generation of a general prosperity. In such situations, it was a great intellectual labor to determine how these values conflict, what trade-offs are possible, and which combination of them maximizes human welfare. Such decisions would be difficult and complex; but they would be made far easier if the fivefold structure were constantly kept in view, so that no essential human value would be totally ignored, no end of political society completely sacrificed.[37]

In speaking to the American people about the need to reevaluate U.S. foreign policy in light of the precepts of natural law, Murray recognized that he was proposing a criterion which would at times conflict with the national interests of the United States, at least as they were usually conceived. Murray explicitly asserted that the existence of an international community demanded that the international common good be followed even when it seemed to conflict with American interests. "Self-interest is a valid category . . . but it is not an adequate category. What is good for us must somehow be subsumed under and made part of a higher good, the good that is higher because it is more universal."[38] And, as Murray made clear, when a nation as wealthy as the United States formulated its policies, the international common good would demand significant sacrifices. "The urgencies and the necessities of the international situation are greater than those of the domestic scene and therefore they have to be pursued even at the cost of sacrifice on the domestic front."[39] Always the true realist, Murray did not believe that any nation would consistently place its own interests second to the common good of the international community. But as a realistic idealist, he believed that the United States must strive to incorporate the notion of the international common good into its process of foreign policy formulation. For in the ideological and spiritual combat that was the cold war, the nation that would win the minds and hearts of the world's people was the nation which was willing to demonstrate that it truly took the interests of those people into account in choosing its own actions.

The Question of Force

Murray believed that the central challenge of the Soviet Union to the United States was a challenge of the spirit, rather than of arms. Yet he recognized that the Soviet arsenal was large and growing, and that the U.S. could not ignore the military peril which was posed by the largest standing army in the world. Moreover, Murray recognized that any effort by the U.S. to advance the international common good would at times require the use of force to repel injustice and aggression directed against smaller nations. For these reasons, Murray undertook a reexamination of the traditional just-war theory in light of the realities of the nuclear age; and he applied the just-war principles to the American situation in the 1950's and 1960's.

In approaching the question of American foreign policy and the use of force, Murray was highly critical of the manner in which war had been visualized during most of the history of the United States. Most explicitly, he was critical of the manner in which the U.S. had prosecuted World War II. In 1944, Murray had been subjected to heated criticism for publishing an article in *Theological Studies* written by John C. Ford on "The Morality of Obliteration Bombing."[40] It was the thesis of Ford's article that American military policy during the war almost certainly violated fundamental moral standards in its disregard for the principles of discrimination and proportionality. Murray agreed with Ford's analysis, and he saw it as part of a much larger pattern of American misperceptions regarding the true nature of war:

> The American attitude towards war has tended to oscillate between absolute pacifism in peacetime and extremes of ferocity in wartime. Prevalent in American society has been an abstract ethic, conceived either in religious or in secularized terms, which condemns all war as immoral. No nation has the *ius ad bellum*. On the other hand, when a concrete historical situation creates the necessity for war, no ethic governs its conduct. There are no moral criteria operative to control the uses of force. There is no *ius in bello*. One may pursue hostilities to the military objective of unconditional surrender, and the nation may escalate the use of force to the paroxysm of violence of which Hiroshima and Nagasaki are forever the symbols. . . . These extreme alternatives are no longer tolerable. Our nation must make its way to some discriminating doctrine—moral, political, and military—on the uses of force.[41]

America's oscillation between pacifism and ferocity had been bad enough when the United States was a relatively isolationist nation. But in the post-war era, when the U.S. was to be the world's great power, this unnuanced view of the use of military force could not be allowed to continue. Using the just-war tradition, Murray set out to revise the American ethic for the use of force in the nuclear age.

Murray believed that there were three central issues which provided the context for an American doctrine on the uses of force in the post-war era. The first issue concerned the nature of the communist threat facing the United States and the free nations of the world. Borrowing from Pius XII, Murray characterized the cold war as "a line of rupture which divides the entire international community into opposed blocs," blocs which can admit of no "coexistence in truth" because of the uncompromising attack which communism made upon the *res sacrae hominis*.[42] Thus the first reality which any valid doctrine of the uses of force would have to take into account was the immense threat to the core of Western values posed by the Soviet Union and its satellites. But important as this reality was, it had to be complemented by a second consideration: the availability of peaceful means with which the United States could meet the Soviet threat.

> A whole array of means is available, in correspondence with the multi-faceted character of the conflict itself. It is a matter of understanding both the usefulness and the limitations of each of them, from spectacular summit meetings across the gamut to the wholly unspectacular work, say, of agricultural experts engaged in increasing the food supply of underdeveloped nations. This whole complex question of the means of conflict must be fully explored antecedently to the consideration of the problem of war. The basic reason is that otherwise one can give no concrete meaning to the concept of war as *ultima ratio*.[43]

The third issue which had to be considered in evaluating the context for a doctrine on the just use of force was the nature of war itself in the nuclear era. The immense technological changes in warfare which had occurred both during and after World War II had dramatically altered the way in which subsequent wars would be fought. In formulating a policy on the recourse to war, these technological changes would have to play a large role.[44]

After considering these three issues, Murray concluded that, contrary to the Scholastic theory of the just war, all wars of aggression (i.e. wars initiated for the vindication of national rights and legitimate interests), whether just or unjust, would fall under the ban of moral prescription in the post-war era.[45] Two reasons could be cited for this alteration of the traditional doctrine. The first was that the increased violence inherent in twentieth century warfare made war disproportionate for the redress of even just grievances. The second concerned the alternative means available for settling international disputes; since the United Nations already existed, to admit the legitimacy of war as a means of redressing grievances would be to retard the juridical organization of the international community. In proscribing all wars of aggression, Murray believed he was following the logic of Pius XII's 1944 Christmas Message, which denied that military force was "a legitimate solution for international controversies and a means for the realization of national aspirations."[46] But even if Pius' 1944 Allocution had not intended to outlaw all aggressive war, Murray believed that the circumstances of twentieth century life made it necessary to do so.

The same could not be said of defensive warfare to repress injustice, however. In a 1953 Allocution to military doctors, Pius XII had defended "the absolute necessity of self-defense against a very grave injustice that touches the community, that cannot be impeded by other means, that nevertheless must be impeded on pain of giving free field in international relations to brutal violence and lack of conscience."[47] Murray fully subscribed to this sentiment, and he argued that warfare was indeed justifiable at times when the brutality of Soviet policy was taken into account. Always, however, and with a new urgency in the nuclear age, Murray declared the questions of proportionality would have to be taken into account in deciding to go to war and in selecting the means to be utilized in war. Murray believed that it was possible in the 1950's to wage a limited nuclear war which did not target enemy populations. Thus he held out the possibility that such a war might genuinely be moral according to just-war criteria. But he argued that if there should ever come a time when the employment of nuclear weapons would in all probability generate a war which "entirely escapes the control of man," then even such an otherwise moral use of nuclear weapons would become immoral.[48]

In Murray's view, the traditional Catholic doctrine on the just use of military force, when modified to reflect the new exigencies of twentieth century life, could perform a critically important function in the formation of United States foreign policy. This doctrine could, in the first place, solve the false dilemmas which saw America as having to choose between pacifism and a cynical realism, between nuclear annihilation and a total surrender to the forces of communism in the world.[49] The just war theory provided the American people with a way of applying military force in those truly extreme situations where fundamental human values were irretrievably at stake, while simultaneously recognizing that technological advances in warfare and the establishment of the United Nations made the legitimate recourse to war less and less frequent. In addition, the theory could limit the escalation of violence even in those situations where war was justified by invoking its clear and stringent guidelines on the *ius in bello*. In Murray's view, the traditional just-war theory served American society in the twentieth century through its capacity to set the right terms for the public debate on the use of force to accomplish foreign policy objectives. "The single inner attitude which is nourished by the traditional doctrine is a will to peace, which, in the extremity, bears within itself a will to enforce the precept of peace by arms. But this will to arms is a moral will; for it is identically a will to justice. It is formed under the judgment of reason."[50] It was the job of reason to steer between the twin dangers of total surrender and nuclear annihilation in the post-war era, and the just war tradition aided this effort not only by the careful distinctions which it brought to bear, but also by its insistence on the need to surrender neither the will to peace nor the will to justice in formulating American foreign policy.

The Spiritual Mission in the International Order

When he first undertook the fight against secularism and injustice in the international order in 1944, Murray assumed that the horrors of World War II had generated a consensus within the world community about the need to reconstruct the international system on a foundation rooted in God's order of justice. "The moral conscience of mankind has been outraged, its sense of justice violated, and above all its belief in human fraternity and solidarity shocked by the present state of affairs; together these three human and Christian sentiments have created a common will to establish a new and better order."[51] In the statements of Pius XII, Murray found both the spiritual impetus and the moral guidance for the creation of such an order, one which would be founded upon "a spirit of truth, justice, and love."[52] As a consequence, Murray's writings during the 1940's betray a pervasive sense of confidence that the post-war era would be markedly different from the previous century, and that a mass-based regeneration of the moral bases of international politics was not only possible, but likely.

The Murray of the 1950's and the 1960's is a much more sober man. The great hopes which Murray had for worldwide collaboration of people of good will through the United Nations were dashed upon the factional disputes and national jealousies which prevented the U.N. from ever becoming the "juridical organization of the international community" which he had envisioned. The moral leadership which he had hoped America would bring to the post-war world was increasingly being destroyed by a purely negative anti-communism which skewed all of American foreign policy and misperceived the core of the communist threat. Most distressingly of all, even within the Catholic community, the stirring words of Pius XII on the need for a new internationalist order based upon the defense of the *res sacrae* were falling on deaf ears, as the suspicions of all truly internationalist thought grew within the United States.[53]

Thus it was a chastened Murray who wrote for the American people during the 1950's and 1960's. But it was a Murray who had lost none of his conviction that the moral law of God must be the foundation for true justice and true peace in society. And as he indicated in his commentary on *Pacem in Terris*, it was a Murray who had never lost hope that humankind could indeed build a new and better world:

> I think that the Pope wishes to make a strong stand against the myth of history as the master of man. I think that this intention stands behind his confident assertion that "the fundamental principle on which our present peace depends must be replaced by another. . . ." We must not, he seems to be saying, feel ourselves to be trapped in history, unable to change its course, unable to control world events, unable to avoid the disaster that waits for us if the world continues on its present course. At least in this respect, the Pope will command the agreement of all men of good will who believe that there are energies in the human spirit whereby man may fulfill his destiny on earth, which is to be, not God, but the image of God. All men who believe in God are agreed that he is the master of history. Man, therefore, manifests himself as the image of God chiefly by his intelligent, confident efforts to

master the course of historical events and direct it toward the common good of the peoples of the earth.[54]

Manifesting himself as the image of God "by his intelligent, confident efforts to master the course of historical events and direct it toward the common good of the peoples of the earth." There could be no better words to describe John Courtney Murray's lifelong effort to construct a public theology for America in the twentieth century, not only in the international order, but in the domestic sphere as well.

5

"THE LIFE-WORK OF
JOHN COURTNEY MURRAY:
FOUNDATIONS FOR AN
AMERICAN PUBLIC THEOLOGY?"

A generation has passed since John Courtney Murray wrote his last prescription for the renewal of American society, and many of the individual prescriptions which he advanced in his writings and lectures now seem anachronistic as a basis for social ethics and public discourse. Murray's description of the communist menace, his conviction that a limited nuclear war could indeed be fought, and his commentaries on the role of government in the economy were powerful analyses in the 1950's, but today they appear more as objects for purely historical inquiry rather than as elements which can contribute to the formation of a contemporary public theology.

How, then, can one account for the tremendous hold which Murray's writings continue to have on those interested in public theology in the United States, a hold which extends both to those who are professional theologians and to those in the public policy community who wish to reconcile their policy positions with their religious faith? How can one explain the frequency and intensity with which religiously-minded writers on economic justice, defense issues, and Church-state relations cite Murray as their guide and inspiration?[1] The answer lies in the vision and design of Murray's life project. For Murray's projection of the Catholic theological tradition onto the American stage was not designed to address merely passing questions of social and political policy;

it was framed within the grand sweep of his perspective on the historical development of Western culture, and it sought to guide the American people in answering the most pressing questions which would be put to them again and again throughout the twentieth century: Will American society acknowledge God as the foundation for its social order? Will the United States continue to adhere to a conception of justice that is transcendent in origin? Will the *res sacrae hominis* be enhanced and protected by the cultural, political, and international life of the American people? It is because Murray's social writings were consistently conceived within this larger perspective that, even when he was commenting on questions which are hopelessly outdated, his writings have a continuing validity and vibrancy.

Precisely because he operated from this larger perspective, Murray's work deserves to be labeled as one of the most articulate, incisive, and enduring public theologies ever produced in the United States. As previously noted, the concept of "public theology" was originated by theologian Martin Marty in a path-breaking article on civil religion written in 1974.[2] Marty argued that in the United States civil religion had taken two different forms. The first, which he labeled "the cultic mode," fused the symbols of mainline religious faith with autochthonous patriotic sentiments. In this form of civil religion, God was seen as the guide and protector of the nation, but substantial religious convictions were not allowed to interfere with national policy. The "high priest" of this cultic form of civil religion was usually the president of the United States, who could inspire in the American people the conviction that they were being faithful to God's will without having to bother about the often troublesome question of just what that will demanded. Contrasted with this "cultic" form of civil religion, according to Marty, had been a "prophetic mode" in American religious history. Participants in this prophetic tradition, exemplified by Jonathan Edwards and Reinhold Niebuhr, sought to create genuine and substantial public theologies which simultaneously validated and critiqued the American historical tradition.

> The prophetic mode has to be dialectical. If it comes unilaterally from outside or is totally rejective from within, it does

not belong to the civil religion, which is an expression of a somehow-covenanted group of insiders. The dialectician says "both/and": God both shapes a nation and judges it, because he is transcendent in both circumstances.[3]

The essence of a true public theology, then, is to maintain this difficult dialectical balance—to retain membership and credibility with the national community by acknowledging God's participation in the life of the nation, while at the same time using religious truth to critique the policies and direction of the nation.

It would be hard to construct a better definition of what John Courtney Murray accomplished through his writings on the social, political, and international life of the United States. For Murray's use of the myths and symbols of American patriotism was masterful; his reconstruction of the American cultural consensus, his reinterpretation of the American political tradition, and his evaluation of America's role in the post-war world all reveal a deep pride in the national history of the United States, and a conviction that God had indeed given America a mission in the world which was of major importance. In part this theme in Murray's works flowed from his need to establish his own patriotic credentials and those of the Catholic community within the larger American society; one of the great achievements of Murray's work was to help overcome the suspicion which many Americans, especially many intellectuals in America, had always had of the Catholic community. But it would be a severe mistake to believe that Murray's use of the myths and symbols of American civil religion was merely artifice, that he did not believe deeply in the patriotic sentiments which he preached. Murray was a true believer, and he could write so effectively about the national heritage of the United States precisely because he believed in the fundamental goodness of the American proposition and the American dream. Murray operated, on grounds of both conviction and strategy, "within the national covenanted community," to use Marty's terminology, and for this reason his writings evoked an automatic sympathy among the broad range of the American public and an automatic credibility with the nation's social, political and economic elites.

But if Murray subscribed to the fundamental themes of American civil religion, he did so with a significant reservation which not only prevented his work from becoming merely an endorsement of the status quo in the United States, but also allowed it to function as a highly effective critique of the most deleterious trends in American society: the reservation which stated that all societies, all cultural and political endeavors, must be evaluated in the light of God's enduring order of justice. The over-arching theme of Murray's life-work was the conviction that all human values must be subjected to transcendent truth, and that any society which built its moral identity upon exclusively this-worldly principles would inevitably succumb to relativism, then to chaos, then to totalitarianism. This was the great lesson of the growth of secularism in the Western world, and Murray was convinced that it was necessary to apply this lesson consistently and rigorously to every problem which he confronted in American society. It was this conviction which allowed Murray to argue, in Marty's terms, that "God both shapes the nation and judges it, because He is transcendent in both circumstances." It was this conviction which made Murray a true public theologian, and not a mere votary of civil religion.

But even if it is granted that Murray's writings on social and political questions constituted an articulate and forceful public theology, and even if it is further granted that this public theology functioned admirably in the immediate post-war era, the question still remains: Does Murray's effort to combat the secular crisis in the United States still represent a comprehensive and effective public theology for the present day? Murray was preeminently a man who appreciated both the dynamism of history and the necessity for any public theology to be rooted in the concrete historical realities of the day. For this reason, he would have rejected outright any attempt to assume automatically that his work on faith and society continues to represent a valid public theology. Instead, he would have insisted that his work be subjected to comprehensive scrutiny and challenge, in order to determine whether its frame of analysis still constitutes a good starting point for the renewal of American society in the last decades of the twentieth century.

In undertaking such a scrutiny, three central questions must be asked. The first is methodological: Does Murray's choice of natural law language still represent the most effective way for Americans to speak to one another about the public role of religion in society? The second question is topical: Do the fundamental questions and categories which Murray addressed still constitute the significant issues facing American society? And the third question which must be asked is prescriptive: Does Murray's application of the principles of natural law to the problems of the present day still hold, or have these problems and American society changed so much that natural law would now render different answers for America's ills? Only in answering these three questions can the enduring validity of Murray's social writings be determined, and only in answering these three questions can one establish whether the Murray corpus represents a sound foundation for a contemporary American public theology.

A QUESTION OF METHOD

In addressing the fundamental problems facing America in the post-war era, Murray returned time and again to the principles of natural law as the source for his evaluations and his prescriptions. In the cultural order, in the political sphere, and in the world of international relations, the answer to America's most pressing ills was the same: revivify the tradition of natural law which had been alive and well at the time of the nation's founding, and the most serious obstacles to a national renaissance will have been overcome. It is not difficult to understand why Murray chose to frame his discourse in natural law terms. The tradition of reason was the matrix within which the social teachings of the Catholic Church had been conceived for centuries, and all of the great thinkers who were instrumental in Murray's intellectual development were natural law thinkers: John of Paris, Thomas Aquinas, Robert Bellarmine, Leo XIII, Pius XII, and John XXIII. Moreover, the United States genuinely had a tradition which echoed the principles of natural law; as Clinton Rossiter had brought home, beneath the most dramatic and momentous declarations of the Founding Fathers was a clear recourse to natural law, as it had been handed down throughout the ages. Thus when Murray sought a methodology which could act as a bridge between the Catholic community and the wider American society, the tradition of reason was the obvious candidate.

But in recent years, serious questions have arisen about whether or not the principles of natural law still represent the most powerful foundation for public theology in the United States. In light of the continuing centrality of Scripture for Protestant men and women, and the renewed appreciation which the Catholic Church has had since the Second Vatican Council for the role of biblical theology, the question has been raised: Can a public theology such as Murray's, which almost totally ignores the role of Scripture and revelation, truly represent the social thought of America's religious men and women today? This question has been reinforced by the great emphasis which has been placed in recent years on the role and power of symbols, not only in theology, but in all realms of public discourse. Murray was not afraid to enlist the myths and symbols of American culture in order to identify with and challenge his listeners; does his refusal to utilize the powerful symbols of biblical theology now invalidate his body of writing as a foundation for a contemporary American public theology? These are hard and penetrating questions, and they have been asked in various forms by many of America's public theologians in recent years. In order to deal adequately with the question of Murray's methodology, it is necessary to confront the specific methodological critiques which have been leveled at Murray's work, and then judge their validity.

The first criticism which is made of Murray's exclusive use of natural law is that it generates a dualistic mode of thinking about the world which erects an impenetrable barrier between the sacred and the secular. David Hollenbach, in an article on "Public Theology in America," has aptly summarized this line of thought:

> There is a kind of dualism in Murray's thinking which, despite this stress on the presence of the sacred in the temporal through graced humanity, sets a great divide between the religious and the secular. This divide is not simply a stratagem for gaining a wider audience for Christian moral views which

have been translated into non-religious language. The relation between the sacred and the secular, as Murray understands it, becomes a relation of unity only within the experience of the individual person, not in the public sphere. The social order can protect this unity, and it can provide the possibility for the realization of this unity within the hearts of persons. The relation between the sacred and the secular is attained by the achievement of a "right order within one man, who is a member of two societies and subject to the laws of both." In the world of institutions, structures, power, and corporate action, however, the dualism is sharply drawn.[4]

If this were actually where Murray's writings led, then his entire effort to combat the secularist idea in the modern world would have been in vain. For Murray's goal was to convince the American people that their social, political and economic life should be infused by sacred values in their corporate as well as their individual dimensions. The great threat which Murray saw to the West was the denial of the fundamentally sacred truths which should ground public life: the acknowledgment of God's role as the Lord of creation and the Source of all value, the adherence to the divine order of justice which anchored all collective human activity, and the enhancement of the *res sacrae* in every sphere of societal life. Murray did not speak of a world in which, to cite Hollenbach, all "institutions, structures, power, and corporate action" were deprived of their sacred identities; on the contrary, he spoke of a world where the sacred character of the nation's institutions, structures and power would be acknowledged by all.

Thus the dualism which flows from Murray's use of natural law in no way excludes the sacred from public life and public discourse. What it does exclude, as Hollenbach and others have pointed out, is the appeal to Scripture or revelation as a grounding for claims in the social and political spheres. It was Murray's clear conviction that in a pluralist society it was both divisive and violative of human rights to construct public institutions according to claims which could be justified only on sectarian grounds. There could only be one ground on which a truly just social order should be established: the ground of the common human nature which was shared by all people and which was comprehensible to all people.

But what was the cost of excluding Scripture and revelation from the realm of the public theology? What values of Christian faith had to be sacrificed in embracing the tradition of reason? In John Coleman's view, the cost consisted, at least in part, of skewing the substance of Murray's social analysis toward an individualism that renders it suspect for the present day:

> My purpose is to point out the relative lack in American Catholic social thought, until recent times, of appeals to biblical imagery in discussions of the normative foundations of public life. I also want to suggest that this lacuna skews Murray's writings on public issues too strongly in the direction of liberal individualism, despite his own intentions.[5]

There are several serious problems with such a statement. The first is that Murray's interpretation of society and the state, while it did stress the freedom of the individual to an immense degree, was not an individualistic one. Murray recast the natural law tradition of the Church in light of the American context, but in doing so he remained faithful to the social nature of the human person which had been reflected in the writings of Thomas, Leo XIII, Pius XII and John XXIII. Murray's stress on the fivefold ends of political society is but one clear index of this fidelity. But a second and, from a methodological view, more important problem inherent in Coleman's critique is the implicit assumption that a biblical ethic, properly employed, will generate a different content than the use of natural law would generate. For if, as Coleman asserts, it was Murray's omission of biblical imagery per se which skewed his writings in a falsely individualistic manner, it can only be because there is a distinctly Christian ethical content which reason cannot grasp.

But many theologians have pointed out that the material content of Christian ethics is identical with that of the human ethics produced by reason. The law of Christ did not add formal ethical precepts which were unknown to previous ages; instead, his life, death, and resurrection altered the framework within which that material content is approached by the believer. The superiority of Christian ethics over natural ethics is a superiority of horizon and motivation, not a superiority of action or behavior.

As Joseph Fuchs has written, "The specific and *decisively Christian* aspect of Christian morality is not to be sought first of all in the particularity of categorical values, virtues, and forms of various human activities. Rather, it resides in the believer's fundamental Christian decision to accept God's love in Christ and respond to it as one who believes and loves. . . ."[6] For this reason, it is incorrect to assert that the choice of natural law as a methodology for formulating a public theology skews the material content of that public theology or leads to moral norms which would differ from a biblically-based ethic. If there are costs which Murray paid for employing the tradition to the exclusion of Scripture and revelation, they lie not in the area of material norms, but elsewhere.

Charles Curran understands this, yet he too is highly critical of Murray's exclusive reliance on natural law as a source of theological reflection. For in Curran's view natural law produces a truncated social ethic; because the Christian horizon is omitted, the resulting social ethic is not a complete ethic at all:

> A theological ethic must understand and reflect on (human) realities in explicitly theological terms recognizing all of the aspects of the stance and incorporating a corresponding Christology and anthropology. An ethical approach based exclusively on creation, the natural, and human reason is incomplete. Christian social ethics as such is a theological discipline and must be explicitly theological in its method and reflection on reality.[7]

In raising this question of completeness, Curran is confusing public theology with a comprehensive social theology. It is certainly true that no Christian social theology could be considered complete if it did not include a specific Christological foundation and a Christian horizon of understanding. For these are the elements which underpin and animate the moral life of the believer. But an American public theology does not claim to be a complete Christian social theology; it is directed, first and foremost, toward forming a spiritual coalition between Christian and non-Christian members of American society, and hence it must be evaluated for its completeness on the basis of the task which it sets for itself: namely, to animate and guide American society in creating a just social order founded upon the principles which God has ordained. Public theology should be seen as a branch of social theology, and specific public theologies should not be criticized as incomplete because they do not accomplish all of the goals necessary for a comprehensive social theology.

In addition to this issue of completeness, Curran's critique questions the theological nature of Murray's work. He is not alone on this point. In a 1979 symposium on public theology which focused on the issue of Murray's methodology, John Coleman, David Hollenbach, and Robin Lovin all made the same point: while Murray's corpus of social writings may be labeled a comprehensive public philosophy, it does not constitute a public theology at all, since it appeals to, and is framed in, exclusively philosophical, rather than theological language. "Public theology is the effort to discover and communicate the socially significant meanings of Christian symbols and tradition," Hollenbach writes. "Public philosophy is the effort to discover and communicate the significant meanings of common social and political experience in our pluralistic culture."[8] Murray himself would have sharply disagreed. So the question emerges: Does Murray's work on faith and society constitute a theology at all?

In answering this question, it is instructive to utilize the approach to theology advanced by David Tracy in his work on *The Analogical Imagination.* In Tracy's view, one cannot answer the question "What is theology?" without understanding the "social location" of the theologian who is speaking:

> Each theologian addresses three distinct and related social realities: the wider society, the academy, and the church. Some one of these publics will be a principal, yet rarely exclusive, addressee. The reality of a particular social locus will, to be sure, affect the choice of emphasis. The tasks of theology in a seminary, in a church-related university, in a pastoral setting, in a program for religious education, in a small community, in the secular academy, in an involvement in a particular cultural, political or societal movement—each of these realities and others will affect the self-understanding of any theologian. Sometimes that influence will prove so powerful that it will effectively determine the theology. More often a social location will provide "elective affinities" for a particu-

lar emphasis in theology, including the emphasis on what will count as a genuinely theological statement. The more general question "What is theology?" first demands, therefore, a response to a prior question: 'What is the self-understanding of the theologian?'[9]

The public which Murray chose principally to address was the wider non-Catholic body of American society, and the language and method which he utilized, far from excluding his work from the theological realm, represented an effort to project the strongest realizable theological assertions onto the national stage. Murray's decision to confine himself to the language of natural law in his dialogue was a tactical one, and while it can plausibly be criticized as a poor tactic, it cannot legitimately be labeled "non-theological."

It is in this area of tactics that one can find the principal criticisms of those who believe that Murray's writings cannot, on methodological grounds, be the basis for an effective American public theology in the present day. They see in the masterful and urbane flow of Murray's prose powerful analyses of the human condition and incisive prescriptions for alleviating the ills of American society. But they believe that in the end, men and women in American society will be motivated to pursue a truly just social order not primarily by rational and systematic argumentation, but by a symbolic appeal to concrete notions of justice, freedom, and peace that only biblical imagery can provide. Thus John Coleman notes:

> The final weakness in Murray's strategy for public discourse lies in the nature of the symbols he uses. There is a sense in which "secular" language, especially when governed by the Enlightenment ideals of conceptual clarity and analytic rigor, is exceedingly "thin" as a symbol system. It is unable to evoke the rich, polyvalent power of religious symbolism, a power which can command commitments of emotional depth. The very necessity of seeking a universality which transcends our rootedness and loyalties to particular communities makes secular language chaste, sober, thin.[10]

There is no doubt that this is a very potent criticism. Murray's work is uniformly systematic, rigorous, and profound; it is seldom evocative, symbolically powerful, or inspirational. Murray's writings often have the power to convince; they seldom have the power to move.[11] It was Murray's goal to make Catholic social thought intelligible to a society which was deeply suspicious of the perceived authoritarianism of Catholic faith. In this effort, he succeeded admirably. But the question remains: Does natural law, unaided by biblical imagery, have the power to move American society toward a just social order founded upon the will of God? The answer must be a qualified no.

No, because Coleman is right in saying that a richer inspirational force must be found to motivate American society. A qualified no, because the acknowledgment of the need for biblical symbolism and religious imagery does not lead to the conclusion that a contemporary American public theology should be a biblically-founded theology. As Murray's critics are well aware, the use of biblical images in public discourse has been a two-edged sword in American history. It has undergirded the abolitionism of the nineteenth century and the civil rights movement of the twentieth. But it has also supported the system of slavery, the refusal to extend the vote to women, and the most vicious nativism directed against Catholics, Jews, and blacks. It was for these reasons that Murray was suspicious of allowing biblical mandates into the public discourse of American society, and these suspicions remain equally valid in the present day.

How, then, can one construct a public theology which utilizes the power of religious imagery yet avoids the danger of a fundamentalistic misuse of biblical materials? First of all, by designing the core of that public theology around a natural law base. Murray's fundamental insight was correct: in a pluralistic society it is divisive and illegitimate to base claims for society and the state upon grounds which cannot be justified without sectarian warrants. Second, by using biblical and religious symbols in a manner which is strictly mediated by the precepts of natural law. Scripture and sectarian tradition can indeed add richness, texture, and inspiration to a public theology, but they should always be employed in a way which enhances and brings out the meaning implicit in natural theology. Biblical and religious claims which cannot be substantiated by independent recourse to natural law should have no place in a contemporary public theology. Third, by using scriptural and religious images selectively, depending upon the specific audience which is being addressed. Here Tracy's notion of the social location of the theologian is important. When one is addressing a group of Christians on American foreign policy, the public theologian can profitably use biblical images to enhance his message, since those images are a common frame of reference. But when a public theologian is testifying before Congress, he should omit all sectarian references, lest they be interpreted as grounding social claims *solely* on the basis of revelation or the teachings of a particular church. Such a vision of public theology will use biblical imagery to complement its social and ethical analysis, but not to ground it. In this way of thinking, it might be better to speak of public theolo*gies* with a common core, rather than a set and universal public theology.[12]

But does not such an approach represent a utilitarian concept of biblical theology which disregards the legitimate autonomy of scriptural exegesis? It certainly could, if biblical images were used in a manner which distorted their meanings in Scripture. But giving priority in public theology to the principles of natural law does not automatically entail a distortion of biblical materials. In the first place, if the categorical moral content of revelation is identical with that of natural law, there will be, in principle, no substantive conflicts between the directives pointed to by natural law and those proposed by Scripture. Second, the role of biblical materials in such a conception of public theology performs the same task which revelation performs in relation to natural law: for believers, it provides the horizon and the inspiration within which moral precepts must be seen. Thus such a tactical use of biblical materials does not violate the legitimate autonomy and authority of revelation, even if it does at times omit the language of Scripture in the interests of advancing the categorical moral content which Scripture proposes.

At this point, one must confront a fundamental question about the role of natural law itself in the present day: Does it truly represent an effective bridge between all peoples in speaking about social, cultural, and political issues? This was the question raised by Reinhold Niebuhr in his debates with Murray on the question of natural law:

> The only natural law that almost all of us can accept without presupposition or without creed is that there is a common humanity that makes Christian and non-Christian secularists, etc., feel that what the Boers are doing in South Africa is awfully bad. There is some ultimate concept of human responsibility towards man and acknowledgement of the dignity of man. But when you get to the particular, you find the whole question about the historical relativity of reason.[13]

In our present age, when we are even more aware of the cultural diversity of the world than was true in Niebuhr's day, the question seems even more pressing. How is it possible to establish that, in the words of *Gaudium et Spes,* "In the depths of his conscience, man detects a law which he does not impose upon himself, which holds him to obedience"?[14] And how is it possible to establish that this law corresponds with the principles of natural law as Murray proposed them?

The first step is to recognize two characteristics which Murray emphasized in his description of natural law. One is the historic and dynamic character of the tradition of reason. The application of natural law does not consist merely of deriving unchanging principles of conduct from abstract essences. Natural law must be applied to concrete human reality, and thus its specification will change as human reality changes. The other characteristic of Murray's thought which is essential for demonstrating the validity and universality of the natural law tradition is his notion that all ethical insight is contingent, and that the complexity of the modern world makes ethical decision-making even more difficult than in previous ages.

Beyond this, in order to answer the question which Niebuhr raised one must do something which Murray did not do: namely, engage in a rigorous philosophical exposition of the epistemological roots of natural law. Murray was writing for a general audience. Moreover, one of his primary goals was to convince Americans that natural law represented the common moral heritage of the human community, and that this truth could be perceived by the average person. For this reason, Murray did not engage in the type of epistemological argument necessary to answer Niebuhr's question on a sophisticated intellectual plane. But such an epistemological argument is a necessary component of a complete public theology. It would not have to be included in all presentations of public theology, since for the most part the audiences to which public theology is aimed will not be seeking such a theoretical rigor. But the questions of men such as Reinhold Niebuhr demand that public theology have the demonstrated ability to ground its fundamental assertions in a sophisticated epistemological framework, and this was a demand that Murray himself did not meet.

Having said this, it is important to note that Murray's description of natural law in terms understandable to the average person does point to a method for answering those who say that the tradition of reason does not provide an effective moral and intellectual bridge across cultures, religions, and races. For in the language and methodology employed by the diverse peoples of the world to advance their claims to human rights in the modern era, one can see the very process of moral discernment which Murray describes. One could understand why the early declarations in support of human rights might reflect a natural law mentality, since these were products of the Western nations. But in the more recent formulations of human rights, formulations which were composed in the third world and which in many other ways reflect distinctively third world concerns, there is a consistent appeal to the order of justice which grounds the sacred dignity of the human person, and a consistent recourse to the rights of freedom, equality, human welfare, security, and morality which constitute Murray's fivefold ends of political society.[15] Thus in the very order of human interaction where a transreligious and transcultural language is most imperative, the language and methodology of natural law have emerged alone to occupy the field.

It is because of this very ability of natural law to bridge the gulf between people of different cultures and faiths that it deserves to be the foundation for American public theology. It was Murray's great insight to recognize the fundamental pluralism of American society, and to convey the social aspirations of the Catholic faith in a manner which would not violate that pluralism. In our own time, when both the pluralism and the secularism of American culture are even more pronounced than in Murray's day, it would be ill-advised to sacrifice that insight even to capture the added inspiration which a biblically-centered public theology might generate.

A QUESTION OF SUBSTANCE

Even if it is granted, however, that the natural law methodology which Murray consistently followed in his work still represents the surest foundation for public theology in the United States, an equally pressing question remains: Does the substance of Murray's societal analysis still constitute the optimal basis for public theology in the present day? In essence, two issues are involved here. The first concerns Murray's choice of topics to address: Do the categories singled out as important in his writings still represent the pressing issues which a public theology should address? The second question pertains to the manner in which Murray addressed these topics: Do the prescriptions which resulted from Murray's effort to apply natural law principles to these issues still remain valid despite the many changes which have taken place over the past twenty years? By answering these questions in tandem, it is possible to determine whether the substance of Murray's analysis continues to be an acceptable foundation for public discourse on the role of spiritual values in American society.

The Challenge of Secularism

This issue of secularism was the binding force that united all of Murray's writing on social questions. From questions of the university's role in society to issues of nuclear war, the backdrop which animated and guided his work was a preoccupation with the public role of religion in society. Murray had no doubt that this role was in jeopardy in the United States. And he had no doubt that if America failed to reverse the drift toward secular values in the public arena, then the core values which had made American society healthy and vibrant would atrophy, one by one, until the very principles of freedom and justice which secularism pretended to serve would be no more. Murray believed that the primary agenda of public theology in the United States should be

to reverse the secular drift, and to reinject the sense and substance of the sacred into American public life.

Does this viewpoint remain a valid one? Do the indices of
secularism which Murray pointed to genuinely constitute a corruption of the public sphere, or are they merely facets of the
healthy process of institutional differentiation which is usually
termed the secularizing of society? Even if Murray is correct in
pointing to the growth of secularism, can a public theology help
to reverse the secularist drift, and if so how? These are questions
which must be answered before the analysis of secularism in
American society which Murray presented can be accepted as the
basis for present day theologizing.

There is no more controverted question in the field of sociology than the question of whether or not religion has been in
dramatic decline as a social force in the twentieth century. During
the 1950's, a series of works espoused what has come to be called
"the secularization thesis," namely, the assertion that modernity
had inescapably brought with it the progressive evacuation of religious beliefs from Western societies. By the 1960's an opposing
literature had emerged which argued that religion was not in
broad retreat in Western culture, and that it had in most coun-
tries (especially the United States) retained a vitality and pervasiveness which was incompatible with any blanket form of "the
secularization thesis."[16] In 1967 Larry Shiner significantly clarified what had become an increasingly unproductive argument
between these two camps by pointing out that the term secular
needed to be differentiated into five different meanings: 1. the
simple decline of religion; 2. pressure upon religious bodies and
individuals to conform with the world; 3. the desacralization of
the world; 4. the disengagement of religion from society; 5. the
transposition of behaviors from the religious to the secular
sphere (this last is what is generally called secularization as
opposed to secularism).[17] It is the fourth category, the disengagement of religion from society, which Murray focused upon in his
life work. Murray was quite willing to admit that religion had
remained vibrant and pervasive in America; thus the rise of reli-
giosity in the 1950's did not make him question the validity of his
approach to public theology. What concerned Murray was the
substantive public role of religiously-based values in the life of

American society, the ability of spiritual values to influence and energize the cultural, political and international orders in American life. Murray believed that it was here that modernity had sapped the vitality of religion in Western societies, and that it was the public role of religion that desperately needed to be clarified and reinforced in the United States.

Recent sociological commentaries on this question lend great support to Murray's analysis of trends in American life. Peter Berger has found that the decreasing role of religiously-based values in the public order of American life has brought about a collapse of the moral consensus necessary for the long-term preservation of American society. Interestingly, Berger traces this collapse in large part to the rise of a new and secularized "knowledge class" in the U.S. which dramatically influences the formation of national attitudes; one can see here the clear echo of Murray's concern about the secular drift among Western elites and his desire to form a religiously-formed group of men and women to work in the media, the legal establishment, and the university system.[18] Thomas Luckman, Bryan Wilson, and Hans Mol have detected these same trends, with religion retreating from the substantive institutional life of society and remaining potent only as an integrating force for the individual and for the relationships of family, ethnic group, and neighborhood.[19] As a consequence of these trends, the personal meaning and ultimate significance which formerly attached to larger societal institutions because of their sacred character have evaporated, and in a very real sense, these institutions have become dehumanized. In Luckman's words,

> the primary social institutions have emigrated from the sacred cosmos. Their functional rationality is not part of a system that could be of 'ultimate significance' to the individuals in society. . . . (One is) justified in describing this process as a process of dehumanization of the basic structural components of the social order. The functional rationality of the primary social institutions seems to reinforce the isolation of the individual from his society, contributing thereby to the precariousness inherent in all social orders.[20]

It would be hard to find a better summary of Murray's analysis of the secularist drift in the United States. The sacred character of the public institutions of society is no longer recognized; it has been delegitimized. As a result these institutions take on a purely functional character, and the primary values which they seek to realize are those of economic efficiency, technical rationality, and democratic proceduralism. The substance of these public institutions, which in previous ages had been rooted in their ability to serve the transcendent dignity of the human person, can now only be rooted in processes. As a result the individual feels alienated from these institutions, and the social fabric of modern life has an aridness that easily leads to dehumanization and despair.

Of course Murray spoke of these processes as they were just beginning in the United States; the America which he knew was far from being a society in which the individual felt totally alienated from the public institutions of social life. The same is true of America today. But the warning signs of secularism in the public square which Murray spoke of, the danger signals which he gleaned from the works of Voegelin, Guardini and Sturzo, can be clearly discerned in the decreasing public role which religion plays in American public life, and in the increasing emptiness of religious symbols as they are used in public discourse. Peter Berger has found that:

> Religion manifests itself as public rhetoric and private virtue. In other words, insofar as religion is common, it lacks reality, and insofar as it is real, it lacks commonality. This situation represents a severe rupture of the traditional task of religion, which was precisely the establishment of an integrated set of definitions of reality that could serve as a common universe of meaning for the members of society.[21]

Assaults upon the integrating role of religion in society continue to proliferate. The growing number of Supreme Court cases which enforce an absolute separation between religion and government, the increasing consensus among the nation's intellectual elite that religious claims should not be inserted into public discourse, and the tremendous uncertainty among the mass of the nation's citizenry about how personal religious and ethical convictions can be appropriately related to societal issues all lead to a situation where the sacred dimensions of public life are clearly in jeopardy.

As a result of this secularist trajectory, many thoughtful commentators have seriously begun to question the ability of the nation to continue to carry on its democratic tradition. Richard Neuhaus argues, "Without a transcendent or religious point of reference, conflicts of values cannot be resolved; there can only be procedures for their temporary accommodation. Conflicts over values are viewed not as conflicts between contending truths, but between contending interests."[22] As Hans Morgenthau noted in his argument that the nation-state system was not an international political society at all, a prerequisite for the healthy functioning of any political society is the willingness of the individuals and subsidiary institutions of the society to occasionally place their own interests second to the good of the society as a whole. In the absence of any transcendent reference which can ground the common good of society, it is difficult to see how such a willingness can be sustained, and how the democratic tradition of the United States can be prevented from falling into a mere calculus of power, no matter how sophisticated a calculus. In such a situation, as Alasdair MacIntyre has written, "politics becomes civil war carried on by other means. . . ."[23]

Nor is this "civil war" limited to matters of politics, although as Murray presciently noted, in such a situation all issues seem to ultimately become matters of politics. In the area of culture, in that very moral fabric which holds society together, the decline of transcendent values has indeed left a vacuum at the heart of American society, and a corrosion in the soul of a nation which once prided itself on virtue. In the words of Robert Bellah,

> It is one of the oldest sociological generalizations that any coherent and viable society rests on a common set of moral understandings about good and bad, right and wrong, in the realm of individual and social action. It is almost as widely held that these common moral understandings must also in turn rest upon a common set of religious understandings that provide a picture of the universe in terms of which the moral understandings make sense. . . . In the eighteenth century,

there was a common set of religious and moral understandings rooted in a conception of divine order under a Christian,
or at least a deist, God. The basic moral norms that were seen
as deriving from that divine order were liberty, justice, and
charity, understood in a context of theological and moral discourse which led to a concept of personal virtue as the essential basis of a good society. How far we have come from that
common set of understandings is illustrated by the almost
negative meaning of the word "virtue" today.[24]

One can almost hear in these words the echo of Murray's warning
that a society which loses its transcendent sense of moral values
has lost the only truly unifying force a people can have, and that
such a society is forced to "lumber about the world, lost and
mad."[25] The "madness" which Murray spoke of was the inability
of a people to construct a common moral frame of reference, and
the resulting inability of social interaction to be based on a foundation anchored in anything more permanent than mere expe-
diency. America is far from succumbing to such madness, but the
warning signs which Murray pointed to have not diminished in
the past twenty years, but have only intensified.

But what of the birth of the religious "new right" in American society—does not that signal a return to the transcendent
values which can anchor the nation? If Murray were alive, he
would answer with a resounding no. And he would be right. For
while the rising social and political activism of fundamentalists
does represent an understandable reaction to the delegitimation
of religious values that has taken place in American society over
the past forty years, the fundamentalist vision of transcendent
values will not lead to the recreation of a unified moral fabric in
the United States. For the U.S. continues to be a religiously pluralistic society; and any effort to recreate the moral order of the
United States on the basis of specifically sectarian warrants will
only succeed in furthering the divisions in American society. The
answer to the secularist drift does not lie in the imposition of a
literal biblical morality upon the nation as a whole, but in the
recasting of the "public consensus" which guided America's
vision, if not always its practice, for most of its history.[26]

It is precisely in aiding this reformulation of the "public consensus" that Murray's public theology can provide an answer to

the growth of secularism in twentieth century America. For the United States stands as a divided society in the present age. On one side, there is a secularized, often more intellectual core which believes that religious values have no place in American society and that religion should merely be a private matter. On the other side stands a group of some twenty million fundamentalist Christians who see in the growth of secularism an attack upon their most cherished values, and who see in the Bible a mandate for the reform of American life. In the middle stands the great majority of Americans, who personally hold to religious values and who in some vague manner want to have those values reflected in American public life without violating the pluralist structure of the United States. The public theology which Murray began to enunciate almost fifty years ago has the capacity to teach this broad middle group in American society how to begin constructing a society and a state which reflect the sacred dimensions of American public life without trespassing upon the moral and religious freedom of the individual. For Murray's work, with its clear affirmation of the *res sacrae* as the foundation for every element of social life, skillfully roots public values in a transcendent order of justice which appeals only to the law which is written in the hearts of all people, and proposes a public religion whose only tenets are the acknowledgement of the God of creation. On both sides of the spectrum, there are some who will object to such a formulation, but as a foundation for a renewed American moral consensus, Murray's public theology succeeds far better than any other in providing what America needs most: a lens through which to examine itself and restructure its cultural, political, and international identity.

The Order of Culture

The starting point for such a reexamination and restructuring, according to Murray, lay in the order of culture. Specifically, it lay in confronting the three cultural strains which were becoming dominant in twentieth century America and in laying bare their fundamental bankruptcy. The first of these strains Murray identified as technological secularism, the tendency of the modern person to define all problems as rational and functional and to place his trust in the ability of science and technological innovation to create, if not a perfect society, at least the best society. The second corrupting theme which Murray had pointed to in American culture was practical materialism, the preoccupation with economic competition and the accumulation of wealth that had always been present in American society, but which had taken on a new forcefulness in the post-war era. And the final and in many ways the most ominous secular formative principle of culture which Murray had detected in American life was that of philosophical pluralism, the belief that respect for the social, political, and religious diversity of American society demanded an ordering cultural principle for the United States which was explicitly relativist. In evaluating Murray's commentary on the order of culture and its applicability for the present day, it is necessary to inquire whether technological secularism, practical materialism and philosophical pluralism still constitute the dominant formative principles of culture in American society, and, if so, how Murray's presentation of natural law can act as a corrective.

It might seem that the bankruptcy of technological secularism which Murray pointed to in his "Frankensteinian" description of the unbridled scientific ethic would now be apparent to most, if not all, in American society. The specter of nuclear war stands as the most awesome threat to survival which humanity has ever faced. Environmental pollution poses enormous, and in some cases irreversible, health hazards for the entire world. And the limits of the natural resources which are necessary for sustaining a technological society are becoming more and more apparent every year. In the face of these developments, technological secularism as an articulated cultural principle can now be seen by the American people for what it is, the prime example of *hubris* in the modern world, and a purely instrumental conception of human life which—precisely because it is not related to any transcendent conception of the human person—cannot serve as a legitimate formative principle of culture at all.

But the problem is that technological secularism has never operated as an articulated principle of culture for the American people; it has always functioned as an unreflective strain in social and political life in the United States, a tendency to devote greater attention to questions of "how to?" than to questions of "toward what?" It is precisely because technological secularism has functioned in this unphilosophical and unarticulated manner in American society that the inherent link between a purely scientific world-view and the problems of nuclear holocaust, environmental pollution and dwindling natural resources is seldom explicitly made.

Murray's analysis of technolgical secularism can help to make that linkage explicit. It can point out that the benefits which science has produced are a result of the legitimate autonomy of scientific thought in the modern world, but that the efforts of science to free itself from responsibility to a transcendently-based frame of values has led to a situation where, to cite Murray's prediction of thirty years ago,

> man (has) an experience of great impersonal forces that he has not quite got control of, and . . . (he somehow feels) that the whole course of human events is not only uncertain, but that man's hold upon the course of events is extremely precarious.[27]

Murray's use of natural law to critique the purely scientific world-view can help to bring a balance to the technological orientation in American culture by exposing its limitations, and by providing a method for grounding the work of science and industry in values which will reflect the sacred dignity of the human person. In an age of in vitro fertilization and recombinant D.N.A. research, there are few greater priorities for American society than that of positioning the American genius for practicality within a framework of ethical values which can encourage the scientific urge to seek new knowledge, but which can also channel that urge in a direction which ultimately leads to increases in human well-being rather than threatening it.

Like technological secularism, practical materialism has always functioned as an unarticulated principle of culture within the United States. But unlike technological secularism, which has been chastened by the specters of "nuclear winter" and "the greenhouse effect," practical materialism seems only to be growing stronger as a formative principle for the cultural life of the

American people. The 1980's have been a period in which the stress on financial accumulation and material success has risen dramatically among all elements of the population, and it has been particularly noticeable among the generation of young people which is now entering the job market.

Murray's application of natural law to American social and economic life can act as a corrective to this preoccupation with material accumulation and financial success. In assessing the impact of practical materialism on American life, Murray argued that the stress on economic competition in the United States was leading to a situation where America would become "a body without a soul . . . that is literally without a spiritual principle to animate its program of economic and material organization."[28] When Murray wrote those words, he was dealing with a period in which rising American economic power threatened to create a material surplus which would overwhelm the social and cultural life of the nation. Now the situation is reversed; while the economy of the United States continues to grow in absolute terms, America's relative role in the world economy is declining, and adjustments will have to be made in the domestic economic priorities of the United States. In making these adjustments, it is imperative that America be guided by cultural principles which reflect the breadth and richness of the human person. Practical materialism cannot provide such cultural principles. Murray's public theology can.

For Murray's theology recognizes, first of all, that material progress is a tremendous human good, and that economic activity constitutes one of the primary ways in which people exercise their role as co-creators in the world. But it also recognizes that material progress constitutes but one element in the building of a balanced cultural order, and that in the end the spirit of a society is far more important than its material structures. This means that the preoccupation of America's youth with achieving financial success must be challenged by a wider vision of human life. It also means that the period of economic readjustment which the United States is undergoing as a result of new economic competition from Japan, Korea and Taiwan must not lead to changes in the U.S. economy which balance the trade deficits on the backs of the poor through layoffs of the unskilled and decreases in social programs. This period of readjustment does not mean the end of the American dream of an ever more prosperous world. In fact, it can lead to a restructuring of the American dream in which growing prosperity continues to have a prominent role, but in which the complementary spiritual values of justice, honesty, and charity occupy a larger place. Murray's life-work constitutes just such a version of the American dream, and for this reason its critique of practical materialism may well be even more appropriate in the present day than it was when it was first written some thirty years ago.

The third secular principle of culture which Murray combatted during his lifetime—that of philosophical pluralism—is, like technological secularism and practical materialism, still very much with us. Indeed, as a basis for social and governmental policies, the creed of ethical relativism has become the dominant perspective of the American people. The 1960's was a period in which the United States came to a deeper level of tolerance in society; the triumph of the civil rights movement brought with it a recognition that many of the narrow prejudices which had marred American society needed to be discarded if the U.S. was truly to become a just society. One result of this has been the effort to incorporate formerly marginalized elements of American society into the mainstream—ethnic and racial minorities, the handicapped, the uneducated. A less satisfying result of this same drive toward tolerance has been the growing conviction in American society that all strongly held moral proscriptions constitute a form of intolerance, and that there is no such thing as a universally binding moral code which should be reflected in societal life. Robert Bellah has spoken of "the derogation of virtue" in the U.S., the "erosion of common meanings . . . which takes the form, which is by now statistically well documented, of a decline of belief in all forms of obligation: to one's occupation, one's family, and one's country."[29]

This "erosion of common meanings" does not, as Murray argued so forcefully a generation ago, represent the logical extension of America's commitment to racial, ethnic, and religious pluralism. Rather, it represents an apostasy from the only secure foundation upon which a pluralistic and tolerant society can be founded. For as Bellah has pointed out, the core of ethical discourse lies in the concept of obligation; and if there is no body of shared moral meanings in a society, there is no sense of moral obligation, either. In such a situation, tolerance, justice, charity, and all the other civic virtues which are essential to the functioning of a truly pluralistic society will wither away, leaving only pure self-interest as the determinant of public policy. And there is little which is more intolerant than pure self-interest.

Fortunately, philosophical pluralism, as an articulated public philosophy, would be rejected by the American people as a whole. However, philosophical pluralism does not function as an articulated public philosophy for most of the people of the United States. Rather, like technological secularism, it functions as an unconscious orientation which is eating away at the roots of American society. In exposing the premises and the ramifications of philosophical pluralism, Murray's public theology can help to bring the people of the United States to see that it is possible to embrace a meaningful ethical code for social life which is not in any way intolerant or parochial, and that the alternative to embracing such a code is not tolerance and pluralism, but chaos and the domination of self-interest.

In summary, then, Murray's public theology still stands as an incisive and balanced critique of the three major cultural trends which threaten to corrode American society. Each of these trends operates more as a practical orientation than as a thoughtfully considered public philosophy in American life, and it is precisely for this reason that Murray's dogged insistence on exposing the ultimate ramifications of these cultural principles can assist the people of the United States in choosing a formative principle of culture which does not lead to the purely instrumental world of the scientific mentality, or the shallowness of the materialist mentality, or the ethical confusion of the philosophically pluralist mentality. Murray's public theology can guide the American people toward a culture which enhances the sacred dignity of the human person because his theological outlook rests upon the central basis for affirming that sacred dignity: the recognition that God has given to the cultural order a code of justice which all people can recognize and which all people are called to follow. To use Bellah's phrase, there can be no firmer foundation for "shared meanings" in a society than this.

The Order of Politics

In every period of American history, certain political issues emerge at the center of American political life and challenge the ability of the constitutional system to adapt to changed circumstances and new human realities. During the early years of the Republic, those issues concerned the ability of the former British colonies to establish an independent national government which was strong enough to be effective, yet limited in nature so as to protect the freedom of America's citizens and its mediating social institutions. In the post-war era during which Murray formulated his public theology, the focal issues in American politics concerned the ability of the nation to sustain civil liberties in the face of communist subversion, the willingness of the United States to face up to its immense problems of racial intolerance, and the expanding role of the federal government in providing aid to education, health care, and social welfare programs. In the present day, the critical issues at the center of America's domestic political agenda are twofold: the question of how the United States should reflect in its legal structures a respect for the broad moral beliefs of its people without violating individual rights, and the issue of at what level the national government should fix its expenditures on social welfare programs. Taken together, these constitute the social agenda and the economic agenda of "the Reagan Revolution," and in the post-Reagan years America will have to grapple with what has been wrought in the 1980's.[30] Regarding the social agenda, Murray's public theology provides a powerful tool of analysis; regarding the economic agenda, it is woefully inadequate.

There is perhaps no more divisive set of political issues in contemporary American society than those colloquially labeled "the social issues," and among these none are more divisive than the questions of abortion, pornography, and the regulation of private sexual conduct. The common thread which runs through all of these issues is that they present to the American people difficult cases in which it must be determined how public morality should be reflected in public law. For each issue, there is a core constituency which argues that a respect for the proper role of morality in national life demands legal proscriptions, while there

is an equally vocal group which argues that any such legal proscriptions constitute a wrongheaded attempt to legislate morality
and an invasion of personal privacy. How are the citizens of the
United States to differentiate between these issue areas and confront the question of morality and public law in a way which will
respect both the need to enhance the tradition of public morality
in America and the need to respect freedom within society?

John Courtney Murray's public theology constitutes a good
first step in this process. For Murray's initial assertion about the
nature of public morality is that it resides, first and foremost, in
the order of society rather than in the realm of public law. Thus
the attempt to solve the issues of abortion, pornography, and sexual promiscuity cannot begin in the order of politics, but must
take place overwhelmingly in the order of culture, in those
mediating institutions of society which have the primary responsibility for education and moral formation: the family, the
churches, and the schools. It is these institutions which must
engender in the American people a respect for the right to life,
for the virtue of chastity, and for public morality as a whole, and
if these institutions are not performing their tasks well, no government legislation will promote a truly just and moral public
order.

Having established that morality is not primarily a matter of
the political order, Murray's theology argues, nonetheless, that
part of the responsibility for maintaining public morality does fall
within the purview of government. The concept which Murray
used to define that limited purview was "the public order," that
minimum threshold of public morality which is essential for the
healthy functioning of society. Using such a concept, it is possible
to differentiate between the broad issue areas of the "social
agenda" now facing the American people, and to propose that
the three questions of abortion, pornography, and private sexual
conduct stand in three different relations to the public order; as
a consequence, they call for three different approaches to legal
proscription.

The issue of abortion, without any doubt, falls entirely within
the scope of the public order; for what is involved in abortion is
the question of whether the state will legally protect the life of
every one of its citizens. If the public order is to have any mean-

ing and integrity whatsoever, the equal protection by the state of every human life must constitute a central function of both law and government, and even the most legitimate questions of personal privacy and personal rights must remain secondary to this overriding governmental responsibility.

The issue of pornography is one of those issues which lies partly within the domain of the public order, according to Murray's schema, and partly outside the power of government. In approaching such issues, it is necessary to keep three things in mind: the need for the state to come down squarely on the side of public morality rather than on the side of public immorality, the need to continuously respect the right to freedom in society, and the need for prudence in constructing any law which limits that freedom. In light of these principles, it is possible to see that pornography constitutes a part of the public order insofar as it touches upon the state's responsibility for the protection of minors, or the government's duty to insure that people on the streets are not accosted by pornographic materials on news-stands, or the government's responsibility to insure that those who participate in the production of pornographic materials are not coerced. But beyond this, as Murray notes, American society has opted to maximize the principle of freedom, and the decision of individuals to privately read pornographic materials is one that can be interfered with by government only at great peril.

The issue of private sexual conduct, the third element of the social agenda in contemporary America, is an area which lies entirely outside the scope of the public order. It is certainly possible to construct an argument which establishes ties between private sexual acts by consenting adults and that part of the common good which is entrusted to the state; but the logic required to establish such ties would completely eviscerate what Murray labored his entire life to defend: the distinction between state and society. If there are to be any meaningful limits to the public order whatsoever, then private sexual activity must fall outside that order, and the present day attempts to retain laws against homosexuality and sexual promiscuity must be rejected.

In summary then, the social agenda facing the United States is a complex one. It can only be addressed productively by employing carefully-crafted and soundly-based distinctions between the roles which should be assigned to the state and those which should reside in society. One of the great strengths of Murray's public theology is that it devotes considerable attention to the working out of just these distinctions. Murray himself would have forcefully rejected the idea that the precise legal standards for regulating a complicated and community-based issue such as pornography can be derived once and for all from any public theology; for he recognized that historical and cultural factors play an important role in the formulation of such areas of public law. But Murray correctly believed that what mattered most in such issue areas was not precise formulations, but general orientations. And in facing the complex and extremely divisive social agenda which now confronts the United States, Murray's writings provide just the type of orientations which America needs to reach a new social consensus, a social consensus which blends both freedom and moral substance.

Unfortunately, the same cannot be said of Murray's public theology as it touches upon the economic order in American society. For in the contemporary age, when ecclesiastical pronouncements upon the need for justice in all economic relationships have taken on a new concreteness and specificity, Murray's relative inattention to economic issues appears all the more as a glaring lacuna in his public theology. There is no substantive new insight which Murray's thought offers in the economic realm; what little attention he gives to the question of distributive justice is derived from *Rerum Novarum*. And as Murray himself would have been the first to realize, the world of economic relationships has changed immensely since the time of Leo XIII, creating what is truly a new "human reality" which must be reflected upon in the light of the principles of natural law.

There are several reasons for Murray's uncharacteristically poor treatment of economic justice. The first is that Murray recognized the complexity of modern economic theory, and he also recognized that he did not have the knowledge required to conduct sophisticated analyses of the American economic system. Having tackled the questions of religion and government, which required him to master large amounts of information in the fields of history, sociology, and law, Murray felt that the economic arena would require the same degree of work, and he was content

to leave that work to others.[31] A second reason for Murray's decision to avoid an in-depth analysis of the American economic system can probably be traced to the focus of his public theology.
Murray's preoccupation with the distinction between state and
society, and his general approval for the manner in which the
United States had accomplished that distinction, made him reluc-
tant to follow the logic of the Church's teaching and demand a
much wider distributive role for government in American society.
This was unfortunate, because it is precisely in addressing the
problem of state and society as it pertains to the question of economic justice that Murray might have been able to make his most
important contribution to American social thought, by providing
a general orientation for the construction of a society which
blends true equity with the preservation of freedom in the economic order.

As it is, Murray did not make such a contribution, and for
this reason his work cannot provide a full-bodied public theology
for the United States in the contemporary age. Murray's work on
the order of culture, his skillful analysis of the relationship
between morality and law, and his rich reflections upon the need
for incorporating religious values into the public life of the
nation all remain valid, but they must be complemented by a systematic analysis of the economic system of the United States in
the light of recent religiously-based reflections, including the
encyclicals of Pope Paul VI and Pope John Paul II, the declarations of the National Council of Churches, and the study-letters
of the Episcopal, Catholic, Lutheran and Presbyterian Churches
in the United States.

One note should be made about the formulation of an economic analysis to complement Murray's social thought. It has
become commonplace in contemporary debates within the American Catholic community about economic issues to cite Murray's
authority as a source of legitimation for both the liberal and conservative positions.[32] Such claims for legitimacy are extremely
dubious, not only because they tend to degenerate into *argumen-
tum ab auctoritate*, but also because Murray did not write enough
on economic issues to clearly support either the liberal or conservative agendas in the present day. Nonetheless, precisely
because Murray's writings are cited so much in the contemporary

debate about the role of government in guaranteeing distributive justice, a brief application of Murray's stated economic principles to the issues of today can help to clear up this question of where Murray might have stood if he had lived to write in the present context.

The first principle which Murray would have pointed to was the necessity for locating the overwhelming responsibility for economic prosperity and justice in the order of culture rather than in the order of government. Murray was not blind to the increasing pressures for state intervention in the economy in the twentieth century. But precisely because he considered overweaning governmental power to be the great threat of modernity, Murray would have resisted a state-based economic order even at some cost in general prosperity and distributive justice. Thus those who cite Murray's authority in order to advance programs which call for massive state intervention in the functioning of the nation's firms and enterprises fly in the face of the fundamental dictum which was ever on Murray's lips: "as much freedom as possible; as much government as necessary." Having said all this, it is equally clear that Murray would have been highly critical of the retrenchment in social welfare spending which is currently taking place in the United States. Murray argued that the government had a special protective role in guarding the claims of the poor in society, and he recognized that the need for exercising that protective role was growing both because the general prosperity of the nation was growing and because the gap between the rich and the poor was getting larger. Murray would have been sympathetic to those who argue that increasing state intervention in the national economy is counter-productive; he would have been manifestly unsympathetic to those who argue that a love of freedom diminishes the responsibility of government to insure that the just claims of the marginalized in society continue to be met.

Thus even in the few tracts which he devoted to economic questions, Murray demonstrated the characteristic balance which emerges from his entire public theology. Freedom and justice: these were the two values which must be preserved in American economic relations, and no rigid formula or ideology could achieve these twin ends. In refusing to delve deeply into the increasingly important issues of the state and the economy, Murray deprived American society of what might have been a rich source of reflection and unity in the 1980's. But in pointing to the need to always strive for balance in questions of economic justice, Murray has pointed to the way which an effective public theology must go in addressing what promises to be a vexing and divisive question for American society, a question which will not go away.

No analysis of Murray's writings on the political order would be complete without mentioning a second major lacuna in his work, namely, Murray's failure to address in any comprehensive manner the issue of racial justice in America. Murray formulated his public theology during the height of the civil rights movement; yet with only two minor exceptions, he never spoke to the need to redress the racial injustices which had been present through American history.[33] In the present day, when the specific issues of racial justice are different from the 1960's but no less troubling to American society, a complete public theology must include a comprehensive consideration of just what racial justice demands in our society, and how it can best be achieved.

The International Order

In the fall of 1985, George Kennan published an influential and highly controversial article in *Foreign Affairs* on "Morality and Foreign Policy." Conceived as an *apologia* not only for his own position on the relationship between ethics and foreign policy, but also as a defense for the realist approach to foreign affairs in general, Kennan wrote:

> The interests of the national society for which government has to concern itself are basically those of its military security, the integrity of its political life, and the well-being of its people. These needs have no moral quality. They arise from the very existence of the national state in question and from the status of national sovereignty it enjoys. They are the unavoidable necessities of a national existence and therefore are not subject to classification as either "good" or "bad."[34]

Such an assertion from one of America's most distinguished and thoughtful statesmen is not only grounds for questioning the basis on which American foreign policy is formulated, but also constitutes a compelling argument that the confusion about the relationship between morality and foreign policy which Murray pointed to some thirty years ago still represents the major obstacle to the pursuit of an American foreign policy which is both moral and in the national interest of the United States.

When Murray first addressed the question of how ethical norms should be applied to foreign affairs, the dominant theorist in the field of international relations was Hans Morgenthau, whose formulation of the realist creed expressly excluded moral norms from having any substantive role in the formation of foreign policy. Today Morgenthau's precepts are recognizable in the "neo-realist" school of international relations, whose major architects include Kenneth Waltz and Robert Gilpin. In the "neo-realist" world-view, the distribution of power is the sole determinant of international policy, and the search for power is the sole legitimate component of the national interest. There is no room for morality in a neo-realist world, because morality is conceived of as the rigid imposition of utopian norms which leads in the end only to pretense and confusion.[35] In the past decade, "neo-realism" has become the dominant paradigm for international relations in the United States. The proposition that morality has no substantively constructive role to play in foreign policy has become the accepted wisdom among specialists in international affairs, and the effort to blend rigorous ethical thinking and an appreciation for the realities of international life has been largely absent from America's attempts to reshape the world order.

But what of the return to idealism in the human rights policies of President Carter, and the renewed commitment to freedom envisioned in the promulgation of the "Reagan Doctrine"? Do these not constitute a new recognition of the role of ethics in the formation of American foreign policy? In one sense, they do. For both the Carter human rights policies and the Reagan commitment to defend the forces of freedom anywhere in the world do appeal explicitly to moral norms as the guiding force for America's role on the international stage. But, unfortunately, the fact that these policies have too often been formulated in such idealistic terms as to be unattainable and the further fact that these policies are too often utilized merely to give a moral patina to decisions made on other grounds have only confirmed the "neo-realist" view that the injection of morality into the formulation of foreign policy must either lead to utopianism or pretense.

Murray's writings on the role of morality and foreign policy are a powerful refutation of all such thinking. For Murray points out that the alternatives to the "neo-realist" world-view are not confined to either Wilsonian idealism or a moralistic charade. The alternative to "neo-realism" which Murray proposes fully recognizes that the application of ethical analysis to international relations is complex and arduous, and that a simplistic morality which views the morality of the state solely through the prism of the moral norms applicable to individuals cannot assist a nation in forming a just and effective foreign policy. By using the framework of natural law to differentiate between the moral character of the state and the moral character of the individual, Murray has presented to American policy-makers an ethical matrix which is stringent, yet not utopian. And by grounding the use of power in international relations in the fivefold ends of the state, Murray has constructed an analytical perspective which is capable of embracing America's immense power in the twentieth century, and of directing that power toward the enhancement of the *res sacrae* of all peoples.

Thus Murray's central theme in his writings on international relations—that of the relationship between morality and foreign policy—has stood the test of time quite well. In approaching Murray's discussions of the more specific elements of American foreign policy, however, it is necessary to distinguish between his specific policy prescriptions, which are often outdated, and Murray's general orientations toward the major issues of American foreign policy, which have a surprisingly enduring validity.

The need for such a distinction can be clearly seen in Murray's approach to world communism. Murray was no unreflective cold warrior; he appreciated the subtleties of Marxist thought, the difficult situation which the Soviet Union confronted after World War II, and the need to appreciate the aspirations of the third world which were often at the root of communism's appeal. But Murray, for all his sophistication, reflected many of the false attitudes toward communism which were prevalent in the 1950's: the tendency to see communism as monolithic, the inclination to equate world communism with the Soviet Union, and the unswerving belief that communist doctrine was rigidly adhered to in formulating the entire foreign policy agenda of the U.S.S.R. As a result of these misconceptions, Murray endorsed specific proposals for American foreign policy which now appear to be incorrect, not only as the basis for policy in the 1980's, but also as a basis for policy in the 1950's. These included the necessity for encircling the Soviet Union through a policy of "continuous engagement," the need to reject the sincerity of all seemingly peaceful steps proposed by the U.S.S.R., and the need to treat communist movements in any part of the world as being controlled by Soviet authorities.[36] Each of these policy proposals is clearly counter-productive as a basis for American foreign policy, and from this one might go on to conclude that Murray's analysis of communism is so skewed that it has little to offer in the present day.

Nothing could be farther from the truth. For the central insight of Murray's approach to communism in the 1950's had little to do with Soviet intentions or the monolithic nature of world communism. The core of Murray's prescription for dealing with the geniune threat of communism to the West lay in challenging America and the other nations of the free world to counter communism with a vision of the world which would speak effectively of freedom, justice, and peace to the former colonial nations which were the principal arenas of confrontation between the United States and the U.S.S.R. Murray was correct in seeing that the central conflict between communism and democracy was not a conflict of force, but a conflict of the spirit; and he was correct in seeing that the United States could not win that conflict if it selected its allies only on the basis of their opposition to communism, rather than on the basis of their willingness to provide justice and freedom to their own peoples. "What kind of order in the world do you want?" This was the question which Murray addressed to the American people, and in arguing that the answer to this question must be centered upon the fivefold ends of peace, freedom, justice, prosperity, and security, Murray pointed to a foundation for American foreign policy which is as valid today as it was at the height of the cold war.

While Murray emphasized the need for American foreign policy to be based upon a positive vision for peaceful and just world development, he also recognized that the United States could not ignore the threat posed by the Soviet military machine to American interests and to world peace. Murray's commentaries on the moral problem of war should be seen as an attempt to guide America's strategic and tactical military planning so that it might reflect a commitment to the use of force which was strong enough to deflect Soviet military encroachments, yet ethical enough to preserve the substance of the just war theory in the nuclear age. Once again, focusing upon the specific policy prescriptions that Murray endorsed can be misleading. Murray not only defended the concept that a limited nuclear war could be fought in the 1950's; he also called for the U.S. to shape its strategic posture in a more flexible manner, so that America would be capable of fighting such a war effectively. But implicit in Murray's endorsement of limited nuclear war in the 1950's was the recognition that if there should come a time when the immense numbers of nuclear weapons in the arsenals of the U.S. and the U.S.S.R. would render it impossible to fight a limited nuclear war which did not violate the principles of discrimination and proportionality, then all nuclear war would be immoral. Certainly the decade of the 1980's is such a time. The heart of Murray's arguments on the use of force was the proposition that the traditional logic of the just war theory, when applied to the changed conditions of the twentieth century, could steer the United States between a perilous pacifism and a cynical realism. That proposition is still a valid one. And the courage with which Murray defended the principles of discrimination and proportionality, even at the height of World War II, stands as a vivid reminder that the morality of any use of force depends not only upon the cause in which it is employed, but also upon the effects which it is likely to produce.

Murray's commentaries on the use of force in warfare are a signal contribution toward clarity in the formulation of U.S. military policies. But his greatest contribution to American thinking on the use of force may lie not in his rearticulation of the just war principles in the light of nuclear realities, but in his assertion that the time to think about the moral restraints on the use of force is not when the battle commences, but in the ongoing construction of American military postures which takes place in peacetime. Murray's whole defense of the concept of limited nuclear war was an attempt to challenge the United States to develop a military posture vis-à-vis the Soviet Union which was both effective and moral. This same challenge confronts the U.S. today, and a public theology which includes Murray's insights could guide American civilian and military planners toward strategic paths which still serve the national interest, but can serve those interests in their fullest dimensions.

The national interest: it seems that in approaching the question of American foreign policy one always returns to this fundamental concept. It was Murray's conviction that the national interest of the United States in the twentieth century could not be defined in isolation, but that it had to be seen within the context of the interest of the international community as a whole. Yet in the forty years which have passed since Murray called for the juridical organization of the world community, there has been little progress in the effort to establish an effective world body or a genuine sentiment among the peoples of the globe that there is a legitimate common good for the international community. It is not that the signs of interdependence which Murray pointed to have disappeared; on the contrary, they have grown stronger with each passing year.[37] It is, rather, that the obstacles which Murray recognized in the 1950's are still present: the unwillingness of sovereign states to sacrifice any of their independence; the reluctance of citizens of the United States and of almost every other nation to look beyond their national identities and see that they are, in some sense, "citizens of the world"; the very legitimate fear that a juridically organized community might degenerate into a monolithic world state. For Americans, these obstacles have been compounded by other developments which have taken place since Murray's death: the rise of anti-Western sentiments in the United Nations and the decreasing power of the U.S. in all international forums. Taken together, these factors have led many in the United States to despair of forming a just international order and have produced a decline in support not only for the United Nations, but for all international bodies.

A corrective for these trends can be found in Murray's articulation of the international common good as an ethical imperative which the United States cannot legitimately ignore. For in his conception of an international society which is pluralistic in structure, and which derives its power from the moral consensus of the human community, one can see the answer for those who see in all schemes of international government a step toward global totalitarianism. And in Murray's description of the increasing interdependence in the twentieth century, one can see the origins of a moral demand placed upon every nation to coordinate its pursuit of the national interest with an appreciation of the international interest. This, then, is the ultimate answer to the question which George Kennan has raised about the relationship of morality and foreign policy. The national interest does indeed have a moral quality which arises from the dignity of the human person in all his social relationships. And the most difficult moral challenge which citizens and policy-makers alike have in formulating American foreign policy in the present day is to insure that in pursuing a phantom "national interest" the interests of the wider human community are not sacrificed. The commentaries of John Courtney Murray, with their respect for both the freedom of American society and the ethical imperatives which result from the existence of a true international community, can help to achieve just such a balance.

CONCLUSION: THE MURRAY LEGACY
AND AMERICAN PUBLIC THEOLOGY

There can be no ignoring the fact that the writings of John Courtney Murray betray significant defects as the foundation for a contemporary American public theology. Murray's refusal to adequately address economic issues, his inattention to questions of racial justice, and his failure to appreciate the fundamentally new "human reality" which was posed by the creation of nuclear weapons all stand out glaringly in his work. But having said this, it is no less true that Murray's life-work should be seen not merely as an indispensable referent for contemporary public theology, but as the most compelling and comprehensive foundation for public theology in the United States today. Murray's natural law methodology, with its ability to project spiritual themes in a non-sectarian way, remains the most promising basis for public discourse on the role of religious values in American society. In addition, the general policy analyses and orientations which Murray proposed still have the power to alert the people of the U.S. to the most disturbing trends in American cultural life—materialism, relativism and a purely technological approach to human life. Murray's overarching belief that America's political decisions must be based not upon self-interest, but upon the sacred dignity of the human person, still offers the best hope for the construction of a truly just social order in the United States. And his dedication to the fivefold ends of political society can lay the foundation for an American foreign policy which is not only humane, but in the long-term best interests of the U.S.

Thus the Murray corpus retains a trenchant and vital quality which uniquely qualifies it to orient the current discussion on the role of religion in American public life. It can, in a phrase Murray himself was fond of using, "set the right terms for the public debate." And while public theology should not rest content with "setting the right terms," the current lack of consensus within American society about the public role of religion demands that the first and most compelling challenge which faces public theologians is to articulate a common set of questions, framed within a common language, that can help the American people to ponder the choices they face. For this task, the life-work of John Courtney Murray remains an unequaled starting point.

NOTES

INTRODUCTION

[1] Chester Jorgenson and Frank Mott, editors, *Benjamin Franklin: Representative Selections* (New York: Hill and Wang, 1962), p. 203.

[2] John C. Fitzpatrick, editor, *The Writings of George Washington* (Washington, D.C.: Superintendent of Documents, 1931–1944), 35: 229.

[3] Lester Cappon, editor, *The Adams-Jefferson Letters* (Chapel Hill: University of North Carolina Press, 1959), 445; 500–515.

[4] Richard Neuhaus, *The Naked Public Square* (New York: Doubleday and Company, 1984), p. 25.

[5] Douglas Wald, pp. 267–270.

[6] For the best summary of the fundamentalist agenda, see Jerry Falwell, *Listen America* (New York: Doubleday and Company, 1980); for a critique see George Marsden, *Fundamentalism and American Culture* (New York: Oxford University Press, 1980).

[7] For two of the most compelling works by Bellah on this subject see Bellah, "Religion and the Legitimation of the American Republic" in Robert Bellah and Phillip Hammond, editors, *Varieties of Civil Religion* (San Francisco: Harper and Row, 1980) and Bellah, et al., *Habits of the Heart: Individualism and Commitment in American Life* (New York: Harper and Row, 1985).

[8] Martin E. Marty, "Two Kinds of Civil Religion," in Russell Richey and Donald Jones, editors, *American Civil Religion* (New York: Harper and Row, 1974), pp. 139–157.

[9] John Coleman, *An American Strategic Theology* (New York: Paulist Press, 1982); Richard Neuhaus, *The Naked Public Square* (New York: Doubleday and Company, 1984).

[10] Richard McBrien, *Caesar's Coin: Religion and Politics in America* (New York: Macmillan Publishing Company, 1987); A. James Reichley,

Religion in American Public Life (Washington, D.C.: The Brookings Institution, 1985); Robert McAfee Brown, *Saying Yes and Saying No: On Rendering to God and Caesar* (Philadelphia: Westminster Press, 1986); Michael Novak, *Freedom With Justice* (San Francisco: Harper and Row, 1984).

[11]National Conference of Catholic Bishops, *The Challenge of Peace: God's Promise and Our Response* (Washington: National Conference of Catholic Bishops, 1983); United Methodist Council of Bishops, *In Defense of Creation: The Nuclear Crisis and a Just Peace* (Nashville: Graded Press, 1986); General Assembly of the United Presbyterian Church, *Toward a Just, Caring and Dynamic Political Economy* (New York: United Presbyterian Church, 1985); The Tenth Biennial Convention of the Lutheran Church in America, *Economic Justice: Stewardship of Creation in Human Community* (New York: Lutheran Church in America, 1980); United States Catholic Conference, *Economic Justice For All* (Washington: United States Catholic Conference, 1986); House of Bishops of the Episcopal Church in the U.S.A., *Economic Justice and the Christian Conscience* (Marquette, Michigan: Urban Bishops' Coalition, 1987).

[12]In the truest sense, public theology is neither specifically Christian, nor specifically confined to mainstream Christian churches. But in practice, the term has come to apply to the effort by non-evangelical Christian theologians to steer a course between the fundamentalist approach to social reconstruction and the secular notion that spiritual values should not influence public policy or the constitution of society.

[13]Robin Lovin, editor, *Religion and American Public Life* (New York: Paulist Press, 1986), p. 9.

[14]Numerous works have already been published on the life and work of John Courtney Murray. Donald Pelotte's *John Courtney Murray: Theologian in Conflict* (New York: Paulist Press, 1976) is a splendid treatment of Murray's efforts to reform the Catholic doctrine on religious liberty, as is Reinhold Sebott's *religionsfreiheit und Verhaeltnis von Kirche und Staat* (Rome: Analecta Gregoriana, 1977). J. Leon Hooper's *The Ethics of Discourse* (Washington: Georgetown University Press, 1986) creatively examines Murray's moral methodology, but is flawed by its erroneous central thesis that Murray was dramatically influenced by the work of Bernard Lonergan. George Weigel's *Tranquilitas Ordinis* (New York: Oxford University Press, 1987) outlines many of Murray's arguments on war and peace, but is limited as a synthetic treatment because its presentation of Murray's writings is at times selective and tendentious. Thus despite the increasing attention paid to Murray in the theological and public policy communities, there exists no systematic treatment of

his efforts to reform the cultural, political and international orders of American life.

1. A SPIRITUAL CRISIS

[1] John Courtney Murray, "A Spiritual Crisis in the Temporal Realm," An Address to the Scheil School, March 1945; The John Courtney Murray Papers, Archives of the Georgetown University (hereinafter referred to as JCM Papers.)

[2] John Courtney Murray, "Towards a Theology for the Layman: The Pedagogical Problem," *Theological Studies* V (March 1944): 349.

[3] John Courtney Murray, "Saint Robert Bellarmine on the Indirect Power," *Theological Studies* IX (March 1948): 491.

[4] John Courtney Murray, "Address to the Catholic Evidence League," 1940, JCM Papers.

[5] Henri de Lubac, *Le drame de l'humanisme athee* (Paris: Spes, 1945): 7. The translation is Murray's and is taken from "Notes: 1947," JCM Papers.

[6] John Courtney Murray, "Reversing the Secularist Drift," *Thought* XXIV (March 1949): 36.

[7] Jacques Maritain, *Education at the Crossroads* (New Haven: Yale University Press, 1943), p. 46.

[8] John Courtney Murray, "A Spiritual Crisis in the Temporal Realm," An Address to the Scheil School, March 1945, JCM Papers.

[9] Pius XI, "Laetus Sane Nuntius." This translation is taken from the Benziger edition of *Two Basic Social Encyclicals* (1943) and was the translation used by Murray in his "Towards a Theology for the Layman," *Theological Studies* V (March 1944): 65.

[10] John Courtney Murray, "Towards A Theology for the Layman: The Problem of Its Finality," 66.

[11] Pius XII, "Christmas Allocution of 1942" in Harry Koenig, editor, *Principles for Peace* (Washington: National Catholic Welfare Conference, 1943), p. 798.

[12] John Courtney Murray, "The Pattern for Peace and the Papal Peace Program" (Washington: Catholic Association for International Peace, 1944), pp. 4–5.

[13] Pius XII, "Christmas Allocution of 1945." The English translation is Murray's own and is taken from Murray's "The Papal Allocution: Christmas," *America* LXXVI (January 5, 1946): 371.

[14] *Ibid.*

[15] Murray, "Reversing the Secular Drift": 37.

[16]John Courtney Murray, "The Catholic, Jewish, Protestant Declaration on World Peace," 1943, JCM Papers, p. 8.

[17]John Courtney Murray, "America's Four Conspiracies," *The Catholic Mind* LVII (May–June 1959): 240.

[18]Murray, "Towards A Theology for the Layman: The Pedagogical Problem": 352.

[19]Paul Blanshard, *American Freedom and Catholic Power* (Boston: The Beacon Press, 1948), pp. 248–263.

[20]John Courtney Murray, "Paul Blanshard and the New Nativism," *The Month*, New Series, V (April 1951): 218–219.

[21]*Ibid.*, 220.

[22]John Courtney Murray, "Christian Humanism in America," *Social Order*, III (May–June 1953): 237.

[23]John Courtney Murray, "The Catholic Position: A Reply," *The American Mercury* LXIX (September 1949): 637.

[24]John Courtney Murray, "The Yale University Lectures," 1951, JCM Papers, III, 22. (The Yale University Lectures were the four formal addresses which John Courtney Murray gave as a Visiting Professor at Yale University during the 1950–1951 academic year. They represent a critically important unpublished survey of Murray's views on the role of religion in society.)

[25]John Courtney Murray, "The American Proposition," 1954, JCM Papers, p. 24.

[26]Alexander Passerin D'Entreves, *The Medieval Contribution to Political Thought* (Oxford: Oxford University Press, 1939).

[27]Luigi Sturzo, *Church and State* (New York: Longmans, Green and Company, 1939).

[28]J. L. Talmon, *The Rise of Totalitarian Democracy* (Boston: Beacon Press, 1952).

[29]Christopher Dawson, *Beyond Politics* (New York: Sheed and Ward Company, 1939); Eric Voegelin, *The New Science of Politics* (Chicago: University of Chicago Press, 1952); Romano Guardini, *The End of the Modern World* (New York: Sheed and Ward Company, 1956).

[30]Text from "The Yale University Lectures," I, 11.

[31]Murray, "The Yale University Lectures," I, 12–15; Murray's interpretation of this key text relied heavily on the work of Robert and A. J. Carlyle in their *A History of Medieval Political Theory in the West* (Edinburgh: William Blackwood and Sons, 1930) and on R. H. Hull's *Medieval Theories of the Papacy* (London: Burns, Oates, and Washbourne, 1932).

[32]John Courtney Murray, "Contemporary Orientations of Catholic Thought on Church and State in the Light of History," *Theological Studies* X (June 1949): 196.

[33]Murray, "The Yale University Lectures," I, 16.

[34]*Ibid.*, I, 25.

[35]Murray, "Contemporary Orientations on Church and State in the Light of History": 198.

[36]John Courtney Murray, "On the Structure of the Church-State Problem," in Waldemar Gurian and M. A. Fitzsimons, editors, *The Catholic Church in World Affairs* (Notre Dame, Indiana: University of Notre Dame Press, 1954), p. 14.

[37]*Ibid.*

[38]Murray, "The Yale University Lectures," II, 11.

[39]John Courtney Murray, "Leo XIII: Separation of Church and State," *Theological Studies* XIV (June 1953): 148–49.

[40]Murray, "Contemporary Orientations": 186–87.

[41]*Ibid.*, 187, fn. 28.

[42]*Ibid.*

[43]Murray, "Yale University Lectures," II, 10.

[44]*Ibid.*, II, 48.

[45]Murray, "Leo XIII": 147.

[46]*Ibid.*

[47]*Ibid.*, 147.

[48]Murray, "The Yale University Lectures," IV, 12.

[49]John Courtney Murray, "The Church and Totalitarian Democracy," *Theological Studies* XIII (December 1952): 528.

[50]*Ibid.*, 533.

[51]*Ibid.*, 540.

[52]*Ibid.*, 541.

[53]John Courtney Murray, "The Natural Law," in R. M. MacIver, editor, *Great Expressions of Human Rights* (New York: Harper and Company, 1950), 85–86.

[54]John Courtney Murray, "How Liberal Is Liberalism?" *America* LXXV (April 6, 1946): 282–283.

[55]Murray, "Leo XIII: Separation of Church and State": 145.

[56]John Courtney Murray, "Leo XIII and Public Religion," JCM Papers, p. 11. (This manuscript constituted Murray's final part of a four article discussion of the teachings of Leo XIII. It was never published because shortly after it was written Murray was asked by Father Vincent McCormick, S.J., the American assistant to the Father General, not to publish anything further on the subject of Church and state without prior approval from the Jesuit curia. [Correspondence between JCM and Vincent McCormick, S.J., JCM Papers]) For a later discussion of this same critique of nineteenth century liberalism see John Courtney

Murray, "The Declaration on Religious Freedom: Its Deeper Significance," *America* XIV (April 23, 1966), 6–7.

[57]Murray, "Leo XIII on Church and State: The General Structure of the Controversy": 9–12.

[58]John Courtney Murray, *We Hold These Truths: Catholic Reflections on the American Proposition* (New York: Sheed and Ward, 1960), pp. 301–02.

[59]Murray, "Freedom of Religion I": 284.

[60]John Courtney Murray, "Church, State and Political Freedom," *The Catholic Mind* LVII (May–June 1959): 227. The concept of "modernity" is one of those fertile terms which becomes used in so many ways by so many different people that its precise meaning is difficult to establish. The core of the concept, captured in Weber's notion of a functionalist and technical mastery of the world by the human person and the institutions he has built, certainly reflects the *hubris* and shallowness which Murray saw as dangerous in the spirit of "modernity." And Murray would have found satisfaction in the increasing suspicion with which contemporary sociology approaches "modernity." [See Peter Berger, *Facing Up to Modernity* (New York: Basic Books, 1977]. Throughout the present work, the term "modernity" is used as Murray used it, namely to designate the tendency in the modern era to see the *res sacrae* as immanent in the individual and to ignore the active role of God in human life.

[61]Murray, *We Hold These Truths*, pp. 198–200.

[62]Murray, "On the Structure of the Church-State Problem": 25.

[63]Murray, "Church, State, and Political Freedom": 225.

[64]Murray, "On The Structure of the Church-State Problem": 25.

[65]Murray, *We Hold These Truths*, p. 202.

[66]*Ibid.*, pp. 202–03.

[67]John Courtney Murray, "The Return to Tribalism," *The Catholic Mind*, LX (January 1962): 8.

[68]Murray, "The Yale University Lectures," I, 4.

[69]Murray, "Towards A Theology for the Layman: The Problem of Its Finality": 70.

[70]John Courtney Murray, "The Vatican Declaration on Religious Freedom," in *The University and the American Experience*, (New York: Fordham University Press, 1966), p. 9.

[71]John Courtney Murray, "The One Work of the One Church," *Catholic Mind* XLVIII (June 1950), 363.

[72]Murray, "The Construction of a Christian Culture," JCM Papers, I-1.

2. RECLAIMING THE CULTURAL ORDER

[1]John Courtney Murray, "Leo XIII: Two Concepts of Government: Government and the Order of Culture," *Theological Studies* XV (March 1954): 32.

[2]*Ibid.*, 33.

[3]John Courtney Murray, "The Construction of a Christian Culture," A Lecture Series at Loyola University in 1940, JCM Papers, I-2.

[4]John Courtney Murray, "The Yale University Lectures," IV, 55.

[5]John Courtney Murray, *We Hold These Truths* (New York: Sheed and Ward Company, 1960), pp. 145–47.

[6]John Courtney Murray, "Lecture at Harvard Summer School," 1952, JCM Papers.

[7]John Courtney Murray to Robert MacIver, February 4, 1954, JCM Papers.

[8]Murray, *We Hold These Truths,* pp. 51–53.

[9]Murray, "The Construction of a Christian Culture," I-1.

[10]Murray to Robert MacIver, February 4, 1954, JCM Papers.

[11]Murray, "Spokane Lectures," March 1962, p. 6; JCM Papers.

[12]John Courtney Murray, "America's Four Conspiracies," *The Catholic Mind* LVII (May–June 1959): 230–231. The four "conspiracies" Murray saw inherent in American society were Protestantism, Catholicism, Judaism, and Secularism.

[13]John Courtney Murray, "The Catholic University in a Pluralistic Society," *The Catholic Mind* LVII (May–June 1959): 258.

[14]Murray, *We Hold These Truths,* p. 89.

[15]John Courtney Murray, "The Return to Tribalism," *The Catholic Mind,* LX (January 1962): 6–7.

[16]Murray, "The Catholic University in a Pluralist Society," 258.

[17]John Courtney Murray, "Commencement Address at the Carnegie Institute of Science," June 26, 1948, JCM Papers.

[18]John Courtney Murray, "The Contemporary Devaluation of Intelligence," 1952, JCM Papers, p. 12.

[19]John Courtney Murray, On the Future of Humanistic Education," in Arthur A. Cohen, editor, *Humanistic Education and Western Civilization* (New York: Holt, Rinehart, and Winston, 1964), pp. 241–242.

[20]John Courtney Murray, "Commencement Address at Manhattanville College of the Sacred Heart," June 5, 1957.

[21]*Ibid.*

[22]John Courtney Murray, "Address at Georgetown University," 1956, JCM Papers, p. 16.

[23]Murray, "The Construction of a Christian Culture," I-3.

[24]John Courtney Murray, "Harvard Summer School Lecture," JCM Papers.

[25]Murray, "The Construction of a Christian Culture," I-7.

[26]John Courtney Murray "The Colleges in the Present Crisis," An Address to the Association of American Colleges, January 28, 1951, JCM Papers, p. 7.

[27]John Courtney Murray, "The State University in a Pluralist Society," *The Catholic Mind* LVII (May–June 1959): 243.

[28]*Ibid.*, 245.

[29]*Ibid.*

[30]John Courtney Murray, "Memorandum to Robert MacIver Reviewing the Draft Statement of the Academic Freedom Project," February 4, 1954, JCM Papers.

[31]Murray, "The State University in a Pluralist Society," 246.

[32]Murray, *We Hold These Truths*, p. 130.

[33]Romano Guardini, *The End of the Modern World*, (New York: Sheed and Ward Company, 1956); William Ernest Hocking, *The Coming World Civilization* (New York: Harper Brothers, 1956); Eric Voegelin, *The New Science of Politics* (Chicago: University of Chicago Press, 1952); Geoffrey Barraclough, "The End of European History."

[34]Murray, *We Hold These Truths*, pp. 131–132.

[35]Murray, "The State University in a Pluralist Society," 248.

[36]John Courtney Murray, participating in a 1960 roundtable discussion at the Center for the Study of Democratic Institutions entitled *Two Faces of Federalism*, p. 78; the Archives of the Center for the Study of Democratic Institutions, Santa Barbara, California.

[37]Murray, *We Hold These Truths*, p. 281.

[38]John Courtney Murray, "The Natural Law," in R. M. MacIver, editor, *Great Expressions of Human Rights* (New York: Harper and Company, 1950), pp. 72–75.

[39]John Courtney Murray, "Natural Law and the Public Consensus," in John Cogley, editor, *Natural Law and Modern Society* (Cleveland: World Publishing Company, 1963) p. 62.

[40]Murray, "The Natural Law," 71.

[41]Murray, *We Hold These Truths*, p. 320.

[42]*Ibid.*, 310.

[43]*Ibid.*, 310–311.

[44]Murray, "Two Faces of Federalism," pp. 83–84.

[45]Murray, *We Hold These Truths*, p. 113.

[46]*Ibid.*

[47]Murray, "Two Faces of Federalism," pp. 82–83.

[48]Murray, *ibid.*, p. 80.

[49]Murray, "Natural Law and the Public Consensus," 66.

[50]Murray, "The Natural Law," 89.

[51]*Ibid.*, pp. 97–98.

[52]*Ibid.*, pp. 100–103.

[53]See Richard Hofstadter, *The American Political Tradition* (New York: Alfred Knopf Company, 1948); Daniel Boorstin, *The Genius of American Politics* (Chicago: University of Chicago Press, 1953); Seymour Martin Lipset, "The End of Ideology," in his *Political Man* (Cambridge: Harvard University Press, 1960).

[54]Walter Lippmann, *Essays in the Public Philosophy* (Boston: Little, Brown and Company, 1955).

[55]*Ibid.*, p. 115.

[56]John Courtney Murray, "The United States and the Public Philosophy of the West," JCM Papers, pp. 9–15.

[57]Adolf A. Berle, Jr., *Power Without Property,* (New York: Harcourt, Brace and Company, 1959). Both Murray's article on "Natural Law and the Public Consensus" and his personal notes on the preparation of this article confirm that it was Berle's contribution which was critical in the development of Murray's approach to the "American consensus" (JCM Papers).

[58]*Ibid.*, 22.

[59]*Ibid.*

[60]Murray, "Natural Law and the Public Consensus," 61.

[61]*Ibid.*, 62.

[62]*Ibid.*, 76–77.

[63]*Ibid.*, 79.

[64]Murray, *We Hold These Truth,* 21.

[65]Murray, "The United States and the Public Philosophy of the West," 13–15.

[66]John Courtney Murray, "Address to the John Carroll Society," February 19, 1961, JCM Papers, p. 24.

[67]John Courtney Murray, "Barriers in the Cultivation of Individual Excellence," February 10, 1958, JCM Papers, pp. 9–10.

[68]John Courtney Murray, 1954 Memorandum to Robert MacIver Regarding the Academic Freedom Project, JCM Papers.

[69]Murray, "Natural Law and the Public Consensus," 77–78.

[70]Murray, *We Hold These Truths,* p. 134.

[71]John Courtney Murray, "The Catholic University in a Pluralist Society," *The Catholic Mind* LVII (May–June 1959): 257.

[72]John Courtney Murray, "Freedom, Responsibility and the Law," *The Catholic Lawyer* II (July 1956): 214.

[73]*Ibid.*, 215.

[74]Murray, "Address to the John Carroll Society," p. 11.

[75]*Ibid.*, 223.

[76]John Courtney Murray, "Catholics in America—a Creative Minority?" *Catholic Mind* LIII (October 1955):594–595.

[77]John Courtney Murray, "Memorandum: Catholic Defects," 1955, JCM Papers.

[78]Murray, *We Hold These Truths*, p. 53.

[79]Murray, "Catholics In America," 594.

[80]*Ibid.*, 596–597.

[81]Murray, "The Two Faces of Federalism," p. 23.

3. RENEWING THE POLITICAL ORDER

[1]The correspondence between Murray and Father Vincent McCormick, S.J., the ranking American in the Jesuit curia at the time, clearly indicates that Murray was told by McCormick not to publish any new articles dealing with Church and state without prior approval from McCormick, an approval that was not given in the two instances in which Murray did submit articles. (Vincent McCormick–John Courtney Murray Correspondence, JCM Papers.)

[2]John Courtney Murray, "Two Concepts of Government," *Theological Studies* XIV (December 1953), 551–567.

[3]John Courtney Murray, "On Religious Liberty," *America* CIX (November 30, 1963):706.

[4]Heinrich Rommen, *The State in Catholic Thought* (Saint Louis: Herder Book Company, 1945); Thomas Gilbey, *Between Society and Community* (New York: Longmans, Green and Company, 1953).

[5]John A. Coleman, "Vision and Praxis in American Theology: Orestes Brownson, John A. Ryan, and John Courtney Murray," *Theological Studies* 37 (1976):34. In one sense, it is misleading to call Murray a "reinterpreter of the Thomist position on politics and the state." For Murray never looked upon his work as a systematic effort to reformulate the Thomistic tradition of politics. Murray fashioned a theory of politics as a tool with which he could address the questions of religious liberty and the renewal of American society which preoccupied him during his lifetime. Thus his approach to politics was instrumental, rather than comprehensive. Fortunately, by reading through the various texts in which this theory of politics was presented, it is possible to reconstruct Murray's thought on politics in a more comprehensive way, and thus to appreciate the degree to which Coleman is absolutely correct in hailing Murray as a great reinterpreter of the Thomistic political tradition.

[6]John Courtney Murray, *We Hold These Truths* (New York: Sheed and Ward, 1960), p. 315.

[7]*Ibid.*

[8]Murray, *We Hold These Truths*, 315.

[9]*Ibid.*

[10]John Courtney Murray, "The Problem of State Religion," *Theological Studies* XII (June 1951), 158.

[11]*Ibid.*

[12]Murray was certainly an eclectic reader, and the sources which were influential in his intellectual development regarding the nature of politics included not only philosophers and theologians, such as Robert Bellarmine, John of Paris, and Francisco Suarez, but also commentators in the fields of law, political science, and sociology. In spite of this, Thomas Aquinas remains far and away the most important source for Murray's sustained reflections on the nature of politics.

[13]*Ibid.*

[14]John Courtney Murray, "Analysis For the Rockefeller Brothers' Project," JCM Papers, p. 28.

[15]*Ibid.*

[16]*Ibid.,* 29.

[17]*Ibid.*

[18]See, for example, John Courtney Murray, "The Problem of Religious Freedom," *Theological Studies* XXV (December 1964): 519-521; Murray, "The Matter of Religious Freedom," *America* CXII (January 9, 1965): 40.

[19]*Ibid.,* 40.

[20]Murray, "The Problem of Religious Freedom," 520.

[21]Letter of Samuel Cardinal Stritch to John Courtney Murray, November 17, 1956, JCM Papers.

[22]John Courtney Murray, "Questions of Striking a Right Balance: Literature and Censorship," *The Catholic Mind* LIV (December 1956): 671.

[23]*Ibid.*

[24]John Courtney Murray, "Leo XIII: Two Concepts of Government," *Theological Studies* XIV (December 1953): 554-555; Murray, "Questions of Striking a Right Balance," 671-672.

[25]John Courtney Murray, Leo XIII: Two Concepts of Government: Government and the Order of Culture," *Theological Studies* XV (March 1954):14.

[26]*Ibid.,* 12.

[27]Interview with Monsignor George Higgins.

[28]John Courtney Murray, "Two Concepts of Government," 551.

[29]*Ibid.,* 552.

[30] *Ibid.*

[31] *Ibid.*, 553.

[32] *Ibid.*, 556.

[33] *Ibid.*, 557.

[34] John Courtney Murray, "The American Proposition," JCM Papers, p. 23.

[35] *Ibid.*, 24.

[36] *Ibid.*, 27

[37] John Courtney Murray, "The Declaration on Religious Freedom: A Moment in Its Legislative History," in JCM, editor, *Religious Liberty: An End and a Beginning* (New York: Macmillan, 1966), p. 41.

[38] John Courtney Murray, "The Issue of Church and State at Vatican II," *Theological Studies* XXVII (December 1966): 593.

[39] *Ibid.*, 598.

[40] John Courtney Murray, "The Garden and the Wilderness," *Yale Law Review* (March 1967): 1035.

[41] John Courtney Murray, "Religious Freedom and the Atheist," An Address at the University of Connecticut, May 15, 1965, JCM Papers.

[42] John Courtney Murray, quoting *Dignitatis Humanae* in his Address on Religious Freedom and the Atheist; the original text of *Dignitatis Humanae* reads: "et ipsa societas fruatur bonis iustitiae et pacis quae proveniunt ex fidelitate hominum erga Deum Eiusque sanctam voluntatem." (*Acta Apostolicae Sedis* 22, 934.)

[43] John Courtney Murray, "Address to the John Carroll Society," February 19, 1961, JCM Papers, p. 30.

[44] John Courtney Murray, "Hopes and Misgivings for Dialogue," *America* CIV (January 14, 1961): 460.

[45] *Ibid.*

[46] It is always difficult, of course, to reconstruct the precise thinking behind a man's work. But as one reads through John Courtney Murray's writings, looks at his lecture notes, and examines the personal notes which he took on the books he read, what emerges clearly is the picture of a man who thought in an utterly systematic way, but who did so in order to answer specific questions. This is particularly true of Murray's thought on the nature of politics. He could have easily written a comprehensive treatise on the subject, but he never did. His thought on the state and government appears only in a derivative fashion, as it was applied to the issues of religious liberty and the renewal of American society. This does not make this thought any less coherent or significant, although it does make it much harder to reconstruct.

[47] Murray, "The United States and the Public Philosophy of the West," p. 7.

[48]Clinton Rossiter, *Seedtime of the Republic* (New York: Harcourt, Brace and Company, 1953), pp. 369–370.

[49]Murray, "The United States and the Public Philosophy of the West," p. 5.

[50]Murray, *We Hold These Truths,* pp. 42–43.

[51]John Courtney Murray, "Leo XIII: Separation of Church and State," *Theological Studies* XIV (June 1953): 160.

[52]Murray, "Leo XIII: Separation of Church and State," 152; see also Murray, "The Problem of Pluralism in America," 207.

[53]Murray, "The American Proposition," pp. 14–15.

[54]*Ibid.,* 19.

[55]Murray, *We Hold These Truths,* pp. 57–58.

[56]Murray, "The American Proposition," p. 10.

[57]John Courtney Murray, "The Philosophy of the First Amendment," A Memorandum for the National Catholic Welfare Conference, 1948, JCM Papers, p. 9.

[58]Murray, "The American Proposition," 11; see also Murray, "Leo XIII: Separation of Church and State," 153.

[59]Murray, "Leo XIII: Separation of Church and State," 153.

[60]John Courtney Murray, "The School and Christian Freedom," *Proceedings* of the National Catholic Educational Association, XLVIII (August 1951): 64.

[61]*Ibid.,* 63.

[62]Murray, "The School and Christian Freedom," 63.

[63]John Courtney Murray, "Freedom, Responsibility and the Law," *The Catholic Lawyer,* II (July 1956), 217.

[64]Murray, *We Hold These Truths,* p. 308.

[65]John Courtney Murray, "Lecture Notes, 1953," JCM Papers; Murray, "Commentary," in *The Elites and the Electorate,* an occasional paper of the Center for the Study of Democratic Institutions, Archives of the Center for the Study of Democratic Institutions.

[66]John Courtney Murray, "On the Structure of the Church-State Problem," in Waldemar Gurian and M. A. Fitzsimons, editors, *The Catholic Church in World Affairs* (Notre Dame, Indiana: University of Notre Dame Press, 1954), p. 16.

[67]Murray, "The School and Christian Freedom," 64.

[68]*Ibid.,* 63.

[69]John Courtney Murray, "The Yale University Lectures," IV, p. 58.

[70]Murray, *We Hold These Truths,* p. 202. Murray's quotation of "One there is . . ." is not actually taken from any other source. It is his personal invention, an inversion of Pope Gelasius' "Two there are . . ."

quotation; Murray often cited this inversion as a mark of the distortion of the political tradition of the West wrought by democratic monism.

[71] John Courtney Murray, "Catholicism and Democracy," An Address at Georgetown University, March 6, 1950.

[72] Murray, *We Hold These Truths*, p. 156.

[73] Murray, "The School and Christian Freedom," p. 63.

[74] John Courtney Murray, "Law or Prepossessions," in R. G. McCloskey, editor, *Essays in Constitutional Law* (New York: Alfred Knopf, 1957), p. 341.

[75] *Ibid.*, p. 318.

[76] *Ibid.*, p. 328.

[77] Murray, *We Hold These Truths*, pp. 150–151.

[78] John Courtney Murray, "Separation of Church and State: True and False Concepts," *America* LXXVI (February 15, 1947): 545.

[79] Murray, *We Hold These Truths*, pp. 150–151.

[80] *Ibid.*, 151.

[81] Murray, "Yale University Lectures," IV, pp. 56–57.

[82] Murray, "The School and Christian Freedom," 64.

4. RECONSTRUCTING THE INTERNATIONAL ORDER

[1] *Acta Apostolicae Sedis* XXXIII, 10. The translation is taken from Harry Koenig, editor, *Principles for Peace* (Washington: National Catholic Welfare Conference, 1943), number 1640. This was the translation used by Murray in his "The Pattern for Peace and the Papal Peace Program" (Washington: Paulist Press, 1944): 5.

[2] Murray, "The Pattern for Peace," 10. (A.A.S., XXXIV, 16.)

[3] Murray, "The Pattern for Peace," 11.

[4] Murray, "The Pattern for Peace," 22.

[5] Murray, "World Order and Moral Law," 581.

[6] John Courtney Murray, "Principles for Peace," *Theological Studies*, IV (December 1943), p. 635.

[7] For the classic critique of the utopian position in the inter-war period, see E. H. Carr, *The Twenty Years' Crisis: 1919–1939* (New York: Harper and Row, 1945).

[8] Hans J. Morgenthau, *Politics Among Nations: The Struggle for Power and Peace* (New York: Alfred Knopf, 1948), pp. 13–21.

[9] Reinhold Niebuhr, *Christianity and Power Politics* (New York: Charles Scribner's Sons, 1940), p. 4.

[10] John Courtney Murray, "Morality and Foreign Policy, Part I" *America*, CII (March 19, 1960), p. 280.

[11] Murray, "Morality and Foreign Policy," 730.

[12] Murray, "Morality and Foreign Policy," 731.

[13] John Courtney Murray, *We Hold These Truths* (New York: Sheed and Ward, 1960), p. 272.

[14] Actually, the moral perspectives inherent in the writings and actions of Woodrow Wilson and John Foster Dulles are more supple and complex than either the "realists" or Murray gave them credit for in their various critiques. Ample evidence of this is presented in Arthur Link's *Wilson the Diplomatist* (Baltimore: Johns Hopkins University, 1957) and Michael Gushin's *John Foster Dulles: A Statesman and His Times* (New York: Columbia University Press, 1972).

[15] Murray, *We Hold These Truths*, p. 274.

[16] *Ibid.*, p. 268.

[17] Morganthau, 162.

[18] John Courtney Murray, "Challenges Confronting the American Catholic," *The Catholic Mind*, LVII (May–June 1959), p. 199.

[19] John Courtney Murray, "The Juridical Organization of the International Community," 1944, JCM Papers.

[20] *Ibid.*

[21] John Courtney Murray, "World Order and Moral Law," *Thought*, XIX (December 1944): 585.

[22] Murray, "The Juridical Organization of the International Community," p. 9.

[23] Murray, "World Order and Moral Law," 582.

[24] Murray, "The Juridical Organization of the International Community," 7.

[25] Murray, "A Presentation For the Hearings of The Rockefeller Brothers Project," JCM Papers, p. 37.

[26] Murray, "Challenges Confronting the American Catholic," 198.

[27] John Courtney Murray, "Things Old and New in 'Pacem in Terris,'" *America* CVIII (April 27, 1963): 614. (A.A.S., 55, p. 293.)

[28] Murray, "World Order and Moral Law," 586.

[29] John Courtney Murray, "Address to the John Carroll Society," February 19, 1961, JCM Papers, p. 14.

[30] John Courtney Murray and Walter Millis, editors, *Foreign Policy and the Free Society* (New York: Oceana Press, 1958), p. 26.

[31] Murray and Millis, "Foreign Policy and the Free Society," 36–37.

[32] Murray, "Address to the John Carroll Society," p. 14.

[33] John Courtney Murray, "The Return to Tribalism," *The Catholic Mind*, LX (January 1962), p. 5.

[34] Murray, *We Hold These Truths*, p. 94.

[35] Murray, "Rockefeller Brothers Project," p. 31.

[36] *Ibid.*, p. 33.

[37] *Ibid.*, p. 37.

[38] *Ibid.*

[39] *Ibid.*, p. 38.

[40] John C. Ford, "The Morality of Obliteration Bombing," *Theological Studies*, 5 (1944): 261–309.

[41] John Courtney Murray, "War and Conscience," 1966, JCM Papers, p. 4.

[42] Murray, *We Hold These Truths*, p. 240; A.A.S., 43 (1951), p. 57, and A.A.S., 47 (1955), p. 25.

[43] *Ibid.*, pp. 241–242.

[44] *Ibid.*

[45] John Courtney Murray, "Remarks on the Moral Problem of War," *Theological Studies* XX (March 1959): 45.

[46] *Ibid.*, 47; A.A.S. 37 (1945), p. 18.

[47] *Ibid.*, 48; A.A.S. 45 (1953), p. 748.

[48] *Ibid.*, 51.

[49] Murray, *We Hold These Truths*, pp. 253–254.

[50] *Ibid.*, p. 256.

[51] Murray, "The Pattern for Peace," 9.

[52] *Ibid.* The text Murray quoted here is from Pius XII's 1942 Christmas Message, A.A.S. 35 (1943), p. 18.

[53] Murray, "Challenges Confronting the American Catholic," 198.

[54] Murray, "Things Old and New in *Pacem in Terris*, 614; A.A.S. 55 (1963), p. 288.

5. "THE LIFE-WORK OF JOHN COURTNEY MURRAY

[1] For a sampling of those who have used Murray's insights extensively in their own attempts to formulate a public theology for contemporary America see Martin Marty, *Religion and Republic: The American Circumstance* (Boston: Beacon Press, 1987); Richard McBrien, *Caesar's Coin* (New York: Macmillan Publishing Company, 1987); Richard Neuhaus, *The Naked Public Square* (Grand Rapids: Eerdmans Publishing Company, 1984); John Coleman, *An American Strategic Theology* (New York: Paulist Press, 1982). For a glimpse of the ways in which Murray's work has functioned in contemporary debates over economic and defense issues, see David Hollenbach, "The Growing End of an Argument," *America* CLIII (November 30, 1985): 363–366; George Weigel, *Tranquilitas Ordinis* (New York: Oxford University Press, 1987); Lay Commission on Catholic Social Teaching and the U.S. Economy, *Toward the Future:*

Catholic Social Thought and the U.S. Economy (New York: American Catholic Committee, 1984); Michael Novak, "Economic Rights: The Servile State," *Catholicism in Crisis* (October 1985): 9–16.

[2]Martin E. Marty, "Two Kinds of Civil Religion," in Russell E. Richey and Donald G. Jones, editors, *American Civil Religion* (New York: Harper and Row, Publishers, 1974), pp. 139–157.

[3]*Ibid.*, p. 149.

[4]David Hollenbach, "Public Theology in America: Some Questions for Catholicism After John Courtney Murray," *Theological Studies* 37 (1976): 300.

[5]John Coleman, "A Possible Role for Biblical Religion in Public Life," in David Hollenbach, editor, "Theology and Philosophy in Public: A Symposium on John Courtney Murray's Unfinished Agenda," *Theological Studies* 40 (December 1979): 702. See also John A. Coleman, *An American Strategic Theology* (New York: Paulist Press, 1982), pp. 193–198.

[6]Joseph Fuchs, *Personal Responsibility and Christian Morality* (Washington, D.C.: Georgetown University Press, 1983), p. 55. Certainly there are many theologians such as Coleman who would disagree with Fuchs, but even most writers who postulate a material distinctiveness to Christian ethics fail to specify any distinctiveness on the societal plane. For a sampling of contemporary thought on both sides of this issue, see Charles Curran and Richard McCormick, editors, *The Distinctiveness of Christian Ethics* (New York: Paulist Press, 1980).

[7]Charles Curran, *American Catholic Social Ethics: Twentieth Century Approaches* (Notre Dame, Indiana: University of Notre Dame Press, 1982), p. 286.

[8]Hollenbach, editor, "Theology and Philosophy in Public," 714.

[9]David Tracy, *The Analogical Imagination* (New York: Crossroad Publishing Company, 1981), p. 5.

[10]John A. Coleman, "A Possible Role for Biblical Religion in Public Life," 706.

[11]It must be noted that Murray's writings on spirituality are *often* evocative and symbolically powerful, a reality which only points all the more clearly to the fact that Murray's exclusion of biblical and religious imagery from his social writings was a deliberate choice dictated by his audience and his objectives.

[12]One can discern just such an audience-centered approach to public theology in the language which Murray used in his speeches and writings. When Murray was addressing groups who were entirely Christian, he would often speak of the need to create a "Christian culture" or a society founded upon "Christian values." When he was speaking to

groups which included non-Christians, or when he was writing for American society as a whole, he would consistently speak of creating a "spiritual culture" of a society founded upon the *"res sacrae."* No matter which terms he employed, Murray consistently respected the pluralistic structure of American society in formulating his prescriptions, and he never advanced public policies that could not be justified without recourse to sectarian warrants.

[13]Robert M. Hutchins, editor, "Two Faces of Federalism," an occasional paper of the Center for the Study of Democratic Institutions, 1961, Archives of the Center for the Study of Democratic Institutions.

[14]*Gaudium et Spes*, 16. Translation taken from Walter M. Abbott, S. J., editor, *The Documents of Vatican II* (New York: Guild Press, 1966), p. 212.

[15]This trend is notable in the Charter of the Organization of African Unity, the Program of Action on the Establishment of a New International Economic Order, and the Algiers Declaration on the Rights of Peoples. For a compilation of these documents, see Burns Weston, editor, *International Law and World Order* (Saint Paul, Minnesota: West Publishing Company, 1980).

[16]For a fine discussion of the history of the "secularization thesis," see John Coleman, "The Situation for Modern Faith," *Theological Studies* XXXIX (December 1978): 601–632.

[17]Larry Shiner, "The Meanings of Secularization," in James F. Childress and David B. Harned, *Secularization and the Protestant Perspective* (Philadelphia: Westminster Press, 1970), pp. 30–42. The terms "secularization" and "secularism" are also controverted; "secularization" was used by Murray to denote the legitimate freeing of the temporal sphere from the overweening authority of religious institutions, while secularism meant for Murray the evacuation of spiritual values from the temporal sphere of public life.

[18]Peter Berger, "From the Crisis of Religion to the Crisis of Secularity," in Mary Douglas and Steven Tipton, editors, *Religion and America: Spiritual Life in a Secular Age* (Boston: Beacon Press, 1983), pp. 14–24.

[19]Thomas Luckman, *The Invisible Religion* (New York: The Macmillan Company, 1973); Bryan Wilson, "Secularization: The Inherited Model," in Phillip Hammond, editor, *The Sacred in a Secular Age* (Berkeley: University of California Press, 1985), pp. 9–20; Hans Mol, *Identity and the Sacred* (New York: Free Press, 1977).

[20]Luckman, *ibid.*, p. 116.

[21]Peter L. Berger, *The Sacred Canopy* (Garden City, New York: Doubleday and Company, 1969), p. 134.

[22]Richard J. Neuhaus, *The Naked Public Square* (Grand Rapids, Michigan: Eerdmans Publishing Company, 1984), p. 110.

[23]Alasdair MacIntyre, *After Virtue* (Notre Dame, Indiana: Notre Dame University Press, 1981), p. 236.

[24]Robert N. Bellah, *The Broken Covenant* (New York: The Seabury Press, 1975), ix–x.

[25]John Courtney Murray, "America's Four Conspiracies," *The Catholic Mind* LVII (May–June 1959): 231.

[26]For an outline of the Fundamentalist agenda for the United States, see Jerry Falwell, *Listen, America!* (New York: Doubleday and Company, 1980); for a critique see George Marsden, *Fundamentalism and American Culture* (New York: Oxford University Press, 1980).

[27]Murray, "Address at Georgetown University," 1956, JCM Papers, p. 16.

[28]Murray, "The Construction of a Christian Culture," A Lecture Series at Loyola University, 1940, JCM Papers, I-2.

[29]Bellah, *The Broken Covenant*, x.

[30]For conflicting presentations and evaluations of this agenda, see George F. Will, *Statecraft as Soulcraft* (New York: Simon and Schuster, 1983); Daniel P. Moynihan, *Family and Nation* (New York: Harcourt Brace Jovanovich, 1986).

[31]Author's interview with Monsignor George Higgins.

[32]See, for example, John A. Rohr, "John Courtney Murray and the Pastoral Letters," *America*, CLIII (November 30, 1985): 373–379; Michael Novak, "Economic Rights: The Servile State," *Catholicism in Crisis* (October 1985): 9–16; David Hollenbach, "The Growing End of An Argument," *America* CLIII (November 30, 1985): 363–366.

[33]In 1945 Murray responded to an inquiry from the Jesuit Assistant's office about the social justice dimensions of continuing to refuse to admit blacks to some Jesuit high schools. Murray replied that since no one had a right to attend a Jesuit high school, there was no violation of individual justice in such a policy, but that the requirements of social justice in the 1940's demanded that the Society take some action on behalf of black equality and the admission of blacks in segregated schools would be a good start (Letter to Father Zaccheus Maher, April 30, 1945, JCM Papers). In 1963, Murray gave an address supporting the substance of the civil rights agenda; see "Making the News Good News," *Interracial Review* XXXVI (July 1963): 34–35, 130–131.

[34]George F. Kennan, "Morality and Foreign Policy," *Foreign Affairs* (Spring 1985): 198.

[35]For a sampling of the major works of the "neo-realist" school, see Kenneth Waltz, *Theory of International Politics* (New York: Random

House, 1979); Robert Gilpin, *War and Change in World Politics* (Cambridge: Cambridge University Press, 1981).

[36]To get a sense of the intellectual atmosphere from which Murray made these recommendations, compare two works written by a man whom Murray relied on substantially in his own analysis: Raymond L. Garthoff, *Soviet Strategy in the Nuclear Age* (New York: Frederick Praeger, Publishers, 1958); Garthoff, *Detente and Confrontation: American-Soviet Relations from Nixon to Reagan* (Washington, D.C.: The Brookings Institution, 1985).

[37]See Robert Keohane and Joseph Nye, *Power and Interdependence* (Boston: Little, Brown and Company, 1977).

SOURCES CONSULTED

PRIMARY SOURCES

Archives of the Woodstock College Library, Georgetown University, Washington, D.C. The Woodstock Archives contain the personal papers of John Courtney Murray, including his class notes, unpublished manuscripts, formal addresses, and personal correspondence. These materials are vital in establishing the linkages between Murray's published works and in demonstrating how Murray's public theology developed during the post-war years.

Archives of the United States, Washington, D.C. John Courtney Murray served as a member of the Presidential Commission on Military Education in the 1950's and the Presidential Commission on Selective Service in the 1960's, during the war in Vietnam. The Proceedings of both of these Commissions, which convey much of Murray's insights about the relationship of morality to foreign and military policy, are contained in the National Archives.

Archives of the Center for the Study of Democratic Institutions, Santa Barbara, California. From 1953 until his death, John Courtney Murray served on the Board of Trustees of the Center for the Study of Democratic Institutions (originally called the Fund for the Republic). During this time, Murray participated in a series of seminars which the Center held on topics of interest in domestic and foreign policy. The tapes and transcripts of these seminars are especially helpful in understanding Murray's approach to natural law as the basis for building a moral consensus in society.

FROM THE PUBLISHED WORKS OF JOHN COURTNEY MURRAY (IN CHRONOLOGICAL ORDER)

Murray, John Courtney. "Current Theology: Christian Cooperation." *Theological Studies* III (September 1942): 413–431.

———. "Current Theology: Cooperation, Some Further Views." *Theological Studies* IV (March 1943): 100–111.

———. "Current Theology: Intercredal Cooperation: Its Theory and Its Organization." *Theological Studies* IV (June 1943): 257–268.

———. "Principles for Peace." *Theological Studies* IV (December 1943): 634–638.

———. "The Pattern for Peace and the Papal Peace Program." Washington, D.C., Catholic Association for International Peace, 1944.

———. "Towards a Theology for the Layman: The Problem of Its Finality." *Theological Studies* V (March 1944) 43–75.

———. "The Juridical Organization of the International Community." *The Wall Street Journal* (October 9, 1944): 16–18.

———. "World Order and Moral Law." *Thought* XIX (December 1944): 581–586.

———. "On the Problem of Cooperation: Some Clarifications: Reply to Father Paul H. Furfey." *The American Ecclesiastical Review* CXII (March 1945): 194–214.

———. "Current Theology: Freedom of Religion." *Theological Studies* VI (March 1945): 85–113.

———. "Freedom of Religion I: The Ethical Problem." *Theological Studies* VI (March 1945): 229–286.

———. "God's Word and Its Realization." *America* LXXIV (December 8, 1945), supplement: xix–xxv.

———. "The Papal Allocution: Christmas." *America* LXXIV (January 5, 1946): 370–371.

———. "How Liberal Is Liberalism?" *America* LXXV (April 6, 1946): 6–7.

———. "Operation University." *America* LXXV (April 13, 1946): 28–29.

———. "Separation of Church and State." *America* LXXVI (December 7, 1946): 261–263.

———. "The Court Upholds Religious Freedom." *America* LXXVI (March 8, 1947): 628–630.

———. "What Does the Catholic Church Want?" *Catholic Mind* XLVI (September 1948): 580–588.

———. "Dr. Morrison and the First Amendment." *America* LXXVIII (March 6, 1948): 627–629, 683–686.

————. "The Role of Faith in the Renovation of the World." *The Messenger of the Sacred Heart* LXXXIII (March 1948): 15–17.

————. "Saint Robert Bellarmine on the Indirect Power." *Theological Studies* IX (December 1948): 491–535.

————. "On the Necessity for Not Believing: A Roman Catholic Interpretation." *The Yale Scientific Magazine* XXIII (February 1949): 11–12.

————. "Reversing the Secularist Drift." *Thought* XXIV (March 1949): 36–46.

————. "Towards a Theology for the Layman." *Jesuit Educational Quarterly* XI (March 1949): 221–228.

————. "Free Speech in Its Relation to Self-Government." *Georgetown Law Journal* XXXVII (May 1949): 654–662.

————. "Review of: Paul Blanshard's *American Freedom and Catholic Power.*" *The Catholic World* CLXIX (June 1949): 233–234.

————. "Contemporary Orientations of Catholic Thought on Church and State in the Light of History." *Theological Studies* X (June 1949): 177–234.

————. "The Catholic Position: A Reply." *The American Mercury* LXIX (September 1949): 274–283, 637–639.

————. "Law or Prepossessions." *Essays in Contemporary Problems* XIV (Winter 1949): 23–43.

————. "The Natural Law." In *Great Expressions of Human Rights,* pp. 69–104. Edited by R. M. MacIver. New York: Harper and Company, 1950.

————. "The One Work of the One Church." *Catholic Mind* XLVIII (June 1950): 358–364.

————. "Paul Blanshard and the New Nativism." *The Month* V (April 1951): 214–225.

————. "The School and Christian Freedom." National Catholic Educational Association. *Proceedings* XLVIII (August 1951): 63–68.

————. "For the Freedom and Transcendence of the Church." *The American Ecclesiastical Review* CXXVI (January 1952): 28–48.

————. "The Church and Totalitarian Democracy." *Theological Studies* XIII (December 1952): 525–563.

————. "Leo XIII on Church and State: The General Structure of the Controversy." *Theological Studies* XIV (March 1953): 1–30.

————. "Christian Humanism in America." *Social Order* III (May–June 1953): 233–244.

————. "Leo XIII: Two Concepts of Government." *Theological Studies* XIV (December 1953): 551–567.

————. "Leo XIII: Two Concepts of Government: Government and the Order of Culture." *Theological Studies* XV (March 1954): 1–33.

————. "The Problem of Pluralism in America." *Thought* XXIX (Summer 1954): 165–208.

————. "Catholics in America — A Creative Minority — Yes or No?" *The Catholic Mind* LIII (October 1955): 590–597.

————. "The Catholic University in a Pluralist Society." (Saint Louis University Address delivered in November 1955) *The Catholic Mind* LVII (May–June 1959): 253–260.

————. "Special Catholic Challenges." *Life* XXXIX (January 13, 1956): 144–146.

————. "The Religious School in a Pluralist Society." *The Catholic Mind* LIV (September 1956): 502–511.

————. "Freedom, Responsibility and the Law." *The Catholic Lawyer* II (July 1956): 214–220, 276.

————. "The Bad Arguments Intelligent People Make." *America* CXVI (November 3, 1956): 120–123.

————. "Literature and Censorship." *The Catholic Mind* LIV (December 1956): 665–677.

————. "The Christian Idea of Education." In *The Christian Idea of Education,* pp. 152–163. Edited by Edmund Fuller. New Haven: Yale University Press, 1956.

————. "How to Think Theologically About War and Peace." *Catholic Messenger* LXXVI (December 1958): 7–8.

————. "America's Four Conspiracies." In *Religion in America,* pp. 12–41. Edited by John Cogley. New York: Meridian Books, 1958.

————. "Foreign Policy and the Free Society." New York: Oceana Publications, 1958.

————. "State University in a Pluralist Society." *The Catholic Mind* LVII (May–June 1959): 242–252.

————. "Remarks on the Moral Problem of War." *Theological Studies* XX (March 1959): 40–61.

————. *We Hold These Truths: Reflections on the American Proposition.* New York: Sheed and Ward, 1960.

————. "Morality and Foreign Policy, Part I." *America* CII (March 19, 1960): 729–732.

————. "Morality and Foreign Policy, Part II." *America* CII (March 26, 1960): 764–767.

————. "The American Proposition." *Commonweal* LXXIII (January 20, 1961): 433–435.

————. "What Can Unite a Religiously Divided Nation." *Catholic Messenger* LXXIX (April 27, 1961): 1–4.

————. "The Return to Tribalism." *The Catholic Mind* LX (January 1962): 5–12.

————. "Making the News Good News." *Interracial Review* XXXVI (July 1963): 34–35; 130–131.

————. "Natural Law and the Public Consensus." In *Natural Law and Modern Society*, pp. 67–92. Edited by John Cogley. Cleveland: World Publishing Company, 1963.

————. "Things Old and New in *Pacem in Terris*." *America* CVIII (April 27, 1963): 612–614.

————. "Key Themes in the Encyclical." In The American Press edition of *Pacem in Terris*, 1963, pp. 57–64.

————. "On the Future of Humanistic Education." In *Humanistic Education*, pp. 231–255. Edited by Arthur A. Cohen. New York: Holt, Rinehart, and Winston, 1964.

————. "Religious Freedom." In *Freedom and Man*, pp. 131–140. Edited by John Courtney Murray. New York: P. J. Kennedy and Sons, 1965.

————. "The Problem of Religious Freedom. *Theological Studies* XXV (December 1964): 503–575.

————. "The Declaration on Religious Freedom." In *Vatican II, An Interfaith Appraisal*, pp. 577–587. Edited by John Miller. Notre Dame, Indiana: Association Press, 1966.

————. "Freedom, Authority, Community." *America* CXV (December 3, 1966): 734–741.

————. "A Will to Community." In *Theological Freedom and Social Responsibility*, pp. 111–116. Editied by Stephen F. Bayne. New York: Seabury Press, 1967.

————. "Freedom in an Age of Renewal." *American Benedictine Review* XVIII (September 1967): 319–324.

WORKS WHICH WERE CRITICAL IN JOHN COURTNEY MURRAY'S INTELLECTUAL DEVELOPMENT

Ecclesial Documents

Pope Leo XIII. *Diuturnum*. (An encyclical on the origin of civil power delivered June 29, 1881.) *Actae Sanctae Sedis*, 14: 3–14.

————. *Immortale Dei*. (An encyclical on the Christian constitution of states delivered November 1, 1885.) *Actae Sanctae Sedis*, 18: 161–180.

————. *Libertas.* (An encyclical on the nature of human liberty delivered June 20, 1888.) *Actae Sanctae Sedis,* 20: 593–613.

————. *Rerum Novarum.* (An encyclical on labor and capital delivered May 15, 1891.) *Actae Sanctae Sedis* 23: 641–670.

————. *Au Milieu Des Sollicitudes.* (An encyclical on the Church and State in France delivered February 16, 1892. *Actae Sanctae Sedis,* 24: 219–529.

————. *Longinqua Oceani.* (An encyclical on Catholicism in the United States delivered January 6, 1895.) *Actae Sanctae Sedis,* 27:387–399.

Pope Piux X. *Il Fermo Proposito.* (An encyclical on Catholic Action in Italy delivered June 11, 1905.) *Actae Sanctae Sedis* 37: 741–767.

————. *Singulari Quadam.* (An encyclical on labor organizations delivered on September 24, 1912.) *Acta Apostolicae Sedis,* IV (1925): 657–662.

Pope Pius XI. *Quas Primas.* (An encyclical on the feast of Christ the King delivered December 11, 1925.) *Acta Apostolicae Sedis,* XVII (1925): 593–610.

————. *Mortalium Animos.* (An encyclical on religious unity delivered January 6, 1928.) *Acta Apostolicae Sedis,* XX (1928): 5–16.

————. *Laetus Sane Nuntius.* (An apostolic letter on Catholic Action addressed to Cardinal Segura on November 6, 1929.) *Acta Apostolicae Sedis,* XXI (1929): 664–668.

Pope Pius XII. "Nuntius Radiophonicus A Summo Pontificie Die XIV Mensis Decembris A. MCMXLI." (The Christmas Allocution of 1941.) *Acta Apostolicae Sedis* XXXIV (1942): 10–21.

————. "Nuntius Radiophonicus A Summo Pontificie Die XIV Mensis Decembris A. MCMXLII." (The Christmas Allocution of 1942). *Acta Apostolicae Sedis* XXXV (1943): 9–24.

————. "Nuntius Radiophonicus A Summo Pontificie Die XIV Mensis Decembris A. MCMXLIV." (The Christmas Allocution of 1944.) *Acta Apostolicae Sedis* IIIVII (1945): 10–23.

————. "Sermo a SSMO D.N. Pio PP XII Habitus Die XXIV Mensis Decembris A. MCMXLV." (The Christmas Allocution of 1945.) *Acta Apostolicae Sedis* XXXVIII (1946): 15–25.

————. "Nuntius Radiophonicus Universi Orbis Episcopis et Christifidelibus" (The Christmas Message of 1950.) *Acta Apostolicae Sedis* XLIII (1951): 49–59.

————. "Iis Ovi XVI Conventui Oficii Internationalis Inquisitionis de Medicina inter Milites Exercenda Interfuerunt." *Acta Apostolicae Sedis* (1953): 744–754.

Pope John XXIII. *Pacem in Terris.* (An encyclical letter on peace in the modern world delivered April 11, 1963.) AAS 55, p. 293.

Other Works

Bellarmine, Robert, *De Laicis,* in C. Pedone Lauriel, editor, *Opera Omnia* (Naples: 1872): volume II, pp. 312–343.
Bevenot, M. "No Common Basis?" *Clergy Review* XI (June 1942): 266–269.
Berle, Adolf A. *Power Without Property: A New Development in American Political Economy.* New York: Harcourt, Brace and Company, 1959.
Blanshard, Paul. *American Freedom and Catholic Power.* Boston: Beacon Press, 1949.
Butterfield, William. "Cooperation with Non-Catholics." *Clergy Review* XXI (1942): 152–171.
Carlyle, Robert and A. J. *A History of Medieval Political Theory in the West.* New York: Barnes and Noble, Inc., 1953.
Dawson, Christopher. *Beyond Politics.* New York: Sheed and Ward Company, 1939.
D'Entreves, Alexander Passerin. *The Medieval Contribution to Political Thought.* Oxford: Oxford University Press, 1939.
Ford, John C. "The Morality of Obliteration Bombing." *Theological Studies* IV (1945): 261–309.
Garthoff, Raymond. *Soviet Strategy in the Nuclear Age.* New York: Frederick Praeger, Publishers, 1958.
Gilbey, Thomas. *Between Society and Community.* New York: Longmans Green and Company, 1953.
Guardini, Romano. *The End of the Modern World.* Translated by Joseph Theman and Herbert Burke. New York: Sheed and Ward, 1939.
Hocking, William Ernest. *The Coming World Civilization.* New York: Harper and Brothers, 1956.
Kennan, George. *American Diplomacy, 1900-1950.* Chicago: University of Chicago Press, 1951.
Kern, Fritz. *Kingship and Law in the Middle Ages.* New York: Harper and Row, 1942.
Kissinger, Henry. *Nucear Weapons and Foreign Policy.* New York, Harper and Brothers, 1957.
Leclercq, Jean. *Jean de Paris et l'ecclésiologie du XIIIe siècle.* Paris: J. Vrin, 1942.
Lefever, Ernest. *Ethics and United States Foreign Policy.* New York: Meridien Books, 1957.

Lippmann, Walter. *Essays in the Public Philosophy.* Boston: Little, Brown and Company, 1955.

de Lubac, Henri. *Le drame de l'humanisme athée.* Paris: Spee, 1945.

Maritain, Jacques. *Christianity and Democracy.* Translated by Doris Anson. New York: Charles Scribner's Sons, 1944.

————. *Education at the Crossroads.* New Haven: Yale University Press, 1943.

————. *Man and the State.* Chicago: University of Chicago Press, 1951.

McIlwain, C. H. *The Growth of Political Thought in the West.* New York: Harper and Company, 1932.

Meyer, Alfred. *Leninism.* Cambridge: Harvard University Press, 1957.

Morgenthau, Hans. *Politics Among Nations: The Struggle for Power and Peace.* New York: Alfred Knopf, 1948.

Niebuhr, Reinhold. *Moral Man and Immoral Society.* New York: Charles Scribner's Sons, 1932.

Riviere, J. *le probleme de l'Eglise et de l'Etat au Temps de Philippe le Bel.* Louvain: Spicilegium Sacrum Louvaniense, 1926.

Rommen, Heinrich A. *The State in Catholic Thought.* Saint Louis: Herder Book Company, 1945.

Rossiter, Clinton. *Seedtime of the Republic.* New York: Harcourt Brace, 1953.

Sturzo, Luigi. *Church and State.* New York: Longmans Green and Company, 1939.

Talmon, J. L. *The Rise of Totalitarian Democracy.* Boston: Beacon Press, 1952.

Troeltsch, Ernst. *The Social Teachings of the Christian Churches.* London: George Allen, Ltd., 1931.

Thomas Aquinas. *Commentaria in X Libris Ethicorum Ad Nicomachum.* (Parmae) Edited by Vernon Burke. New York: Musurgia Publishers, 1949.

————. *Politicorum Seu De Rebus Civilibus.* (Parmae) Edited by Vernon Burke. New York: Musurgia Publishers, 1949.

————. *De Regimine Principum.* Marietti edition, Turin, 1924.

————. *De Veritate Catholicae Fidei Contra Gentiles.* Edited by I. Bertrand. Paris, 1881.

————. *Summa Theologica.* Edited by the Fathers of the English Dominican Province. London: Burns, Oates, and Washbourne, Ltd., 1920.

Voegelin, Eric. *The New Science of Politics.* Chicago: University of Chicago Press, 1952.

Watkins, Frederick. *The Political Tradition of the West.* Cambridge: Harvard University Press, 1948.

SECONDARY WORKS

Articles

Aubert, Jean-Marie. "Dèbats autour de la morale fondamentale." *Studia moralia* 20 (1982): 195–222.

———. "La spécificite' de la morale chrétienne selon saint Tomas." *Le Supplement* vol. 92 (1970): 55–73.

von Balthasar, Hans Urs. "Nine Theses in Christian Ethics." In *Readings in Moral Theology Number Two: The Distinctiveness of Christian Ethics,* pp. 190–206. Edited by Charles E. Curran and Richard McCormick. New York: Paulist Press, 1980.

Berger, Peter. "Secular Theology and the Rejection of the Supernatural: Reflections on Recent Trends." *Theological Studies* XXXVIII (March 1972): 39–56.

Caldera, Rafael. "The Universal Common Good and International Social Justice. *The Review of Politics* 38 (January 1976): 27–39.

Childress, James. "Just-War Criteria." *War or Peace? The Search for Answers,* pp. 40–58. Maryknoll, New York: Orbis, 1980.

Coleman, John. "The Situation for Modern Faith." *Theological Studies* XXXIX (December 1978): 601–632.

———. "Vision and Praxis in American Theology: Orestes Brownson, John A. Ryan, and John Courtney Murray." *Theological Studies* XXXVII (1976): 3–40.

Congar, Yves. "The Sacralization of Western Society in the Middle Ages." *Concilium* 7 (September 1969): 55–71.

Curran, Charles. "The Changing Anthropological Bases of Catholic Social Ethics." *The Thomist* 45 (April 1981): 284–318.

Degnan, Daniel. "Two Models of Positive Law in Aquinas: A Study of the Relationships of Positive Law and Natural Law." *The Thomist* 46 (January 1982): 1–32.

Finnis, John. "Natural Law and the 'Is-Ought' Question." *The Catholic Lawyer* 26 (Autumn 1981): 266–277.

Fiorenza, Francis Schüssler. "Political Theology as Foundational Theology." *Proceedings of the Catholic Theological Society of America* 32 (1977): 142–177.

Goerner, E. A. "John Courtney Murray: Historicism as Antidote." In Goerner, editor, *Peter and Caesar,* pp. 169–184. New York: Herder and Herder, 1965.

Haring, Bernard. "Dynamism and Continuity in a Personalistic Approach to Natural Law." In *Norm and Context in Christian Ethics,* pp. 199–218. Edited by Gene Outka and Paul Ramsey. New York: Charles Scribner's Sons, 1968.

Hehir, J. Bryan. "The Just War Ethic and Catholic Theology: Dynamics of Change and Continuity." In *War and Peace; The Search for New Answers*. Edited by Thomas A. Shannon. Maryknoll, New York: Orbis, 1980.

———. "The Unfinished Agenda." *America* 153 (November 30, 1985): 386–387.

Higgins, George. "John Courtney Murray: Some Personal Recollections." *America* 153 (November 30, 1985): 380–385.

Hollenbach, David. "Public Theology in America: Some Questions for Catholicism After John Courtney Murray." *Theological Studies* XXXVII (1976): 290–303.

Hollenbach, David, editor. "Theology and Philosophy in Public: a Symposium on John Courtney Murray's Unfinished Agenda." *Theological Studies* XL (December 1979): 700–715.

Joblin, Joseph. "Diritti Dell' Uomo, Ateismo e Instituzioni Culturali Cristiani." *La Civiltā Cattolica* Anno 132, vol. 3, 118–132.

Johnson, James T. "Natural Law as a Language for the Ethics of War." *The Journal of Religious Ethics* 3 (Fall 1975): 217–242.

Kennan, George. "Foreign Policy and Christian Conscience." In *The Moral Dilemma of Nuclear Weapons*, pp. 69–78. Edited by William Clancy. New York: Church Peace Union, 1961.

———. "Morality and Foreign Policy." *Foreign Affairs* (Spring 1985): 195–213.

Langan, John. "Should Decisions Be the Product of Reason?" *Personal Values in Public Policy*, pp. 48–72. Edited by John C. Haughey. New York: Paulist Press, 1979.

Lorenzetti, Luigi. "Il pluralismo sociale nello stato democratico." *Rivista di teologia morale* 48 (ottobre-decembre 1980): 589–600.

Martina, Giacomo. "The Contribution of Liberalism and Socialism to a Better Self-Conception of the Church." In *The History and Self-Understanding of the Church*, pp. 93–101. Edited by Roger Aubert. New York: Herder and Herder, 1971.

Marty, Martin E. "Two Kinds of Civil Religion." *American Civil Religion*, pp. 139–157. Edited by Russel E. Richey and Donald G. Jones. New York: Harper and Row, 1974.

McCormick, Richard. "Does Religious Faith Add to Ethical Perception?" In *Personal Values in Public Policy*, pp. 155–173. Edited by John C. Haughey. New York: Paulist Press, 1979.

Moschetti, Stefano. "La Legittima Autonomia Delle Realta Terrene: Riflessioni sulla 'Gaudium et Spes'." *La Civiltà Cattolica* Anno 135, vol. 4 (1984): 428–440.

Administrative Board of the National Catholic Welfare Conference. "On Secularism." *The Catholic Mind* LVI (January 1948): 1–8.

Novak, Michael. "Economic Rights: The Servile State." *Catholicism in Crisis* III, number 10 (1985): 8–15.

von Ouwerkerk, Coenraad. "Secularism and Christian Ethics: Some Types and Symptoms." In *Understanding the Signs of the Times,* pp. 97–142. Edited by Franz Bockle. New York: Paulist Press, 1967.

Ramsey, Paul. "The Vatican Council on Modern War." *Theological Studies* XX (1966): 179–203.

Rohr, John A. "John Courtney Murray and the Pastoral Letters." *America* 153 (November 30, 1985): 373–379.

Scully, Edgar. "The Place of the State in Society According to Thomas Aquinas." *Thomist* 45 (July 1981): 407–429.

Shiner, Larry. "The Concept of Secularization in Empirical Research." *Journal for the Scientific Study of Religion* 6 (1967): 207–220.

Weigel, George. "John Courtney Murray and the American Proposition." *Catholicism in Crisis* 3 (November 1985): 8–13.

———. "The Margin Makes the Difference: John Courtney Murray on Morality and Foreign Policy." *Catholicism in Crisis* II (December 1985): 6–9.

Whelan, Charles. "Religious Belief and Public Morality." *America* 151 (September 29, 1984): 159–163.

Books

Bainton, Roland. *Christian Attitudes Toward War and Peace.* New York: Abingdon Press, 1960.

Bellah, Robert, et al. *Habits of the Heart: Individualism and Commitment in American Life.* Berkeley: University of California Press, 1985.

Berger, Peter. *The Sacred Canopy.* Garden City, New York: Doubleday and Company, 1969.

Cogley, John. *Catholic America.* New York: Dial Press, 1973.

Coleman, John A. *An American Strategic Theology.* New York: Paulist Press, 1982.

Cross, Robert. *The Emergence of Liberal Catholicism in America.* Cambridge, Massachusetts: Harvard University Press, 1958.

Curran, Charles. *New Perspectives in Moral Theology.* Notre Dame, Indiana: Fides Publishers, 1974.

————. *American Catholic Social Ethics*. Notre Dame, Indiana: University of Notre Dame Press, 1982.

————. *Directions in Catholic Social Ethics*. Notre Dame, Indiana: University of Notre Dame Press, 1985.

d'Entreves, A. P. *Natural Law: An Introduction to Legal Philosophy*. London: Hutchinson University Library, 1964.

Douglas, Mary and Tipton, Steven, editors. *Religion and America: Spirituality in a Secular Age*. Boston: Beacon Press, 1983.

Finnis, John. *Natural Law and Natural Rights*. Oxford: Clarendon Press, 1980.

Fuchs, Joseph. *Personal Responsibility and Christian Morality*. Washington, D.C.: Georgetown University Press, 1983.

————. *Christian Ethics in a Secular Arena*. Washington, D.C.: Georgetown University Press, 1984.

Garthoff, Raymond. *Detente and Confrontation: American-Soviet Relations from Nixon to Reagan*. Washington, D.C.: Brookings Institution, 1985.

Hammond, Phillip, editor. *The Sacred in a Secular Age*. Berkeley: University of California Press, 1985.

Haring, Bernard. *Faith and Morality in the Secular Age*. Garden City, New York: Doubleday and Company, 1973.

Hoffner, Joseph. *La Dottrina Sociale Christiana*. Rome: Edizioni Paoline, 1979.

Holland, Joe, and Henriot, Peter. *Social Analysis*. Maryknoll, New York: Orbis, 1985.

Hollenbach, David. *Nuclear Ethics: A Christian Moral Argument*. New York: Paulist Press, 1983.

————. *Claims in Conflict: Retrieving and Renewing the Catholic Human Rights Tradition*. New York: Paulist Press, 1979.

Hughes, Gerald. *Authority in Morals*. Washington, D.C.: Georgetown University Press, 1978.

Lefever, Ernest, editor. *Morality and Foreign Policy*. Washington: Georgetown University Press, 1977.

Love, Thomas. *John Courtney Murray: Contemporary Church-State Theory*. Garden City, New York: Doubleday and Company, 1965.

Lovin, Robin. *Religion and American Public Life*. New York: Paulist Press, 1986.

Luckmann, Thomas. *The Invisible Religion*. New York: The Macmillan Company, 1973.

Macquarrie, John. *Three Issues in Ethics*. New York: Harper and Row, 1970.

Marsden, George. *Fundamentalism and American Culture.* New York: Oxford University Press, 1980.

Marty, Martin. *Religion and Republic: The American Circumstance* (Boston: Beacon Press, 1987).

———. *The Public Church.* New York: Crossroad Publishing Company, 1981.

McBrien, Richard. *Caesar's Coin: Religion and Politics in America.* New York: Macmillan Publishing Company, 1987.

Neuhaus, Richard John. *The Naked Public Square.* New York: Doubleday and Company, 1984.

O'Collins, Gerald. *The Theology of Secularity.* Notre Dame, Indiana: Fides Publishers, 1973.

Pelotte, Donald E. *John Courtney Murray: Theologian in Conflict.* New York: Paulist Press, 1976.

Reichey, A. James. *Religion in American Public Life.* Washington, D.C.: The Brookings Institution, 1985.

Russell, Frederick. *The Just War in the Middle Ages.* New York: Cambridge University Press, 1975.

Tracy, David. *The Analogical Imagination.* New York: Crossroad Publishing Company, 1981.

Waltz, Kenneth. *Theory of International Politics.* New York: Random House, 1979.

Walzer, Michael. *Just and Unjust Wars.* New York: Basic Books, 1977.

Weber, Max. *The Sociology of Religion.* Translated by Ephraim Fischoff. London: Methven and Company, 1965.

Wilson, John. *Public Religion in American Culture.* Philadelphia: Temple University Press, 1979.